Sea Kayaking

NORTHERN
CALIFORNIA

Sea Kayaking
NORTHERN
CALIFORNIA

Demece Garepis

The McGraw-Hill Companies

Camden, Maine • New York • San Francisco • Washington, D.C.
Auckland • Bogotá • Caracas • Lisbon • London • Madrid
Mexico City • Milan • Montréal • New Delhi • San Juan
Singapore • Sydney • Tokyo • Toronto

Ragged Mountain Press

A Division of The McGraw·Hill Companies

10 9 8 7 6 5 4 3 2 1

Library of Congress Cataloging-in-Publication Data

Garepis, Demece.
  Sea kayaking Northern California / Demece Garepis.
    p. cm.
  Includes bibliographical references (p.   ).
  ISBN 0-07-040596-4 (paper)
    1. Sea kayaking—California, Northern.   2. California, Northern—Guidebooks.   I. Title.
  GV788.5G37   1998
  797.1'224'09794—DC21   98-4019
                                                                 CIP

Questions regarding the content of this book should be addressed to:

Ragged Mountain Press
P.O. Box 220
Camden, ME 04843
www.raggedmountainpress.com

Questions regarding the ordering of this book should be addressed to:

The McGraw-Hill Companies
Customer Service Department
P.O. Box 547
Blacklick, OH 43004
Retail customers: 1-800-262-4729
Bookstores: 1-800-722-4726
www.books.mcgraw-hill.com

WARNING

Sea kayaking can take paddlers into harm's way, exposing them to risks of injury, cold-water exposure and hypothermia, drowning, and other hazards that can lead to serious injury or death.

This book is not intended to replace instruction by a qualified instructor or to substitute for good personal judgment. In using this book, the reader releases the author, publisher, and distributor from liability for any injury, including death, that might result. It is understood that you paddle at your own risk.

✺ This book is printed on 60-pound Renew Opaque Vellum, an acid-free paper that contains 50 percent recycled waste paper (preconsumer) and 10 percent postconsumer waste paper.

Printed by R.R. Donnelley, Crawfordsville, IN
Design and Production by Faith Hague
Edited by Pamela Benner; Kathryn Mallien
Photography by Michael Powers
Maps by Cartisia and Martha Dean

*To my father, who introduced me to the power of the sea,
and to my mother, who introduced me to the love of language.*

))))) Contents

〰️ Foreword

By Steph Dutton

I first met Demece in Sitka, Alaska, in 1994. I was visiting a friend who ran a kayak tour operation for the cruise lines calling there. She put me to work guiding because she was shorthanded. I'm the first to admit that I have no business leading tours, and my friend Heidi was quick to recognize that. One morning she was getting her group, fresh from the ship, outfitted. She told them that a well-known kayaker would accompany them and gave them my name. That's how I met Demece and her mother. I implored my friend to cut me loose from the group so I could paddle alone with the two women. We spent the most delightful couple of hours together, ghosting along in Camp Cougan Bay. It was a burst of freedom for me; I had neither to fake answers to questions about the flora and fauna nor try to explain to the cruising passengers that Sitka Sound was not a large lake. We drifted along, oblivious to everything but that comforting shroud of familiarity and mysticism that only Alaska provides. Since then Demece and I have seen each other often. Our meetings are never planned, and that makes them even more special. Paddling with Demece takes me back to when I first began to paddle, and reminds me that kayaking is just a sport—a fine way to recreate.

I was lured into sea kayaking in 1990 when I was a ski instructor in northwest Washington. I stood out a bit as a leg amputee teaching the sport to able-bodied people. A group of very tough and competitive disabled athletes calling themselves Team USAble gathers once a year for the grueling Ski to Sea relay race. They are the only amputees in a field of more than 200 able-bodied teams. Looking to grow, they cast about and hooked me. The final leg of the race, crossing Bellingham Bay, could at the time be done either by Hobie Cat or sea kayak. For years, I had been an avid, though not good, sailor. Crewing on the Hobie sounded like great fun, but paddling a kayak sounded even better. I drove to Bellingham and picked up my loaner Ocean Kayak Scupper Pro. I loved that boat and the way it made me feel.

Skiing gave me a sense of the fluid motion I had lacked since I'd lost a leg in a car accident. Two years and several operations after the accident, it was clear that the fractures would not heal. It took me two weeks, but I finally convinced the doctor to amputate. While I never regretted the decision, I had never really reconciled myself to the consequences. Paddling that old boat, though, gave me the feeling of grace I had been looking for and allowed me to accept who I was.

When, in 1993, I announced to a friend on Team USAble that I was going to paddle from Victoria, British Columbia, to Ensenada, Baja California, he didn't join in the chorus of others who told me I was crazy. His words—"You'll never be the same"—almost caressed me. It was what I needed to hear. After BC to BC '93 came a 1994 trip with Van Hicks in the first unsupported circumnavigation of the northern chain of the California Channel Islands. That led to a "class-V saltwater adventure" with a couple of Oregon whitewater paddlers. Five days into the 1995 Oregon Coast Winter Challenge, they left. My Alaskan friend Heidi Tiura was running shore support for the expedition. A licensed 100-ton-vessel master, she had run charter boats on the Oregon coast in winter and knew what was out there waiting for me: 30 days of paddling, two broken boats, and two near-drownings. But I finished. In 1996, when Heidi and I were paddling off Point Pinos near Monterey, we found ourselves surrounded and enchanted by gray whales. That day gave rise to our current project, a multiyear sea-kayaking documentary and research project on the California gray whale called In the Path of Giants.

I have enjoyed using the sea kayak to achieve firsts and now to utilize it in assisting with valuable research, conservation, and education. There have been some heavy tolls to pay, however. I can no longer romanticize the ocean. I've become a destination- and reason-driven paddler. When I leave the beach in the morning, I know that I have a certain number of miles to paddle that day to make my landing spot, or that the whales are my reason for paddling. I pay attention to what I'm doing out there and little else. This is why I have enjoyed Demece's book so much. While reading, I can close my eyes and see the deep emerald color of the water off Trinidad Head; I can see a kayak slicing through a low-lying fog that shrouds Freshwater Lagoon. And I can see myself in that kayak.

I'll bare teeth over politics and conservation, but I won't argue about kayaking. As you read this book, don't think about what the technical experts tell you about your forward stroke. Practice and be safe, but not a fanatic. Don't pay the slightest attention to whether your boat has a rudder or not, and no one should care if it's rotomolded plastic or Kevlar. Go to these places and take advantage of the painstaking research Demece has done. Paddle some, and enjoy the wonderful spirit that guided you there.

STEPH DUTTON
Monterey, California, 1998

⁑⁑ Preface

The first time I went kayaking, rain fell on Monterey Bay. It calmed the waters, and as I watched thousands of drops make unique, light concentric circles on the low swells, I heard a symphonic inhalation of breath. I had never heard that long, low inhalation before, and seeing nothing, I paddled on. A few seconds later, a gray whale and her baby breached, fins glistening in the soft rain. As they quietly emerged from the slate flat surface only a few yards away, I gasped, realizing that these two giant travelers were aware of my presence and were gently moving around me. Then, without thinking, I leaned over, and capsized. The capsize didn't scare me; I simply scrambled back into my boat. But in those few moments I suddenly knew I had fallen in love with the sport. A sport so interactive that you become part of a constantly changing environment—swells rise and fall, waves that are following become beam waves, wind directions change, fog rolls in, storms appear without warning when you're not looking. Because you are in harmony with the environment, however, you learn to respect it and the vital interdependence of marine life on its surroundings. Kelp beds are vertical columns of nutrients for thousands of creatures, as well as calm resting places where otters teach their young the delectable art of shell cracking. Smooth limestone cliffs offer cragged entries into mysterious caves and rock gardens. Salt-covered rocks are comfy sunlit lounge chairs for harbor seals, whose barking is comparable to the cacophony of a thriving city tenement community.

Kayaking often brings out the best in people and exposes them to the most magical intricacies of marine life. It can also involve the deadly consequences of wrong decisions. Beyond managing your own safety, you must be mindful of the fragile ecosystems you will encounter. But this fragile ecosystem is stressed—to an extraordinary degree. From deformities in starfish to the migration of whales, the signs are clear: What we do can profoundly undermine the continuation of this interdependence. Paddle in these precious areas and do something to preserve them, now.

What other message do I have for readers of this book? You'll probably find that the folks you kayak with are kindred spirits. I have never felt such closeness. You'll watch for each other, develop a signal and communication system to let each other know your condition or conditions ahead. You move as a group, endeavoring to experience an unpredictable adventure together. You will come to know each other's skill level, and most importantly, you'll become more honest in assessing your own skills and realize the need to learn and practice. For the good of your fellow kayakers—practice your skills; for yourself—practice your skills. The fellow paddlers I trust most are the ones with whom I've practiced rolls, as well as self- and team rescues, at a local reservoir evenings after work. Why? You can't trust folks who don't practice their skills.

Northern California offers so many wonderful, easy-to-access paddles. Head out and watch a sunset shimmer across the water or go kayak surfing at a local beach after a hard day at work. The explosion and fall of fireworks launched off Santa Cruz or Treasure Island are an exhilarating, heavenly light show—best seen from your kayak. Full moon paddles bring out a magical time of setting sunlight and iridescence emerging from the bay's surface. These evening jaunts offer the escape from daily affairs and the relaxation typically experienced only on weekends. And, of course, weekend paddles offer extended adventures along sloughs, to coastal rock gardens, to bay points. Overnight camping trips provide extended paddling adventures with other kayakers and enable you to spend more time in pristine areas.

Kayaking brings together environmentally focused communities attempting to turn the tide against overwhelming odds. It brings together people who would otherwise never meet and who are nevertheless somewhat dependent on each other for survival. It extends the historic use of kayaks—for hunting and gathering—and lends modern paddlers the experience and challenge of close contact with the water and wildlife. How can one sport offer so much? Go paddle and find out.

☷ Acknowledgments

Several expert kayakers and naturalists contributed their advice and wisdom to this book. Big kudos to Ken Mannshardt, Tamara Borichevsky, Jeanne Coffey, Lang Craghill, Richard Dudzinski, Steph Dutton, Don Frey, David Holmes, Doug Huft, Bob Licht, John Lull, Phyllis Mace, Fred McCollum, John McKay, Mike McNulty, Gary Malyn, David Martinovich, Michael Powers, John Reed, Hal and Liz Schmidt, Roger Schumann, Jean Severinghaus, Debrah Volturno, and Beth and Dale at Rivers and Mountains. Very special thanks to Fred Gillam and Mark Rauscher for reviewing the manuscript and providing much-needed technical advice, and to George Gronseth for his advice on the trip rating system and his reading of an earlier version of the manuscript. Special thanks also to Sally Holland, for living through countless impromptu trips and my obsessive checking of details.

⌇⌇ How to Use This Book

The trips listed in Part 2 are organized by county. There are 17 counties in all; those along the coast are presented first, from north to south, followed by inland counties, which are also presented from north to south. Each county section opens with a detailed map for all of the trips in that county, including highways, major cities and towns, and numbered launch sites. Under each trip heading in the text, you'll find a map key indicating the specific trip number/launch site as labeled on the county map, followed by the page number for that map. Note that different trips within a county sometimes launch from the same site but are assigned different numbers; alternate launch points for the same trip are assigned the same number as the main launch site, followed by a letter (1A, for example).

Under each map key is a list of trip specifics: preferred NOAA chart(s), estimated paddle time *(round trip unless otherwise noted)*, trip rating (see below for a full description of the SK rating system), special hazards, directions to the launch site and nearest campsite, and best paddle time/tide. A summary of what you can expect to see and do on the trip wraps up each trip description. All mileage information is round-trip, unless otherwise noted.

Following the county trips is a list of areas especially suited to kayak surfing. These are not accompanied by a map or launch points; launches are described in the text only.

George Gronseth, the founder of The Kayak Academy, a school for state-of-the-art sea kayaking instruction, is among the world's leading experts on kayaking safety. He has helped to develop a classification system that rates sea kayaking trips according to the conditions usually encountered along the route. Like the rating system that has been used for years by whitewater kayakers, this new SK (for "Sea Kayak") system greatly simplifies the problem of describing the relative difficulty of different trips. It is used for all of the trips in this book.

> **SK 1:** Insignificant current; short fetch in an area protected from waves by surrounding land formations. Paddling conditions are generally calm.

SK 2: Maximum predicted current may be up to 1 knot; fetch is less than 10 nautical miles, unless it is possible to land and walk out. Crossings in this semiprotected area are less than ½ nautical mile. Choppy water is unlikely, as are winds over 10 knots.

SK 3: Maximum predicted current may be up to 3 knots, fetch may be more than 10 nautical miles, and your crossings may be up to 2 nautical miles. This area commonly has 10-knot or stronger winds and waves that wash over a kayak's deck.

SK 4: Predicted currents are between 2 and 4 knots, fetch may be more than 10 nautical miles, and crossings may be up to 5 nautical miles in this unprotected area. Steep waves and/or swells, and steady winds of at least 15 knots for most of the day are common. The route may cross areas with strong turbulent currents, and may have 1- to 2-foot waves at launch and landing sites.

SK 5: Predicted currents may be too fast for some kayakers to paddle against, and the hazards due to currents may be extreme. Fetch may be more than 10 nautical miles. Whitecaps, surf in the 2- to 4-foot range at launch and landing sites, fast currents, and winds over 15 knots are common.

SK 6: Predicted currents may exceed paddling speed and may cause extremely rough waters. Fetch may be more than 10 nautical miles, and there may be few or no safe landing sites along the route. Rough weather, breaking whitecaps, continually strong winds, and surf greater than 4 feet are common. Kayak reentry rescues may not be possible.

Trips with different SK ratings naturally require different skills. But paddling skills alone are no substitute for good judgment based on experience and knowledge, common sense, and trip planning. The important thing is to assess your skills honestly, to build experience in increments, and to stay within your limits. Before setting out, make an honest evaluation of conditions and be certain they match your paddling and rescue skills. Be prepared to stay on shore if they don't. There's no embarrassment in safe and sensible kayaking. Following is a list of skills that are widely regarded as necessary for each SK rating:

SK 1 and SK 2

◆ Previous basic instruction (completion of a basic skills class)
◆ Familiarity with paddle strokes, high and low braces, and steering with the paddle
◆ Practice on capsizing and reentry rescues, including assisted T-rescues and self-rescues
◆ Hands-on experience in using all your equipment
◆ Ability to paddle several miles without becoming cranky or exhausted

- Knowledge of shipping lanes, buoys, and signal markers, as well as the boat traffic, tides, currents, and weather in the area you are paddling
- Ability to use your first-aid kit and to identify and treat hypothermia

SK 3 and SK 4

- All of the skills listed for SK 1 and SK 2 trips
- Ability to perform self-rescues with fully loaded kayak
- Ability to rescue others, including emptying water from their cockpits in the T-rescue style
- Ability to brace and steer efficiently in 2- to 4-foot waves hitting sideways
- Ability to paddle efficiently in 15-knot winds while traveling in any direction
- Ability to perform braces and rescues in 2- to 4-foot waves
- Ability to launch and land your boat in surf 2 feet high
- Ability to plan the ferry angle of your paddle route, taking wind and tidal currents into consideration
- Ability to read water conditions, including shoal areas, tide rips, eddies, whirlpools and boils, waves, and opposing currents

SK 5 and SK 6

- All of the skills listed above
- Ability to maintain a pace of at least 3 knots under good conditions, for the duration of the trip
- Ability to launch and land through surf more than 2 feet high
- Ability to paddle with confidence in large seas (6 feet or larger) and strong wind (20 to 30 knots is common in Northern California)
- Ability to maintain good boat control in whitewater, tide rips, and following seas
- Reliable Eskimo roll on both sides
- Tested rescue skills in rough conditions
- Advanced skills in first aid, emergency communication, and boat repair
- Excellent navigation skills

A Note on Safety

The trips presented in this book are rated according to the SK 1–6 system described on pages xiv to xvi. Conditions may vary widely, however, and even relatively easy SK 1 trips can be downright dangerous in extreme weather. Common sense, good judgment, and the discipline to stay out of the water when you're uncomfortable with conditions are the foundations of safe paddling. Be sure to plan your trip wisely by checking the NOAA forecast in advance, checking all your gear, and going over your trip plan with fellow paddlers. Paddle times in this book are estimated generously, with time allowed for breaks, wildlife viewing, and even lunch, but they will naturally vary with conditions and paddlers' individual abilities and temperaments.

⫷⫷⫷ Part 1
Getting Ready

〰〰 A Brief History

Archaeologists tell us the kayak is at least 4,000 years old. Designed by the native peoples of the Far North, these small boats were constructed with frames of driftwood, bones, reeds, and ivory, and covered with the stretched and sewn skins of seals, reindeer, or caribou, and pierced only by the kayaker's small cockpit. Perfectly adapted for use by arctic hunters, they were watertight even in foul weather, fast and maneuverable, easy to portage because they drew little water, and equally at home in ocean swells and whitewater rivers. Virtually all the arctic peoples of North America and Asia built kayaks for hunting and transportation.

The Indians of California built a variety of canoes, but the kayak was unknown there until the mid–nineteenth century, when international trade in sea otter skins brought Russian and North American fur traders to the Arctic. Hundreds of Inuit and Aleut hunters in the traders' employ pursued otters from the Aleutians to Baja California, Mexico. At San Francisco, where Mexican ships guarded the mouth of the bay, otter hunters landed their kayaks by night, portaged over the Marin headlands, and slipped into bay waters, taking thousands of otter pelts in just a few years.

Times have changed, however, and modern kayakers are for the most part outdoors enthusiasts, paddling their boats for sport and relaxation. And fortunately for today's paddlers, the wetland resources of the Northern California coast are under careful management; but it wasn't always so.

Since 1850, half of Northern California's open water and tidal marshes have been filled or obstructed from tidal action by dikes and levees, eliminating 95 percent of the area's original wetland habitats. Rampant filling of the bays has been a particular concern because most of the acreage supporting creeks and rivers that lead into the bays is outside the perimeters of public lands. Wasteful logging practices and urban development have increased the numbers of bay dikes and levees that stop tidal action. In the three major Northern California bays—Humboldt Bay, San Francisco Bay, and Monterey

Bay—this concern has resulted in commissions that regulate bay filling, tidal land and creek reclamation, and shoreline development.

Northern California bays and estuaries contain more than 95 percent of California's remaining coastal wetlands. These waters are critical stops along the Pacific Flyway for millions of migrating waterfowl. Almost the entire population of migrating birds winters in the bays, as do the state's canvasbacks and scaups. In San Francisco Bay and Humboldt Bay, large numbers of shorebirds—including plover, rails, avocets, and stilts—inhabit the marshes. Monterey Bay is distinguished for a comprehensive renewed effort to preserve the California coast's most exposed migratory passage for the California gray whale, as well as for providing a rich refuge for thousands of dolphins and otters.

Major Northern California preserves and shoreline parks include Humboldt Bay National Wildlife Refuge, San Francisco National Wildlife Refuge, and the Monterey Bay National Marine Sanctuary. These areas preserve habitats critical for the entire coast's survival.

Because of these efforts, Northern California's coast is an ideal destination for kayakers.

))))) Sea Kayaking Gear

Although popular images of California feature palm trees and endless summers, the Golden State's climate and water are not quite so uniformly tropical. Many inland waters at high elevations are ice-covered in winter and spring, and cold currents from the northern Pacific keep California's coastal waters chilly year-round. The weather is full of surprises; winter storms in particular can pack a tremendous wallop. Your gear should allow you to paddle comfortably in "normal" conditions and enable you to deal safely with deteriorating weather and water conditions whenever they arise. That means clothing to ward off the cold and prevent hypothermia, safety and signaling devices, equipment that is in proper working condition, and bright colors visible in boat traffic.

Maintaining and checking a gear list is a small discipline; I use one for every trip, and it has enabled me to paddle for years without once forgetting anything essential. I recommend you check your gear list twice—faithfully—each and every time you paddle, whether for a days-long tour or a quick afternoon spin around the lake.

My gear list is actually three lists: (1) basic stuff I always take along, (2) items I take every time I paddle big water, like bays or the open ocean, and (3) items for overnight camping.

The Basics (don't leave home without them)

This is a fairly long list, but with the exception of the boat and the paddles, it all fits in a large laundry basket. After paddling, wash whatever gear has been soiled or exposed to salt and let it dry in the open air. Do a quick inventory and check for any damage that might prevent your equipment from functioning properly on future trips. Stuff everything back into the laundry basket—ready for the next time.

bailer
bilge pump (equipped with a
    float if it's one of the hand-
    held types)
boat with front and rear
    buoyancy
change for pay phone
chart or map of area
Coast Guard–approved Type
    III personal flotation device
    (PFD)
compass
dividers and pencil
dry bag with stuff sack
duct tape and repair kit
EPIRB
fire starter
first-aid kit
flares (or other visual signal aid,
    required for night paddling)
floating tow rope, 50 feet long
food (more than you think
    you'll need)
gloves
GPS
hypothermia kit (extra clothes
    and foil blanket in dry bag)
knife

lip balm
marine whistle or horn
navigation light (required for
    night paddling)
neoprene booties
neoprene farmer john or dry suit
paddle
paddle jacket
paddle leash
polypro top
self-rescue float
signal mirror
spare paddle
sponge
spray skirt
strobe
sunglasses with strap
sunscreen
tide and currents table
VHF radio
warm hat/visor
watch
water bottles
water filter
waterproof chart case
waterproof flashlight
waterproof matches
windbreaker

Always remember that flotation aids and thermal protection equipment work only when you use them. Just because it's a warm day, don't assume you won't need to put on your wet suit, PFD, and booties. You can always take a neoprene top off or partially fold down a wet suit, but not taking it along is a short road to disaster. Most serious sea kayaking accidents—including the majority of fatalities—involve hypothermia. Your thermal protection and PFD are your main defenses. Use them. And remember: you don't have to be in the water to become hypothermic.

If you're paddling big, open water, you'll need a few additional things:

bear bags and line
big and small flashlights
   (and spare batteries)
camp clothes
camp knife
camp shoes
candle
dry bags to pack your stuff in
handkerchief
insect repellent
kitchen utensils
lantern and spare mantles
large plastic garbage bags

matches
rain hat
rain poncho
sleeping bag (and foam
   sleeping pad)
stove and fuel
stove repair kit and extra fuel
tent and guylines (and tarp,
   ground cloth, and stakes)
toiletries
towel
VHF radio spare battery

For Bays or the Open Ocean

backup buoyancy (flotation bags inside bulkhead compartments)
deck compass
helmet
nautical chart

For Camping

Check these lists when planning a trip, and once again before you leave. Naturally, there are at least a few items I haven't listed that can add to your comfort and enjoyment. I like a good book when I'm camping, and a thermos of hot tea is always welcome on a chilly day. I often take a camera and extra film. And lightweight, water-resistant binoculars are great for scouting routes, locating landmarks, and watching wildlife.

More on Safety Equipment

In California, kayakers are required to have a Coast Guard–approved personal flotation device (PFD) in the boat at all times. The most popular PFD among kayakers is a Type III, which provides good mobility and comfort for the wearer, as well as excellent buoyancy. Unlike Type I PFDs, a Type III is not designed to keep the wearer's face out of the water if the wearer is unconscious, but for most paddlers the many advantages of the Type III outweigh this one disadvantage. Besides providing good freedom of movement, Type III PFDs designed for paddlers are available in high-visibility colors and with the extra pockets so useful for the little items that kayakers carry while on the water. The most important thing to remember about your PFD is to wear it—no matter how short the trip, or how calm the conditions, or how warm the weather. It's basic equipment, as essential as your boat and paddle. When I'm out on the water I can pick out the wannabe paddlers—they're the ones with their PFDs stuck in the back of the cockpit or strapped to the deck of the boat. For an extra measure of safety, add a whistle to the zipper tab and reflective tape on the back and shoulders of your PFD.

Between sunset and sunrise, all paddlers must, by law, display a white navigation light and have on hand at least one other visual signal aid, such as flares. Your paddle may also display a glow-in-the-dark light stick taped to your paddle. A whistle or horn is also essential, especially at night.

〉〉〉 Communications and Safety

Advise at least two emergency contacts of your exact trip plans and provide, on paper, a destination plan and a list of your emergency communication equipment to the nearest harbormaster. Leave a copy in your vehicle at the put-in.

Communication with fellow paddlers should be discussed during pretrip planning. Review hand signals, paddle signals, whistle/horn/light signals, emergency communications, and medical skills.

Flares burn with intense light and make excellent emergency signals. Bear in mind, however, that no flare is completely waterproof, and you should stow them in a waterproof container. Flares are available in a dizzying variety. The most commonly used are meteors, parachute flares, smoke flares, and hand-held flares. *Meteors*, which are launched into the air with a simple flare gun, burn very brightly, but as their name suggests, they burn out very quickly. *Parachute flares*, also launched with a flare gun, burn longer than meteors but can drift a considerable distance in wind. *Smoke flares* last longer, but fog or wind will dissipate the smoke. *Hand-held flares* last the longest, about two minutes, but are the least visible at a great distance because they are surface lights. Hand-held flares should not be used while in a kayak because they may drip burning material. Check also for expiration dates; most flares will last for about 3½ years after manufacture. Carry a variety of light flares and smoke flares in your basic equipment. Attach a small battery-powered strobe on your PFD.

Hand-held mirrors and signal mirrors, which have no official USCG approval rating, are effective in signaling nearby boaters and aircraft. Mirrors give a strobelight effect as you keep adjusting the mirror.

Emergency Position Indicating Radiobeacons (EPIRBs) and Very High Frequency (VHF) radios are both effective emergency communications tools. EPIRBs are waterproof, long-range, one-way transmitters, and you must be licensed to use them. Some paddlers use their cellular phones in a waterproof bag, but cell phones enable you to reach land-based emergency help (911) only, and it takes time for 911 to contact the proper marine authorities and the nearest ship. And remember that cell-phone coverage is incomplete in remote areas. VHF radios are coming down in price (around $200), and you can get a distress signal and a weather radio in one. VHF radios provide two-way communication and generally have a range of 5 to 10 miles. VHF radios are the most practical radios for most paddlers, and while not waterproof themselves can be purchased with a special waterproof bag that enables you to operate the radio while it is sealed inside. I highly recommend them.

The important thing is to be visible and to be honest with yourself at all times. A brightly colored PFD, a brightly colored kayak paddle, reflective tape, and signal/light equipment greatly increase your chances of being spotted if you get into trouble. Acknowledge and respond to your body's signals. If you're the least bit hungry, eat. If you're a little chilled, put on an extra piece of water-resistant clothing. Don't get cocky and neglect to use your basic equipment. And above all, let your fellow paddlers know you're hungry, cold, or feeling spacey or dizzy. Sea kayaking is more fun, and safe, when we're honest with ourselves, when we help each other, and when we ask for help without embarrassment.

〰 Planning a Day or Overnight Paddle

Some people like to plan a paddle down to the last stroke. Others I know like to plan the basics but are flexible about other possibilities, from bailout points to surprise snacks. So here's a list for basics planning that can amended to suit your needs.

Bays and Inland Waters

Check equipment.

Check tidelog/tide table.

Check current table.

Check route plan against nautical chart for rips, tide flats, time and distance, etc.

Check weather conditions.

Meet before launch to jointly assess weather conditions and to determine whether group skills confidently surpass maximum expected conditions; review communications signals, trip plan, bailout points, how close together to paddle, and other expectations/concerns/medical preconditions/learning skills; assign leader/sweep.

Check kayak rental/supplier resources.

Check lunch/grog/dinner landing site for group availability.

Check nearest location of emergency resources.

Check transportation route.

Discuss carpooling.

Agree on snacks/meals/drinks to share.

Provide personal emergency contacts and let them know in advance when you'll return, giving them launch site, shuttle takeout, and plan of route.

Hold camper pretrip meeting if you're camping.

Check camping checklist if you're camping.

Leave note in car detailing trip plan and emergency numbers so search team can start looking in the right area.

Check with local paddlers about your destination, conditions, skill level required, and route.

Rough-Water Bays and Open Coast

The above plus:

Determine pretrip scouting route.

Obtain advice from kayakers who have recently paddled this trip, with key factors addressed: currents, eddies, swells, tide rips, whirlpools, fog, winds, traffic, shoals, landing/launching in surf, bailout points, storm conditions, submerged rocks or pilings, marine life dangers.

Check bailout points thoroughly for access in various weather conditions.

Establish criteria for selecting trip guide.

⁌ Tides and Tidal Currents

There are two high tides and two low tides every day. The extremes of high and low are separated by just over six hours. What does that mean for us paddlers? When we paddle in bays, rivers, and sloughs affected by tides, we can use tidal currents to our advantage. But we must also watch out for the hazards they create. *Current velocity* is related to the *tidal range*—the height difference between high and low tide—as well as to the contour of the land near and over which the water is moving. The flow direction of a tidal current depends on whether the current is *flooding* (coming in) or *ebbing* (going out); and the current's strength or speed is related to this ongoing tidal exchange.

If you look at a tidelog, you'll see a graphic representation of the tidal movement and current speed. Where such graphs are not available, you can get the times and levels of high and low tide from tide tables, many of which give not only the times and levels of the tides but also provide tables of ebb and flood currents. These "current tables" predict the time of *slack tide*—when there is no significant tidal current at a given location—as well as the velocity of the maximum ebb and flood currents. It is a common mistake to assume that the current goes slack at the same time that the tide hits its high or low; in fact, slack can occur hours after the high or low tide. In short, to predict the time of slack, you need to use current tables—not tide tables. Unless you will be paddling the eddies near shore, plan to use the direction of tidal flow to your advantage, both going to your destination and returning. Don't paddle into the current unless you have to. Plan your paddle to coincide most efficiently with the changes in tidal currents.

The strength of the tidal flow, and thus the strength of the currents, changes over the course of a tidal cycle. In his book *The Fundamentals of Kayak Navigation*, David Burch describes the change in tidal currents using the "Rule of 12ths":

> The first hour volume is 1/12th of tidal water flow.
> The second hour volume is 2/12ths of tidal water flow.
> The third hour volume is 3/12ths of tidal water flow.
> The fourth hour volume is 3/12ths of tidal water flow.
> The fifth hour volume is 2/12ths of tidal water flow.
> The sixth hour volume is 1/12th of tidal water flow.

When trip planning, you can use the currents associated with the ebb and flood to your advantage. For example, you can start in slack and return with the ebb or flood current, whichever moves with you on your return. Or you can launch as ebb or flood begins, whichever is moving against your destination, and return in full ebb or flood. Another option is to start by paddling the nearshore eddies, going against the direction of the main current, and then use that current on your return. Currents, by the way, are described according to the direction in which they are moving, or *setting*. Winds, on the other hand, are described according to the direction from which they are blowing.

Tidelogs, and the tide tables on which they are based, are not perfect—nor are current tables. Use them as guides for trip planning, but while on a trip, *read the water* and make your own observations. In the back of the tidelog is information that will enable you to adjust the data to your specific trip location. Likewise, the data in tide and current tables are for a central geographic points of tidal exchange; for all other locations, the timing and other aspects of the tides and currents need to be adjusted by factors listed in the "Tidal Differences" and "Current Differences" tables. Also, remember that weather conditions, especially wind velocity, affect the flow of ebb and flood currents, and the stage of the tide. For example, the ebb current may start earlier in a bay because of a strong offshore wind.

Tides can have a remarkable effect on shallow bays and estuaries, with the low tide exposing large areas of the bottom. These places, called *tidal flats*, are a good reason to invest in nautical charts, which show the depth of the water. If a particular passage along your route is a concern, plan to cover it when the current flow will most likely be in the same direction as the wind, and with enough water—at least 2 feet—to paddle efficiently.

⟨⟨⟨ Currents

Rough-water conditions are created by swells, currents, wind, and the shape of the sea floor. In Northern California bays, strong currents can produce areas of turbulence, such as tide rips, eddylines, whirlpools, and boils.

Tide rips occur where water flow is constricted as a result of dramatic topographic changes, or where two currents collide. Sometimes the more extreme tide rips are labeled on nautical charts. Although most tide rips can be negotiated by skilled paddlers, the conservative strategy is to avoid such areas or time your trip to traverse them during slack. If you have developed good paddling skills and know how to keep your boat stable through tide rips, just keep a sharp eye out for them, and determine in advance which ones look too challenging. In calm weather, tide rips are noisy and appear as dark patches on the surface. Try to spot or listen for a "river-rapids" sound. They can also produce foam or appear as an isolated area of whitecaps. In windy weather, choppy water camouflages rips, so study your charts ahead of time. If you do get caught in a rip, paddle in the direction the current is flowing. Keep a fast, short paddle brace cadence through the rip, keeping your boat stable, and it will carry you out the other side.

Eddylines occur where the current either reverses direction or makes an abrupt change in speed. They can be a sharply defined line, but often they are a broad zone of boils and swirls of water moving in different directions. The abrupt and turbulent flows of water within eddy boundaries make them likely places to capsize. Eddylines, which can vary from a few feet to miles in length, develop when flowing water is unable to follow a sharp turn in the shoreline. The water flow then breaks off and continues straight downstream, leaving an eddy of still water. Some of this "separated" water is pulled away by the nearby flow, creating a low-pressure area. To fill in the low area, water flows upstream inside the eddy, causing a *reverse eddy*, or *backeddy*.

When traveling opposite the main current, use eddies to your advantage by finding the eddyline and paddling inside it. When you reach the beginning of the backeddy, you will have to sprint around the point until you reach the next backeddy. This technique is called *eddy hopping*. When crossing the eddyline and entering the main current, keep your bow pointed nearly upstream. Lean and brace on the downstream side until you've caught your balance in the new current. Put your paddling energy into moving upstream; once you're past the point and into the next eddy you can rest until you need to hop around the next point. Eddy hopping builds skill in maintaining a specific direction, strengthens your overall paddling skills, and lets you rest between brief periods of strong, active paddling.

Whirlpools are sometimes found along strong eddylines. If you find yourself in a whirlpool you didn't see or couldn't avoid, be ready to do several quick braces blended with turning strokes to help the whirlpool spin you around. Go with the flow; don't fight it. Do not leave your paddle deep in the water; the changing current may cause you to "trip" over it. Keep paddling with the flow until the whirlpool dissipates farther down the eddyline.

When water moves in different directions along an underwater shelf, it can appear as a *boil*—a dome-shaped upwelling that can stretch several feet over the surrounding surface. They are more frequent in the summer along the Northern California coast, when deep currents flow to the surface. Boils are less common than eddylines and whirlpools, and unlike these phenomena, boils are unpredictable; there's no general rule to tell you which way to lean and brace. When your boat enters a boil, keep your balance by reacting to the tipping forces with short, choppy, bracing strokes.

A strong wind will often interfere with your ability to use currents efficiently, particularly when it blows opposite the current. This creates hazardous situations that you should avoid if you can. For example, a paddler may experience *yaw*, or the action of moving sideways. Or beam waves (waves that hit parallel to the boat) can make a kayak less stable. At a minimum, a paddler can expect bow or stern waves if the wind blows opposite the direction in which the current is moving. Because wind direction and velocity shift quickly, especially when the air pressure is changing—as it does in afternoon fog—it is reasonable to expect several combinations of these effects to occur at once. Be prepared to wait until the wind or current slows down or switches direction. Use the current tables to predict the direction of the main current and when it will change. Before you launch, watch the water and look for clues to the direction of the current. While paddling, watch the surface conditions carefully for the rips, eddylines, whirlpools, and boils mentioned above so you can anticipate when and where the current changes direction and speed. By doing this you can avoid getting caught in opposing wind and current.

))))) Weather Conditions

Northern California is a jigsaw puzzle of microclimates, both overland and at sea, and the weather is changeable from hour to hour. I often start paddling on a cold, foggy day on smooth seas, continue through a bright, windy afternoon, and return in calm winds and hot sunshine—all in the same day. In Northern California's bays, the climate can differ wildly even over short distances. Here, kayakers are advised, "If you don't like the weather, paddle a few miles."

Storms usually occur from November through April. Storms from the south or southwest are usually wet and rainy; those from the north or northwest are usually cold, windy, and dry. Both can produce dangerous kayaking conditions. Be aware, too, that storms in the Gulf of Alaska or off Baja can send huge swells to the Northern California coast. The local weather may be clear and calm as 20-foot waves pound the beaches. If you plan a coastal camping trip, note weather conditions far out in the Pacific that can send big swells your way days after a storm. Strong offshore winds occur in September and October, with hot Santa Ana winds blowing out to sea.

Summer conditions in bays along the coast often include strong winds. Typical summer weather is the result of static high pressure off the coast, protecting us from storms but producing wet coastal fog.

Paddlers new to kayaking in Northern California are often surprised to find the wind blowing in their faces, or at their backs, both going to and coming from a destination on a given day. Get used to it. Along the California coast, morning offshore winds typically reverse by afternoon; you can experience a headwind or a tailwind both ways. And because bays, river mouths, sloughs, and other open-water mouths to the coast cut through the lowest point of a coastal mountain range, paddlers are right in the middle of a dynamic exchange of wind, fog, and pressure. This is the price of beauty.

When a typical storm front comes through, the south wind comes first. The wind then turns and comes from north or east, and finally from the northwest. Fronts signal temperature changes—hotter or colder. When you see and feel a south wind, it means a front is coming through and probably the weather will get bad. It may rain, and high winds are in the offing. Even safe beaches can get dangerous.

Inland valleys also affect bay paddling. Here's why: Pressure zones constantly displace other pressure zones. You can think of a pressure zone as a big sucking sound, or wind. As hot air rises in the valleys (the hotter the air, the lighter the pressure zone, which causes the hot air to rise), the heavier, colder air pushes in to replace it. So, as the coastal fog bank gets warm during the morning, it rises and moves off-coast, thus making the coast "clear of fog." The fog pushes back along the coast in the midafternoons, bringing moisture and heavier, colder air, and stronger winds along the bays.

Learn to recognize the different types of fog and their portents. High night fog, called *radiation fog*, occurs when the sky is clear, the winds are light, and the humidity is high. In Northern California, radiation fog occurs mostly in the northern bay and delta areas, usually during the winter. This fog doesn't occur over open water.

Tule fog is low-lying fog, most common over marshes and bays. It is thickest in the morning and usually dissipates during the day, although in the Central Valley at some times of year it can persist for days or even weeks at a time. Because it's so low to the ground and often very thick, tule fog makes for tricky and sometimes dangerous paddling—poor visibility makes it hard to see and be seen. Stay off the water if you can.

Advection fog forms day or night when warm air blows over cold water. This is the most common fog in the summer along the open coast. It often blows off by late morning, at least near shore, but can persist for days or weeks. Advection fog was responsible for Mark Twain's observation that the coldest winter he'd ever experienced was a summer in San Francisco.

Get to know the clouds and the direction of the winds that move them. When winds are from the southeast and thin cirrus clouds fill the skies, expect a wet frontal system. Bank on it if the barometric pressure falls and the wind

Northern California Weather Tips

◆ If the wind is blowing or gusty in the morning, chances are the conditions will get worse during the day.

◆ A typical summer day along the coast starts with a calm morning and a low overcast, and becomes clear and windy in the afternoon. The wind usually dies after sunset.

◆ If the wind is blowing from the south, the weather will usually deteriorate, and rain is possible. The back side of the pressure front is usually colder and windier than the leading edge.

◆ Listen to the weather radio the night before and the morning of your trip. Never assume that the NOAA forecasts are completely reliable; they are a reliable source of general weather information for your area.

increases. These winds can blow up to 70 miles per hour (mph). If a southwest wind turns around to the northwest, expect a cold, dry storm from Alaska.

Get to know the location of the display flags for weather advisories. Most bays in the region have facilities for posting flags for small-craft advisories. Detailed information on weather conditions can be obtained by tuning into National Weather Radio at local frequencies, or by consulting the nearest mariner resource listed in the trip description. Get a weather radio and listen to it periodically throughout the day. Understand how to interpret the buoy reports and weather forecasts. Following is a list of weather resources:

1) National Oceanic & Atmospheric Administration (NOAA), National Weather Service Forecasts at 162.40, 162.475, and 162.55 MHz can be received 20 to 40 miles from antenna sites. Reception is usually best when you have a direct line of sight to the antenna. This is a pain for the region's kayakers, whose line of sight is so often blocked by coastal cliffs. There are local antenna sites at:

   Redwood City VHF-FM KHB-49, 162.55 MHz
   Monterey 162.40 MHz
   Pt. Arena 162.40 MHz

2) Telephone—prerecorded updated weather conditions

   San Francisco (650) 364-7974 (24 hours)
   Eureka (707) 443-7062 (prerecorded messages); 443-6484 (leave messages on voice mail or speak directly with NOAA staff)
   Santa Maria (805) 925-0246, 6:00 A.M. to 3:00 P.M. weekdays

3) Call local resources, such as harbormasters or marinas, in advance to check out what the conditions are. Also, just before your trip, spend a few minutes on shore to observe conditions for yourself.

Storm Advisory Flags

Storm advisory flags are frequently posted throughout the year in the bays. Those you'll most commonly see on these Northern California trips are *small-craft advisories*, signaled by one red flag during the day. The night signal is two lights, a red light above a white one. Small-craft advisories warn small boats, including kayaks, not to go out, and that winds can be up to 38 mph.

A daytime *gale warning* is marked by two red flags, and its night signal is two lights, a white one above a red one. Gales warnings are for winds from 39 to 54 mph.

A daytime *storm warning* is marked by a square red flag with a black square in its center. The night signal is two lights, both red. Storm warnings alert boaters to winds from 65 to 73 mph.

A daytime *hurricane warning* is signaled by two red flags with black squares in the center of each flag. The night signal is three lights: top red, middle white, bottom red. A hurricane warning is for winds above 74 mph.

Coast Guard stations and many marinas no longer display storm advisory flags, but they are still sometimes displayed at park ranger stations and municipal piers.

Other Flags

Another flag that conveys important information is a red square flag on a motorboat, which tells you that a water-skier is in the area. The skier may be in the water, or a ski line is being extended in the water, or a skier is getting ready to ski.

A red flag with a diagonal white stripe signifies that a diver is in the water. In either case, avoid paddling close to an area where such a flag is flying.

〰〰 Navigation

Kayaks are unique boats: They are very sensitive to wind and surface conditions, they are relatively slow moving, and they can be difficult for other boaters to see. Navigational planning is perhaps even more important for kayaks than for larger boats because kayaks are more dramatically affected by surface conditions. Steep, choppy, 3-foot waves are an annoyance to a 30-foot sailboat but a major navigational factor to a kayak. A 2-knot tidal current can be all but ignored by a powerboat moving at 25 knots, but it may double or halt the progress of a kayak, or carry it 2 miles sideways during a one-hour crossing. Good navigation skills can help a paddler predict the best conditions and times for efficient and safe paddling, and ensure a safe and timely arrival at the desired destination.

For inshore navigation, buy an up-to-date nautical chart with a scale of 1 inch or so per nautical mile. The commonly used chart scale of 1:80,000, for example, shows 1.1 nautical miles per inch. Charts showing smaller areas in greater detail (for example, NOAA's 1:40,000 scale coastal charts, which show about 0.55 nautical mile per inch) are ideal for planning but best left at home, since you don't want to have to pack several charts for a single trip. Check out all the pertinent charts at the store before you buy, looking at the level of detail. For example, are their symbols for dangerous objects (like rocks and shoals) clear and unambiguous?

A simple way to estimate the distance of a trip is by using string and a nautical chart. You'll be better off, however, with a pair of dividers. These enable you to read chart distances without relying on gross estimates. As you "walk" the dividers between two points, you count the number of steps and convert them to nautical miles using the scale on the chart. For the purposes of beginning and most intermediate trips listed here, a navigational chart, tide and current tables, and dividers or string will give you plenty of information for planning your trip.

Because currents affect the speed and direction of your boat, to make sure you get where you want to go you'll need to estimate your *ferry angle*, or the angle at which you will head to ensure that you reach your destination (see accompanying illustration). I recommend the method described by David Burch in *Fundamentals of Kayak Navigation*. If the current is at a right angle to your course, then use the following calculation:

$$\text{ferry angle} = \frac{\text{current speed} \times 60 \text{ degrees}}{\text{paddling speed}}$$

For currents at a 45-degree angle to your bow or stern, simply multiply by 40 degrees instead of 60 degrees.

You'll find *current speeds* (measured in knots, or nautical miles per hour) and directions listed in the current tables for the general areas and times you are paddling. If your launch point differs from the main locations listed in the tables, you will have to make some adjustments to find the current speed and direction at your exact location. You can do this by looking up the main location nearest your launch point. Then flip to the back of the book for tables of differences that will enable you to calculate the necessary adjustments for your specific location. The annual publication, *Tidelog Northern California*, published by Pacific Publishers, is a good source. These tables are readily found in most marine stores.

Once you've determined the current speed, you'll need to determine your paddling speed. *Paddling speed* averages 2 knots for beginners and 3 knots for intermediate paddlers. (Paddling speed is actually determined by the efficiency of your stroke and to a lesser extent by muscle power, boat design, and wind and current speed. You can test your paddling speed with a watch in a preset nautical mile.) With this information in hand, you can solve the equation and find your ferry angle.

Another way to find a ferry angle is by using *vectors*, lines that represent the speed and direction of your boat and the current. In all, you will draw three lines. First draw one line that represents the direction from your launch site toward your destination (course made good). Its length doesn't matter. Now draw

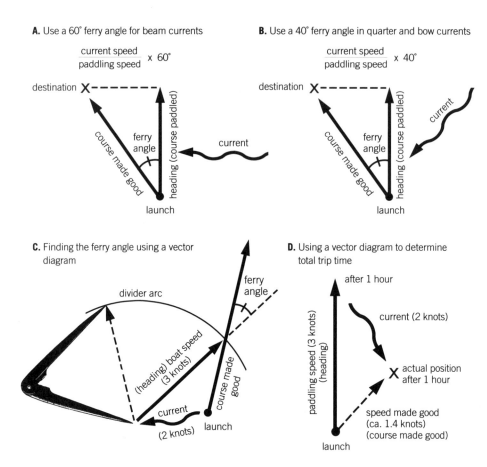

A. Use a 60° ferry angle for beam currents

$$\frac{\text{current speed}}{\text{paddling speed}} \times 60°$$

destination **X**- - - - - - -

course made good

course paddled (heading)

ferry angle

current

launch

B. Use a 40° ferry angle in quarter and bow currents

$$\frac{\text{current speed}}{\text{paddling speed}} \times 40°$$

destination **X**- - - - - -

course made good

heading (course paddled)

ferry angle

current

launch

C. Finding the ferry angle using a vector diagram

divider arc

ferry angle

(heading) boat speed (3 knots)

course made good

current (2 knots)

launch

D. Using a vector diagram to determine total trip time

after 1 hour

current (2 knots)

paddling speed (3 knots) (heading)

X actual position after 1 hour

speed made good (ca. 1.4 knots) (course made good)

launch

a second line from the launch site that represents the current speed and direction. If the current speed is, say, 2 knots, draw a line 2 units long in the appropriate direction. (Choose any convenient unit of length, so long as you are consistent throughout the diagram.) Now set your dividers to a length proportional to your boat speed. If your speed is 3 knots, for example, the divider tips should be open to 1.5 times the length of the current line. Place one divider tip on the end of the current line, and swing the dividers until the other tip intersects the line representing your course made good. The resultant vector is the bearing you need to follow, and its angle with the course made good is your ferry angle (see part C of the accompanying illustration).

You can also determine your ferry angle by taking a compass bearing to a landmark in the direction of your course. The *heading* is the direction your boat is pointed, and the *course made good* is the direction you want to go.

Your best bearing aids for inshore navigation are landmarks near your destination, such as the northern end of a windswept beach, the tree on top of a hill, a house on a headland, etc. If you can hold the compass bearing to the landmark fairly constant, your ferry angle is correct. If the bearing to the landmark changes, then you need to adjust your ferry angle accordingly. Despite your best attempts to maintain your ferry angle, it may alter due to changes in the speed of the current, wind pockets, or other weather and surface conditions. Although a compass bearing to a single landmark will work, the job is easier when you can line up two objects on land near your destination—say, a smokestack behind a prominent bluff. This becomes your *range*, and the bluff and smokestack are your *range marks*. By watching your range marks and compensating for any change, you can judge how far off your course line you are being pushed. When your ferry angle is correct, the landmarks will stay aligned (i.e., the smokestack will stay behind the bluff).

If you want to determine how long it will take you to reach your destination, you can apply this formula:

$$\text{time (hours)} = \frac{\text{distance traveled (nautical miles)}}{\text{boat speed (knots)}}$$

As mentioned earlier, you determine the *distance traveled* ("course made good") using your dividers and the chart, measuring in a straight line from your launch point directly to your destination. *Boat speed* is a combination of your paddling speed and the current speed. When the currently is directly behind or in front of you, you can determine your boat speed quite easily: *Add* the speed of the current to your paddling speed if you are going with the current; *subtract* the speed of the current from your paddling speed if you are going against the current. Knowing both boat speed and distance you can solve the equation.

If the current is running at an angle to your course, however, finding your boat speed and solving for time traveled is no longer a simple matter of addition and subtraction. But vector diagrams provide a fairly simple method of calculating total travel time in these instances (see illustration D). Draw a line from your launch point in the direction of your destination. As you did when solving for the ferry angle, divide the line into units representing your paddling speed (for example, 3 knots or 3 units). This is where you would be after 1 hour if there were no current. From that position, draw a second line representing the current direction and speed, again making the line the appropriate number of units (for example, 2 knots or 2 units). This is your actual position after 1 hour, taking the current into account. Now draw a third line from your launch site so that it intersects with the current line. Using dividers, determine how long the third line is (in our example, it represents roughly 1.4 knots). This amount is your speed made good, or your actual boat speed through the water. Divide the total trip miles (say, 4 nm) by your boat speed to find the number of hours it will take to reach your destination (4 nautical miles ÷ 1.4 knots = 2.9 hours; convert .9 hours to minutes for ease of use).

Kayak navigation is part science, part intuition. When you have paddled long enough, judging your boat speed and using charts and dividers will become second nature. Learn how to use a compass, and how to check the reading. Local classes, kayak navigation books, and practice will be helpful in refining your navigational skills.

Buoys, Lights, and Markers

Buoys and signal lights should be marked on any nautical map you use for trip planning. *Buoys* mark safe lanes in which to cross bays and open water. Buoys that mark channel boundaries are red on one side of a channel and green or black on the other side. Vessels traveling toward inland water should pass the red buoys on their right side (and therefore should pass green or black buoys on their left). When headed toward sea, the opposite is true. A popular mnemonic for remembering this rule is: "red right returning, green going to sea." This rule is particularly valuable for kayakers, because large vessels closely watch these buoys and will generally see you if you stay close to them. Kayakers can predict how large vessels will approach a buoy and can maneuver in advance to keep clear of them. Buoys are also marked by numbers; usually, the farther inland you go, the higher the numbers on the red buoys.

Buoys with red-and-white vertical stripes mark safe water areas for big ships with deep drafts, the midchannel, or indicate that you are approaching a crossing. Buoys that are red *and* green mark the junction of two channels. If the buoy is mostly red except for a green horizontal band in the middle, it means boats expecting a red buoy on that side of their channel are using the preferred channel, while boats expecting a green buoy along that side are in a secondary channel. Yellow buoys indicate a traffic separation, anchorage area, on-going dredging, or fishnets in the area. *Marker buoys* are white and orange, with a signifying word, such as "dam" or other special advisories, written in the center. *Mooring buoys* are white with a horizontal blue stripe, and indicate where boats can be moored.

Markers appear on posts and come in a variety of shapes. The shape, as with traffic signs, reveals the danger. The orange-and-white diamond-shaped signs with an orange cross in their center tell boats to keep out—due to a dam, rapids, or a swimming area. Orange-bordered diamond-shaped signs with a white center indicate a rock, shoal, dam, or such. The word inside the orange border explains the nature of the danger. A circular sign with an orange border indicates a controlled-use area—for example, No Ski or 5 MPH. A rectangular sign with orange boarders and writing inside it displays official information, such as a first-aid station, distance, or locations.

Rules of the Road

Before you paddle where there will be other boat or ship traffic, make sure you know the basic rules of the road. These rules, established by tradition and by legal conventions, govern the behavior of different types of watercraft when the course of one vessel threatens to interfere with the progress of another. The Rules of the Road are essential to boating safety.

Under the California Uniform State Waterway Marking System, buoys, lights, signals, crossing rules, and other aids provide a simple system for safe passage for all boaters. Get a copy of *The ABCs of California Boating Law*, a free publication by the State of California Department of Boating and Waterways. All harbormasters and public marinas, as well as most boating supply stores, carry this short book.

The basic rule for kayakers is easy: Our boats are the smallest and most maneuverable of vessels, and the most difficult to see. *To be safe, yield to all other vessels.* Big ships, like freighters and tankers, move very fast and require several miles to stop. It's madness to cross in front of such large vessels. Give them a wide berth and allow them the right of way.

Crossing rules. When crossing a channel, navigation signals consist of a system of horn blasts. Paddlers not carrying a horn can still cross safely if they know the system. For maximum visibility and safety when crossing, do it as a group instead of stringing out across the channel. When a boat and a kayaker meet, kayakers do not have the right of way. Big boats, especially, often won't see you and may have a difficult time turning or slowing down quickly when they do see you.

When a boat meets a kayaker head on, or bow to bow, it may sound one, two, or three short blasts. One short blast means that the boat intends to cross by you on their port (left) side. Two short blasts mean it will cross by you on its starboard (right) side. Three short blasts mean it is "operating astern propulsion"; its engines are in reverse gear. If you hear a short blast from behind you, a boat is passing you on your port side. If you hear a two short blasts from behind you, a boat is passing you on your starboard side.

))))) Marine Pollution

Under California's Marine Pollution Regulations, the U.S. Coast Guard prohibits dumping of plastic refuse, garbage mixed with plastic, packing materials or linings that float, metals, and any other garbage except dishwater/graywater or fresh fish parts into any lakes, rivers, bays, and sounds within 3 miles of shore.

In recent years, a great deal of needed attention has been focused on the problems caused by human-made debris in the marine environment. Such debris seriously threatens both public health and the habitat of many marine species.

What can you do to help clean up our water and our shores? For one thing, if you pack it in, pack it out, including everything biodegradable. And get involved. When you paddle, pick up trash left behind by others and bring a camera to document polluters. A list of marine wildlife, adopt-a-beach, municipal, and nonprofit agencies that accept pollution reports appears in Part 3 of this book.

))))) The Sum of It Is to Enjoy the Parts of It

Learning in increments is fun and valuable. You will remember the skills you learn, and with the mastery of each new skill you'll get that well-deserved boost of self-confidence that comes with tangible accomplishment. Keep taking classes in surf skills, rolls, bracing, paddle strokes, rough-water rescues, first aid, trip planning, and navigation. Get involved in the kayak clubs in your area. Chances are you'll get more actively involved in the sport, meet great paddling friends, and maybe volunteer to help preserve our wetlands and coastline. Environmental groups need kayaking volunteers to report environmental trouble, and groups that work with physically challenged adults and children through kayaking need help too. Volunteer work from a kayak may be the most rewarding accomplishment of all.

Part 2
The Trips

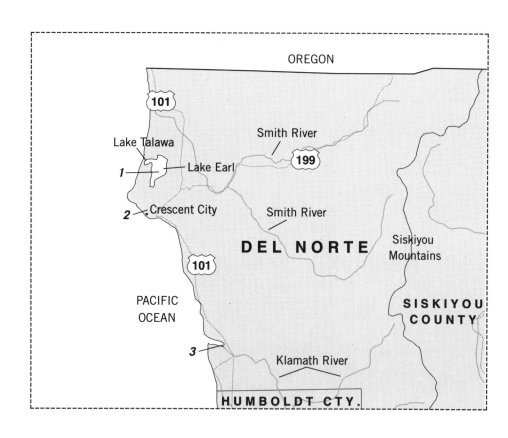

OREGON

101

Lake Talawa

Smith River

199

1 — Lake Earl

2 — Crescent City

Smith River

DEL NORTE

Siskiyou
Mountains

101

PACIFIC
OCEAN

SISKIYOU
COUNTY

3

Klamath River

HUMBOLDT CTY.

Del Norte County

1. Lake Earl to Lake Talawa

2. Crescent City Harbor to Whaler Island

3. Klamath River Estuary: Tour of Redwood Regional Park

Lake Earl to Lake Talawa

Launch site 1, p. 22

Preferred NOAA Chart: 18603, "Crescent City" (subsection of NOAA chart 18600, "Trinidad Head to Cape Blanco")

Estimated Paddle Time: 2 hours

Trip Rating: SK 1

Special Hazards: Afternoon wind

Launch Site: A dirt ramp, on the east side of the end of Lake View Road. There are signs along the road and good parking next to the ramp. Bring an extra set of shoes, since the launch and return can be muddy. Other public launch sites are located in the Pacific Shores subdivision south of Kellogg Road but are hard to find; ask locally for directions. Managed by Jedediah Smith Redwoods State Park (707-464-6101).

Nearest Campsite: Prairie Creek State Park is 5 miles southeast of Lake Earl, off US 101, near Crescent City (707-464-6101, ext. 5301).

Best Paddle Time/Tide: Morning to early afternoon. Not tide dependent.

Practically no one paddles here, but it's a kayaker's paradise. Lakes Earl and Talawa, freshwater lagoons that encompass more than 2,000 acres, are ideal for beginning paddlers. Motorboats are prohibited in these connecting lakes, whose depths range from 6 to 20 feet. You can paddle directly from Lake Earl to Lake Talawa through the connecting 18-foot channel known as The Narrows. Paddling along the edge of Lake Earl is in itself an entire day trip. Unfortunately, in summer most of Lake Earl's surface is covered by sago pondweed, making paddling unenjoyable.

Lake Earl can get foggy and windy, and it's best to paddle with little or no wind to avoid a fierce chop in the shallow lagoon bed. If you have no choice but to paddle in less than ideal conditions, this can be a good place for learning to paddle in wind and fog without much danger of capsize.

This is a true bird-watcher's and photographer's paddle. Surrounded by an ancient dune that offers a rich habitat for a variety of wildlife, the lagoons are major stopover points along the Pacific Flyway. If you paddle in spring or late fall, you'll see thousands of Aleutian geese, peregrine falcons, brown pelicans, and bald eagles—more than 250 species of birds have been sighted here. Lake Earl supports the highest wintering population of canvasback ducks north of San Francisco.

When the pounding Pacific occasionally breaches the sand dunes and floods the coastal lagoon, the resulting nutrient-rich water supports the dense vegetation attractive to the thousands of migratory waterfowl. Lake Earl, fed by Jordan Creek, is mostly freshwater, while Lake Talawa is mostly saline. The creek is a spawning ground for salmon, steelhead, and sea-run cutthroat trout.

Stop and see the rangers at the Department of Fish and Game for the day's forecast and local tips (2591 Old Mill Road in Crescent City, 3½ miles south of your launch site; 707-464-2523, but the rangers are not always in). Their headquarters feature a nature walk and access to other hiking trails. Picnic along the shore or in the nearby picnic area. You'll find more hiking opportunities in the Lake Earl Wildlife Area, which includes sand dunes, ponds, wetlands, and meadows. The Lake Earl Project lands are managed by the adjacent Jedediah Smith Redwoods State Park.

Crescent City Harbor to Whaler Island

Launch site 2, p. 22

Preferred NOAA Chart: 18603, "Crescent City" (subsection of NOAA chart 18600, "Trinidad Head to Cape Blanco")
Estimated Paddle Time: 3 hours
Trip Rating: SK 2
Special Hazards: Afternoon wind
Launch Site: This is a small ramp in Crescent City Harbor, on Anchor Street. Parking and launching from this site are easy. For information call the Chart Room Marina (707-464-5993), which privately maintains the ramp. Although kayaks can usually be launched for free, be prepared to pay the standard $5 fee in the event their policy changes. Observe launch etiquette and avoid the ramp on First Street.
Nearest Campsite: Jedediah Smith Redwoods State Park at 241 Kings Valley Road is 4 miles east of Crescent City off US 101. Call 707-464-6101.
Best Paddle Time/Tide: Morning to early afternoon. Begin at high tide or slack and return with flood—the launch ramp can get muddy.

Paddling Crescent City Harbor gives you a rare glimpse of one of California's last small commercial fishing communities, offering a noisy display of busy freighters loading lumber onto the docks, a small commercial fishing fleet, and a Coast Guard station. Harbor paddling has its own etiquette; as you launch, be mindful of commercial traffic. Stay out of their way and wait your turn, especially during summer weekends.

The harbor is often foggy or windy, so be prepared for a stiff chop. Fortunately, this is probably the safest harbor for boat traffic along the north coast. The harbor facilities were rebuilt in 1987 after tsunami waves generated by an Alaskan earthquake destroyed much of the waterfront and the central business community. The new harbor is well protected by large rock jetties reinforced by 1,600 25-ton concrete tetrapods. One tetrapod is on display on US 101, just south of Front Street. All the restaurants in the harbor are kayaker friendly.

Paddling south of the breakwater, which is called Whaler Island, at the south end of the harbor and along the beach offers you one of the safest areas on the Northern California coast to practice wave-bracing skills. Bracing makes for a much safer and more interesting paddle, and it's important to learn bracing technique before you learn how to roll. Practice moderate bracing in the small waves closest to the breakwater. As you move 50 yards southward, you'll be challenged by gradually larger waves, particularly when there is a north swell.

Klamath River Estuary: Tour of Redwood National Park

Launch site 3, p.22

Preferred NOAA Chart: 18600, "Trinidad Head to Cape Blanco"
Estimated Paddle Time: 4 hours
Trip Rating: SK 1
Special Hazards: Neglecting to make reservations with Redwood National Park; see below
Launch Site: To reach this boat ramp in the Klamath River Estuary, follow signs from US 101 to the Requa Inn, on Requa Road. At the Requa Inn turn left onto Mouth of the Klamath Road and follow it to the end. This trip, sponsored by Redwood National Park and the Yurok tribe, is a bargain at $40 per person. This fee includes kayak, paddle, helmet, PFD, skirt, paddling lesson, and a guide. Because the launch access is owned by the Yurok, who use it for hunting and fishing, this trip can be done only through Redwood National Park/Yurok tours. For more information and to make reservations, call Redwood National Park (707-822-7611, ext. 5267).
Nearest Campsite: Redwood National Park is 5 miles north of the Klamath River Estuary. Call 707-464-6101.
Best Paddle Time/Tide: Ranger-led tour schedule. Tide dependent.

This four-hour beginner's flatwater tour, intrepidly led by rangers, focuses on the natural and cultural history of the Klamath. Paddlers will see seals and sea lions, otters, beavers, ospreys, and bald eagles. Yurok Indians still fish for salmon along the riverbanks and hold traditional ceremonies. The Klamath has the largest salmon and steelhead trout runs in California. The river and estuary also support flounder, lamprey, bass, and prickly sculpin. Dungeness crabs are found near the river mouth. The exposed tidelands of the estuary are feeding areas for large numbers of shorebirds and ducks. Sea lions and harbor seals haul out on the larger offshore rocks just north of the river.

In 1852, 2,500 Yurok Indians lived along the Klamath River, subsisting largely on acorns and fish and living in redwood plank houses. By 1855 many Yurok were forced to relocate to a reservation, and later were again removed, this time to the Hoopa Valley Indian Reservation in Humboldt County. The mouth of the Klamath has seen many settlers and industries come and go—fur trading, gold mining, and salmon canneries. Yet today the estuary's first residents—the Yurok—still live and work at the mouth of the Klamath.

On this tour, Redwood National Park and the Yurok tribe offer paddlers a unique opportunity to experience the natural and cultural richness of the Klamath River.

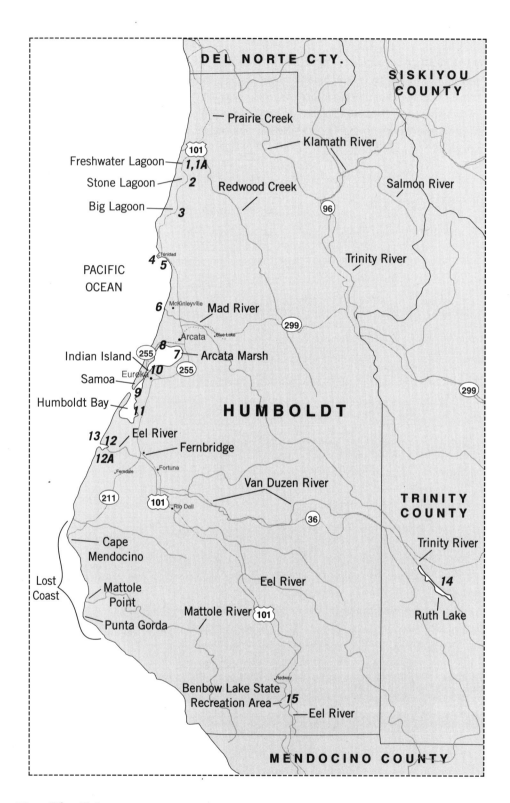

DEL NORTE CTY.

SISKIYOU
COUNTY

Prairie Creek

Klamath River

Freshwater Lagoon — **1,1A**
Stone Lagoon — **2**
Big Lagoon — **3**

Redwood Creek

Salmon River

101

96

PACIFIC
OCEAN

4 **5** Trinidad

Trinity River

6 McKinleyville
Mad River

Arcata Blue Lake

299

Indian Island 255 **8**
7 Arcata Marsh

Samoa **10** 255
Eureka

9

299

Humboldt Bay
11

HUMBOLDT

13 **12** Eel River
12A Fernbridge
Ferndale Fortuna

Van Duzen River

211
101 Rio Dell

36

TRINITY
COUNTY

Cape
Mendocino

Trinity River

Lost
Coast

Mattole
Point

Eel River

14

Punta Gorda

Mattole River 101

Ruth Lake

Redway

Benbow Lake State
Recreation Area **15**
Eel River

MENDOCINO COUNTY

Humboldt County

1. Freshwater Lagoon

2. Stone Lagoon

3. Big Lagoon

4. Surfing and Paddling the Rock Gardens North of Trinidad

5. Indian Beach to Moonstone Beach

6. Mad River Beach

7. Arcata Marsh and Wildlife Sanctuary (Arcata Bay)

8. Samoa Boulevard up Mad River Slough or across to Arcata Marsh

9. North Spit Beach up the Samoa Channel to Indian Island

10. Destinations from the Boat Ramp at the Eureka–Woodley Island Bridge

11. Buhne Drive Beach to Fields Landing Boat Ramp

12. Mouth of the Eel River at Cock Robin Island Road

13. Mouth of the Eel River to Historic Fernbridge

14. Ruth Lake (Trinity County)

15. Benbow Lake State Recreation Area (Eel River)

A Note about Humboldt County Paddling

Even on warm spring days, bring a windbreaker. To avoid strong winds, be out of the water by noon or go for evening or night paddles after the wind has died. Tides significantly affect water depth in Humboldt Bay and along river mouths—high-tide paddles are best for Humboldt Bay, the Eel and Mad River mouths, and all sloughs. Pick up a local tide book in one of the area's many fishing tackle stores.

It's best to lock up your valuables, even your car racks.

Freshwater Lagoon

Launch site 1, p. 28

Preferred NOAA Chart: 18600, "Trinidad Head to Cape Blanco"
Estimated Paddle Time: 1 hour
Trip Rating: SK 1
Special Hazards: None
Launch Site: Dirt ramp. From Eureka, drive 34 miles north on US 101 until you see a sign for Freshwater Lagoon. The sign will direct you to an unidentified road on the east side of US 101. Follow the directions and proceed down this road to the parking lot and launch site at the north end of the lagoon. About 34 miles north of Eureka is a second launch site right on US 101, also at the north end of the lagoon. *(1A)* Redwoods National Park manages Freshwater Lagoon (707-464-6101, ext. 5265).
Nearest Campsite: Patrick's Point State Park (707-677-3570)
Best Paddle Time/Tide: Morning and afternoon. Not tide dependent.

An easy, one-hour paddle, this trip can be combined with picnics, surf fishing, or camping on the west side of the highway. And in this small, quiet lagoon, beginners needn't worry about chop. Freshwater Lagoon was sealed off from the ocean in the 1950s by the construction of US 101. On the south side, the land surrounding the lagoon is wooded and private. The shallow and reedy south end is a good place to observe migratory birds. Most of the lagoon shoreline, which is private property, is exposed grass fields.

Don't paddle here in summer, when RV campers, motorboat enthusiasts, and jet-skiers populate this area. The lagoon floor is rocky, so be sure to wear booties or tennis shoes.

Stone Lagoon

Launch site 2, p. 28

Preferred NOAA Chart: 18600, "Trinidad Head to Cape Blanco"
Estimated Paddle Time: 3 hours
Trip Rating: SK 1
Special Hazards: Moderate afternoon winds; small chop
Launch Site: This dirt ramp is about 50 yards north of the visitor center at the south end of Stone Lagoon Beach. About 32 miles north of Eureka on US 101, Stone Lagoon also has a bank from which you can launch next to the highway, adjacent to the Stone Lagoon Park office. Managed by Humboldt Lagoons State Park (707-488-2041).
Nearest Campsite: Humboldt Lagoons State Park (707-488-2041) is 7 miles south of Stone Lagoon.
Best Paddle Time/Tide: Morning and afternoon. Not tide dependent.

Stone Lagoon is a lovely, quiet beginner's paddle. Here you can spend time at the visitor center to learn about the role of wetlands in the environment and then coast in to one of the many beautiful sand beaches and have a picnic. The lagoon is very wooded, with a thin sandy shoreline frequented by browsing Roosevelt elk. (Remember to enjoy elk and bear from a distance.) It's a great place to observe migratory birds and shorebirds as well.

If the wind picks up, the water can get a little choppy, but not seriously so. Motorboats aren't common here, but in the fog, listen for them.

During summer, the mouth of Stone Lagoon is separated from the ocean by a sandspit—its own beach. In the spring, however, the lagoon breaches, and a high, fast volume of freshwater rushes into the ocean. Keep your eye out for this rush of water, and be very careful not to get too close to the lagoon mouth at this time of year. When the lagoon mouth is open to the ocean, there's a stiff chop. Usually, though, you'll be paddling with the wind—coming from the ocean—while the freshwater currents are streaming out to the mouth.

The lagoon mouth is especially suited for developing paddling skills in wind and small to moderate chop, and for brushing up on bracing skills, when the lagoon is closed to the ocean in summer.

When the sandspit separating the 521-acre lagoon from the ocean is breached, allowing a tremendous influx of salt water, anadromous fish such as silver salmon, steelhead, coastal cutthroat trout, and Pacific lamprey enter the lagoon to spawn in McDonald's Creek, the lagoon's perennial tributary.

As you paddle, you can see and feel how the water turns brackish. In healthy lagoons like this one, where teeming life is hidden, the mixture of salt- and freshwater contains minute plankton and algae. The algae growing in the warm shallows feed the tiny animal plankton, which in turn nourish snails, clams, and crabs that eventually support fish and waterfowl. As plants and animals decay, nutrients are recycled in the soupy water. For many fish, lagoon water is a shelter between oxygen-rich stream and nutrient-rich ocean, a place where their bodies adapt to the mix of fresh and salty waters. Hidden in the mud are burrowing shellfish, gobies, and ghost shrimp. If pollution and land-fills are allowed to destroy coastal marshes, the wealth of lagoon life will dis-appear, as land and ocean animals that depend on the lagoon will have no place to go.

Bordered by forest, a sandspit, and a barely visible highway, Stone Lagoon is the most pristine of the three local lagoons. Like Big Lagoon (the next trip), this body of water is well suited for first-timers, kids, and families. If you paddle southwest, there's a small peninsula, called Ryan's Cove, complete with picnic tables, well-maintained hiking trails, and campsites. It's a beautiful little area for picnics and botany buffs. It's also a good place for a night paddle. At the south-eastern corner of the lagoon is a small creek, where, after paddling a few hun-dred yards, you'll be surrounded by tall green reeds—a great photographic site. Here, Stone Lagoon's plant life far outshines its birdlife.

A campground is situated on the north shore of the lagoon, and environ-mental campsites are accessible by boat from the east shore, where the visitor center is located.

Big Lagoon

Launch site 3, p. 28

Preferred NOAA Chart: 18600, "Trinidad Head to Cape Blanco"
Estimated Paddle Time: 3 hours
Trip Rating: SK 1
Special Hazards: Moderate afternoon winds
Launch Site: This boat ramp is in Big Lagoon County Park off Big Lagoon Beach Road in a parking lot off A Street. Parking costs $2 per day (707-445-7651).
Nearest Campsite: Patrick's Point State Park (707-677-3570). For natural history information, call Harry A. Merlo State Recreation Area (707-445-6547).
Best Paddle Time/Tide: Morning and afternoon. Not tide dependent.

Big Lagoon offers a variety of beginning paddling adventures and conditions. To develop your bracing and paddling skills, move toward the mouth of the la-goon. The north side of the lagoon actually has no mouth, but the portage over to the ocean, which I don't recommend because of the heavy surf, is about 10 feet. Beginners who want to gain experience kayaking against a freshwater cur-rent should paddle through the marsh to Maple Creek. For intermediate pad-dling in freshwater current, paddle up to the north part of Big Lagoon, where you'll face wind and chop along the side facing the ocean. These excursions offer a variety of challenges and a chance to improve and review the skills required for paddling in stream currents and for bracing when wind and chop prevail.

For a quiet, calm paddle, seek out the southern part of the lagoon and also the marsh. This is an especially pretty trip that features an incredible display of endangered and migratory birds. Roosevelt elk also frequent the marsh.

Big Lagoon offers what many consider the North Coast's easiest paddling; everyone feels safe here. This large lagoon is bordered by a sandspit, forest, and the highway. If you travel east toward the highway, you can go under the road and follow the feeder creeks upstream. Elk have been sighted here, too. Since this area is normally calm, it's a good place to practice exit/reentry and rolling skills. Note also that the ocean is a very short walk over the sandspit on the western border of the lagoon.

Wildlife is not spectacular here, and when the wind kicks up in the afternoon, it simply takes the fun out of paddling. The eastern section of Big Lagoon is a popular recreational area, so watch out for boatloads of yahoos who may have a few beers in their bellies; keep your ears open in foggy conditions.

Big Lagoon's long, sandy barrier beach is part of Humboldt Lagoons State Park. The lagoon's wooded eastern shore and extensive salt marsh comprise Harry A. Merlo State Recreation Area. Four Yurok fishing villages existed on the eastern shore, and currently a rancheria occupies the south end.

Big Lagoon's barrier beach is breached often, and its brackish waters support a large marsh community of tule and saltgrass where Maple and Tom Creeks enter the lagoon.

A variety of coastal strand communities inhabit the wetland borders of the north and south sides of the lagoon. Fir and redwood grow on the eastern and northern shores. Some 30 species of fish inhabit the lagoon, including salmon, trout, starry flounder, and crab. Black-tailed deer, black bears, and Roosevelt elk live in the nearby marshlands and uplands.

Surfing and Paddling the Rock Gardens North of Trinidad

Launch site 4, p. 28

Preferred NOAA Chart: 18605, "Trinidad Head" (subsection of NOAA chart 18600, "Trinidad Head to Cape Blanco"
Estimated Paddle Time: 4 hours
Trip Rating: SK 4
Special Hazards: Sneaker waves; sharks (Note: A sneaker wave is an unforeseen wave with a height of 4 feet or more that a paddler does not see coming. These unpredictable waves can be very dangerous and are more common in coastal areas that feature shallow shelves.)

Launch Site: Beach launch. Go north of Trinidad Harbor about 1.5 miles on US 101 and launch on the northern end of College Cove Beach. Trinidad Harbor (707-677-3625).

Nearest Campsite: Patrick's Point State Park, 5 miles north of Trinidad on US 101 (707-677-3570).

Best Paddle Time/Tide: Morning and early afternoon. Begin at high tide or slack and return with flood.

Due to large swells and standing water, capsizing is a real possibility in this area. There's not much to cling to if you capsize, and getting back into your boat and bailing it out could be very difficult . . . and it's a long, cold swim back to the pier. These conditions make this an advanced paddle for kayakers with a reliable roll. Wear a full wet suit or a dry suit to conserve body heat in the event of a capsize. It's best to travel this area with a partner, and bring a flare gun. Be prepared to launch into the surf, keeping mindful of submerged rocks.

This is a truly beautiful cove. You start by going north around Trinidad Head. Stay well away from the rocks when going around Trinidad Head, and note that a sea lion colony just northwest of the head is known to be frequented by great white sharks, whose presence provides additional incentive for local paddlers to perfect their rolls.

Between 1920 and 1926, Trinidad Harbor operated as a whaling station. Now its bays are fished commercially for Dungeness crab and salmon. On 362-foot-high Trinidad Head is a cross that has replaced the one Spanish explorers put up in 1775. Prisoner Rock, one of the larger rocks in the harbor, was so named during the Gold Rush because drunken citizens were deposited there and left overnight. Local historian Ned Simmons at Trinidad Art also reports that Trinidad Head served as a Yurok Indian shelter when tribes from the Bald Hills staged raids on Yurok villages. Pelagic cormorants, pigeon guillemots, and Leach's storm petrels nest on the headlands and rocks.

You can picnic in Moonstone County Park or eat at the Seascape Restaurant in Trinidad Harbor.

Indian Beach to Moonstone Beach

Launch site 5, p. 28

Preferred NOAA Chart: 18605, "Trinidad Head" (subsection of NOAA chart 18600, "Trinidad Head to Cape Blanco")

Estimated Paddle Time: 4–5 hours

Trip Rating: SK 2

Special Hazards: Afternoon winds; submerged rocks; commercial fishing boat traffic; sharks

Launch Site: The beach launch at Indian Beach is in a cove that protects the area from heavy surf. From US 101 in Trinidad, head south on Trinity Street to Edwards Street, south of Trinity Head. There is a small, unmarked road west off Edwards Street, just south of the Seascape Restaurant, that takes you down to the beach for your launch. There is free street parking above the beach, so set your kayak down at the beach first and then park. There is nearby parking for $2 at Bob's Boat Ramp next to the Seascape Restaurant. Trinidad Harbor (707-677-3625).

Nearest Campsite: Patrick's Point State Park is 6 miles north of Little Trinidad Head (707-677-3570).

Best Paddle Time/Tide: Morning to early afternoon. Not tide dependent.

The locals love this stretch of water so much, they call it Lake Pacific. There is rarely enough swell to make paddling in this sheltered cove dangerous. If you kayak along Indian Beach, you can poke around the rocks safely. This is an excellent area to prepare for advanced kayaking around rock gardens. This intermediate paddle runs south 1½ miles to Moonstone Beach and back. The entire journey is flat and protected. Don't go farther south than Moonstone County Park, however; the ocean shelf gets ragged and you'll get into rough water with strong river currents, especially around the mouth of Little River at the southern end of the park.

Conditions at Indian Beach are ideal for beginners. The water is nearly always calm with very little swell. Rock promontories are numerous in this region, and you'll see birds and seals at play here. Please note that this bay is a permanent home to harbor seals; getting too close to them disrupts their feeding, nursing, and digestion. If your presence scares them off the rocks or even makes them turn their heads, you're much too close (marine law dictates that you always stay at least 100 yards from marine wildlife). Here you can also see river otters, an occasional dolphin, puffins, oystercatchers, and sometimes California gray whales. Less than 1½ miles south of the pier is Baker Beach, which has a safe landing area at the north end. Nude sunbathers are common here. Information on the harbor's natural and anthropological history can be found at the Humboldt State University Marine Lab and Trinidad Art, across the street from The Eatery in Trinidad.

Be careful not to go over submerged rocks, which can force you into a balancing act if you're left on top of one when the water surges out. Also, it's best to be out of the water before noon, when the wind whips out of the north. Fortunately, it usually dies around sunset. Keep in mind that seals and sea lions can become aggressive when they're intruded upon, and that great white sharks frequent the area. They haven't hurt anyone, but a kayaker was knocked out of his boat by an aggressively curious shark. Be mindful of fishing boats.

Mad River Beach

Launch site 6, p. 28

Preferred NOAA Chart: 18622, "Humboldt Bay" (subsection of NOAA chart 18620, "Point Arena to Trinidad Head")
Estimated Paddle Time: 3 hours
Trip Rating: SK 1
Special Hazards: Rolling lumber and dislodged branches
Launch Site: To reach this boat ramp, from US 101 north at McKinleyville turn west on Janes Road, then make a sharp right on Janes North Road, then left on Iversen Road and continue until it dead ends at Mad River Road. Turn right on Mad River Road and follow the signs to Mad River Beach County Park and the boat ramp. Managed by the Department of Public Works (707-445-7651).
Nearest Campsite: Clam Beach County Park (707-445-7652), 5 miles north of Mad River Beach County Park.
Best Paddle Time/Tide: Morning and afternoon, in flood.

With virtually no current, these waters are ideal for beginners. Because tides are extreme here, however, be sure to put in when the water level is 5 feet or more above mean tide; otherwise, you'll bottom out in several places. If you head upriver, you'll see many beaver-nibbled trees (and many beavers, too, if you paddle at dusk). Hundreds of migratory waterfowl and shorebirds use the Mad River estuary, and snowy plovers can be seen south of the river mouth. You might spot Aleutian geese, bald eagles, and American prairie falcons in the area. You'll also encounter old bridge pilings, and automobiles that were used as levee fill.

If you head downriver, look for nesting owls in the large holes on the sides of the cliffs. Eventually you'll reach the mouth of the Mad, where the river spills into the ocean. Paddling this extra distance is well worth the extra 2 or 2½ hours (round trip). At the river mouth is a small group of resident seals. Please give them plenty of room. Playing in the waves at the mouth of the river is relatively safe—the water is shallow and the bottom sandy—but wear a helmet.

Common sense tells us to stay out of the river at flood stage. In the mouth, watch for "rolling" trees that can grab your life jacket and pull you under. Stay close to shore at the river mouth until you get a feel for the strength of the flow. If you plan to paddle to the mouth, remember to bring a pair of gloves to prevent blistering and plenty of water.

A Paddler's Introduction to Humboldt Bay

Humboldt Bay is probably the North Coast's most underrated paddling area. It's booming with birdlife in its many wildlife refuges and very rich in history. A good local map shows which areas of the bay are accessible. Paddling is best early in the morning and at moderate to high tides. All of the Humboldt Bay trips are beginner trips, with the exception of paddles around the jetty, which are intermediate excursions.

Little leopard sharks come into the bay to mate in spring. When the water is glassy, you can see their dorsal fins. As the tide goes out, they get trapped in pools, which makes finding a mate easy.

When paddling in the bay, keep in mind that it's subject to tidal changes in water depth. Low tide can leave you stuck in soft, deep mud. If this happens, straddle your kayak with your legs while resting on the cockpit, then use your hands to pull yourself across the mud to the nearest channel. Plan your trip so you're heading south by noon, when that north wind begins to blow. Wear shoes or booties in the bay to guard against submerged sharp objects, and watch out for boats.

Be careful around the jetty. The entire bay empties out through the narrow channel here, and the current can exhaust even a strong paddler. Fishing boats, recreational boats, and oil tankers use the channel, so it can be extremely crowded. And there can be unexpected breakers. The channel is dangerous enough that I prefer to avoid it entirely, except perhaps on a calm, clear day.

Arcata Bay (called Arcata Marsh and Wildlife Sanctuary on some maps and in the trip descriptions below) is the large northern arm of Humboldt Bay, encompassing 8,000 acres. Most of the former marshland surrounding the bay has been diked for dairy production. Nonetheless, these farmed wetlands host a rich variety of habitat for herons, egrets, and waterfowl. The bay's last remaining salt marsh, preserved by the Humboldt Bay National Wildlife Refuge, supports many endangered plants and birds. The bay's extensive intertidal mudflats also host thousands of shorebirds and waterfowl. Cormorants nest on the old Arcata Wharf pilings. Salmon and trout spawn in Jacoby Creek, one of the many creeks that provide riparian habitat for waterfowl, raptors, and river otters. Half of California's commercial oyster production takes place here in the cultured trays located in the mudflats in Mad River Slough.

Arcata Marsh and Wildlife Sanctuary (Arcata Bay)

Launch site 7, p. 28

Preferred NOAA Chart: 18622 "Humboldt Bay" (subsection of NOAA chart 18620, "Point Arena to Trinidad Head")
Estimated Paddle Time: 2 hours
Trip Rating: SK 1
Special Hazards: Afternoon winds
Launch Site: This paved boat ramp is off the end of "I" Street in Arcata. From Eureka, drive north on US 101 7 miles to Arcata. Turn east onto CA 255, or Samoa Boulevard, and make a left onto "I" Street. Follow the signs on

"I" Street for 1 mile. You'll find parking and a dock here, too. The boat launch is managed by City of Arcata Public Works. Nearby Humboldt Bay National Wildlife Refuge can be reached at 707-733-5406. For birdlife information, call the local Audubon Society chapter at 707-822-8542.

Nearest Campsite: Eureka KOA is 5 miles south of Arcata (707-822-4243).

Best Paddle Time/Tide: Calm mornings in mid- to high flood (+3 feet or higher). Combine the paddle with a trail hike.

Check in advance with the refuge manager to coordinate your launch in slack and your return in high tide. You definitely want to return before ebb tide. Humboldt Bay can get rough quickly, especially in winter and spring. The bay gets treacherous in prevailing southeast or northwest winds.

Paddling the 2-mile stretch of wetland in the Arcata Marsh and Wildlife Sanctuary offers a glimpse of one of the major stopover points along the Pacific Flyway. Arcata Marsh is home to more than 200 bird species, including 80 kinds of waterbirds and 4 endangered species. Habitat in Humboldt Bay is extremely diverse. In Arcata Marsh, the northernmost section of the bay, you'll be paddling in mudflats, eelgrass beds, seasonal wetlands, sandspits, and freshwater marsh.

The Arcata Marsh and Wildlife Sanctuary was created in 1979 when the City of Arcata restored 65 acres of sewage-degraded salt marsh. The city built three freshwater marshes and a lake, planted coastal strand communities, and stocked the lake with trout. The City also runs a highly successful salmon ranching project at the nearby wastewater treatment plant. Juvenile salmon are stocked in the plant's oxidation ponds in a nutrient-rich mixture of treated wastewater and bay water.

The marsh provides the only shoreline access in Arcata. Facilities include a picnic area and hiking trails. The local Audubon Society leads nature walks through the marsh each Saturday.

Samoa Boulevard up Mad River Slough or across to Arcata Marsh

Launch site 8, p. 28

Preferred NOAA Chart: 18622, "Humboldt Bay" (subsection of NOAA chart 18620, "Point Arena to Trinidad Head")

Estimated Paddle Time: 3 hours (for each trip)

Trip Rating: SK 2

Special Hazards: Morning and afternoon winds; mud

Launch Site: This boat ramp is off the Samoa Boulevard (CA 255) bridge after you pass over Mad River Slough. Park on the roadside; this is an easy carry down either side of bridge. Near Humboldt Bay National Wildlife Refuge (707-733-5406).

Nearest Campsite: Samoa Boat Launch County Park is adjacent to the Samoa Boulevard boat ramp (707-445-7652).

Best Paddle Time/Tide: Calm mornings in beginning high tide or slack; return in flood.

These are both easy, quiet-water, beginner paddles with plenty of picnic areas along the way. Like virtually all paddling in Humboldt Bay, these trips are best done during calm, windless mornings in slack tide or beginning flood tide, returning in flood tide.

If you paddle north up Mad River Slough, you'll see not only a sample of Humboldt Bay's extraordinary birdlife, but also river otters and beavers. About 1½ miles into your journey, the river divides. If you paddle up the left channel, you'll end up in a farmer's backyard. The channel to the right is the correct one; it leads you to where the slough was cut off from the rest of the Mad River in the 1950s because of sedimentation in Humboldt Bay.

Paddling east from the Samoa Boulevard bridge to the south end of Arcata Marsh provides plenty of paddling through a variety of wetlands. This trip also takes 3 hours (5 miles round trip). With no marked destination point in the marsh, beginners can paddle alongshore for about 2 miles and return. If intermediate paddlers wish to cross the bay, conditions must be calm and the trip should start in the early morning to ensure a calm return; gusty winds start in late morning and increase in the afternoon. Combine afternoon winds with low tide, and the paddle is not enjoyable.

Both trips are great for bird-watching.

North Spit Beach up the Samoa Channel to Indian Island

Launch site 9, p. 28

Preferred NOAA Chart: 18622, "Humboldt Bay" (subsection of NOAA chart 18620, "Point Arena to Trinidad Head")

Estimated Paddle Time: 4 hours

Trip Rating: SK 2

Special Hazards: Rips; afternoon wind

Launch Site: This is an easy beach launch. From US 101 in Eureka, drive west on CA 255 across Humboldt Bay to the Samoa Peninsula. Turn left on New Navy Base Road. Launch from the smooth sandy beach just north of the Coast Guard station (707-443-2213).

Nearest Campsite: Samoa Boat Launch County Park is adjacent to the North Spit beach launch (707-445-7652). To visit the Samoa Cookhouse Museum, call 707-442-1659.

Best Paddle Time/Tide: Calm mornings in beginning high tide or slack; return in flood.

Launching from the beach offers gentler wave action for this intermediate paddle than the tidal actions at the Samoa County Park boat launches. Paddle with the outgoing low/slack tide out the bay mouth. Then head along the north side of the channel to avoid breaking waves. This area is full of seals, sea lions, river otters, and sea birds. You can picnic on Indian Island. Return the same way, on the incoming high tide.

As you would expect when paddling from a bay mouth to the ocean, there is a moderate tide rip. To paddle in the gentler rips, use the north side of the spit for your entry and return from the ocean coasting.

Portions of the 10-mile spit separating Arcata Bay from the ocean have been industrialized for more than a hundred years. Lumber processing facilities and shipping dock construction established the towns of Manila, Samoa, and Fairhaven. At the north end of the Samoa Peninsula Sand Dunes, the Nature Conservancy's Lanphere-Christensen Dune Preserve protects 213 acres of extraordinary undisturbed dunes, some as tall as 80 feet, as well as 125 acres of pristine salt marsh. If you don't want to picnic on Indian Island, Manila Community Park (at Peninsula Drive and Victor Boulevard) provides picnic areas. The Samoa Cookhouse, a former logging cookhouse, serves family-style meals and hosts a logging museum.

Indian Island is a low marsh island. The Wiyot Indians occupied two fishing villages here, and shell mounds dating back 1,500 years have been discovered on the island. The island is the largest single area of salt marsh in Humboldt Bay, and part of the Humboldt Bay National Wildlife Refuge. It supports the northernmost coastal rookery of the American egret. Great blue herons, Virginia rails, and black-shouldered kites can also be seen here.

Destinations from the Boat Ramp at the Eureka –Woodley Island Bridge

Launch site 10, p. 28

Preferred NOAA Chart: 18622, "Humboldt Bay" (subsection of NOAA chart 18620, "Point Arena to Trinidad Head")
Estimated Paddle Time: 5 hours
Trip Rating: SK 2
Special Hazards: Afternoon winds; mud; leisure boats
Launch Site: There are two boat ramps off Waterfront Drive before you cross from Eureka to Woodley Island on CA 255. Going north on US 101 to Eureka, turn left at "L" Street in Eureka, then turn right at Waterfront Drive. The ramps are just under the beginning of the Eureka–Woodley Island Bridge. Samoa launch facilities include parking, rest rooms, and a picnic area.
Nearest Campsite: Samoa Boat Launch County Park (707-445-7652).

Best Paddle Time/Tide: Calm mornings in beginning high tide; return in flood.

I like to paddle east up Eureka Slough and into Freshwater Slough, or west to downtown Eureka; the parking is easy and there are lots of bailout areas in either direction if the winds suddenly pick up and the water gets choppy during this beginner/intermediate paddle.

Check the tide tables. If you want to paddle from the launch site to Eureka Slough or Freshwater Slough, paddle early in the morning with the flood. You can easily pass along the slough islands and discover some of the small finger channels around 7th Street that connect with the channel.

It's a nice paddle to downtown Eureka. Head west 1 mile along the Eureka shore to the Eureka Fishing Boat Basins on Waterfront Drive. You can dock your boat easily at the boat basins or use the boat ramp located there. It's a lovely spot for a picnic, or you can eat at one of the marina restaurants.

Eureka Slough is an intricate lacework of tidal channels and creeks meandering through pastures and marshes. While the wetlands have been diked for pasture, sloughs still support an enormous amount of salt- and freshwater marsh habitat used by birds, seals, and otters. Freshwater Slough is a restored salt marsh in which you'll see water birds, raptures, and songbirds, as well as seals and otters.

You can also dock at the end of the marina on Woodley Island and follow the trail to the wildlife reserve or have lunch at the marina. The area around the island can get congested with leisure and commercial boats.

Buhne Drive Beach to Fields Landing Boat Ramp

Launch site 11, p. 28

Preferred NOAA Chart: 18622, "Humboldt Bay" (subsection of NOAA chart 18620, "Point Arena to Trinidad Head")

Estimated Paddle Time: 3 hours

Trip Rating: SK 2

Special Hazards: Afternoon winds

Launch Site: This is an easy beach launch, but you have to carry your boat over a few rocks. Take US 101 south 3 miles from Eureka to King Salmon Drive. Turn west on King Salmon Drive and follow it around the shore, where it becomes Buhne Drive. Park and launch at the end of Buhne Drive.

Nearest Campsite: Samoa Boat Launch County Park is 2 miles west of the Fields Landing boat ramp (707-445-7652). To visit the Samoa Cookhouse Museum, call 707-442-1659.

Best Paddle Time/Tide: Calm mornings to early afternoons in beginning high tide or slack; return in flood.

This is a beautiful beginner's paddle in and around King Salmon. Kayaking these protected beaches is fun, but be sure to return before ebb, when the mud is exposed. Paddle out the channel and south, following the cove immediately on your left. The cove extends three-quarters of a mile before it opens back to Humboldt Bay. Along the paddle to Fields Landing you'll see a large population of Pacific black brant and many ducks. You can dock at the ramp at Fields Landing, have a nice picnic in the grassy park, and paddle back up to King Salmon.

Like most of Humboldt Bay, this area is subject to rapidly changing winds, so be sure to bail out at one of the beaches along the way if it gets too choppy. Fields Landing has a lot of recreational boat traffic—be careful here and stay away from the docked ships. Fields Landing is a very popular freshwater fishing slough, with salmon being a favorite quarry.

An active shipping port, Fields Landing channel is dredged regularly. Plan ahead for this paddle and return during high tide to work through the shallow slough easily. Paddle another 1½ miles south to the large mouth of Hookton Slough (kayaking from King Salmon to Hookton Slough takes 4 hours round trip), which supports a number of herons, egrets, shorebirds, and ducks. Here you'll paddle through shallow water and along overgrown banks. The mudflats along the slough are major harbor seal haulout areas, and the intertidal zone is both a buffet and a nursery for shorebirds. In the spring, thousands of black brant can be seen here.

Over the years, as the marshlands were diked, the seasonally changing water table could no longer replenish the original wetlands, which became dry and undernourished. Their dry ground made them more susceptible to erosion by wave action. A small community living near Buhne Point restored this marshland by constructing a breakwater. Picnic areas are available here.

Mouth of the Eel River at Cock Robin Island Road

Launch site 12, p. 28

Preferred NOAA Chart: 18620, "Point Arena to Trinidad Head"
Estimated Paddle Time: 4 hours
Trip Rating: SK 2
Special Hazards: Afternoon winds
Launch Site: To get to this dirt bank launch, go 2 miles south of Eureka on US 101, take Hookton Road off the exit ramp, and go south to Eel River Drive. Take Eel River Drive to a right on Cannibal Road, and then left on Cock Robin Island Road. Before you reach the bridge, you'll see a dirt pull-out area on your right—this is the launch site. You can park right there. (Note: Locals warn that cars are sometimes broken into here.) There is an alternate launch site with parking at the end of Cannibal Road. *(12A)*

Nearest Campsite: Eureka KOA is 2 miles north of the mouth of the Eel River (707-822-4243).

Best Paddle Time/Tide: Calm mornings and early afternoons, with flood tide at 5 feet or higher.

This is a safe and accessible beginner's paddle in midflood. With the ocean just downstream, however, be mindful of the tide; a 5-foot or higher tide will slow the rate of river current flow, making the paddle back upstream easier.

Paddle across the Eel River to Cock Robin Island. Follow Cock Robin Island along the shore west less than a mile to the western tip of Cock Robin Island at the mouth of the Eel River. Along the way, marine life abounds, including seals, sea lions, and shorebirds. Before you arrive at the mouth, in about 30 minutes, your nose will tell you that you're about to encounter the area's largest herd of harbor seals. Keep at least 50 feet between you and the seals. You can picnic upriver at the Cock Robin side of the Cock Robin Island bridge, across from your launch site, or farther east—a half-mile upriver to the eastern tip of Cock Robin Island—which also offers a place to picnic.

If you use the alternate launch site *(12A)* from Cock Robin Island, paddle east up the channel to the eastern tip of the island, where there are nice places to picnic. Along the channel, you'll see a diverse array of marine life and migratory birdlife as well. As you paddle up the channel, the water gets shallower and warm, which makes this a good area for practicing group rescue skills.

No matter where you launch from, if you paddle to the mouth, it's best to be conservative as you approach the ocean. Hug the shoreline; if the water flows more quickly than you're comfortable with, you'll be easily able to land on shore. Be especially careful when approaching the mouth, where current and floating trees are a dangerous combination. Stay out during high water, because you'll need to paddle back upstream.

Mouth of the Eel River to Historic Fernbridge

Launch site 13, p. 28

Preferred NOAA Chart: 18620, "Point Arena to Trinidad Head"

Estimated Paddle Time: 3 hours (one way)

Trip Rating: SK 1

Special Hazards: Mild afternoon winds

Launch Site: This boat ramp is at the end of Cannibal Road in Crab County Park in Loleta. Call the Humboldt County Parks Department in Eureka (707-445-7651). Take US 101 to Loleta, which is 17 miles south of Eureka. Turn west on Eel River Road. Follow Eel River Road for 2 miles and turn west on Cannibal Road. Follow Cannibal Road to the

Crab County Park. Follow the road into the park, to the dead end. Park there and launch your kayak from the boat ramp.

Nearest Campsite: Johnny's Marina and RV Park, 3.5 miles south of Eureka on US 101 (707-442-2284).

Best Paddle Time/Tide: Calm mornings in flood

This is a lovely beginner's paddle. Head east from your launch at the mouth of the Eel toward historic Fernbridge. This 7-mile, 3-hour one-way trip is best done on calm mornings with the high tide. Follow the meandering salt marshes where the Eel River, McNulty Slough, and the lower Salt River converge. The Eel River Delta provides essential habitat for birds migrating along the Pacific Flyway. Wildlife you should look for here include tundra swans, ospreys, hawks, kestrels, and threatened peregrine falcons. Stop at the boat launch in Fernbridge, have lunch, and wander through this pretty, artistic town for the afternoon. For an interesting cultural history of the area, check out the Fernbridge Museum at 3rd Street and Shaw (707-786-4466).

Ruth Lake (Trinity County)

Launch site 14, p. 28

Estimated Paddle Time: 2 hours

Trip Rating: SK 1

Special Hazards: Afternoon winds

Launch Site: Ruth Lake Public Marina (707-574-6524) public boat ramp. From the town of Mad River on CA 36, drive 13 miles southeast on Lower Mad River Road. Parking is next to the public boat ramp.

Nearest Campsite: Bailey Canyon State Park at the Mad River Ranger Station (707-574-6233).

Best Paddle Time/Tide: Mornings and afternoons. Not tide dependent.

Ruth Lake is wonderful for day picnics, fishing, and paddling. It's little used, and the marina has plenty of supplies and groceries. When the lagoons and channels are treacherous, Ruth Lake is the place to go. Migratory birds prefer Ruth and Benbow Lakes before they make their official Pacific Flyway stop at Lake Earl. There are lots of bailout areas on the east bank, with several campgrounds.

Benbow Lake State Recreation Area (Eel River)

Launch site 15, p. 28

Estimated Paddle Time: 2 hours

Trip Rating: SK 2

Special Hazards: This is a summer paddle only.

Launch Site: Use the boat ramp at Benbow Lake State Recreation Area (707-923-1380). From Garberville, drive 2 miles south on US 101. Turn west at Benbow Lake State Recreation Area and follow the road to the boat ramp. The launch is just inside Benbow Lake State Recreation Area, adjacent to the parking lot and day-use area.

Nearest Campsite: Benbow Lake State Recreation Area (707-923-3238).

Best Paddle Time/Tide: Summer mornings and afternoons. Not tide dependent.

An arm of the Eel River, Benbow is seasonal—usually after Memorial Day Weekend, a dam is put up and creates this little lake. It's ideal for beginners: no motorized boats are allowed; temperatures are quite warm; and the lake doesn't get much wind. Practice your stroke and rescues here. The lake is long and narrow, covering 230 acres.

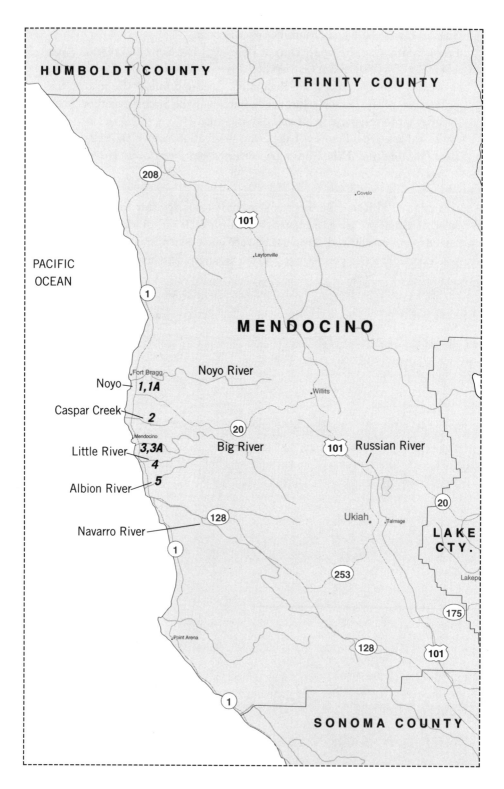

Mendocino County

1. Noyo Bay and Harbor

2. Caspar Creek to Caspar Headlands State Beach
   and Reserve

3. Big River

4. Van Damme State Park: Rock Gardens and Caves

5. Albion Flat

Noyo Bay and Harbor

Launch site 1, p. 46

Preferred NOAA Chart: 18626, "Elk to Fort Bragg"
Estimated Paddle Time: 2 hours (Noyo Harbor)
Estimated Paddle Time: 3 hours (Noyo Bay)
Trip Rating: SK 2
Special Hazards: Leisure boats; choppy, shallow channel with boat traffic from harbor mouth to cove
Launch Site: There are two public boat access sites in Noyo on CA 1:
1. A boat ramp off CA 1, off North Harbor Drive. Follow North Harbor Drive to the end of Basin Street. At crossroads of Basin Street and South Harbor Drive, on the left is Noyo Fishing Access (watch for sign on left) and a concrete boat ramp with adequate parking.
2. Easy beach access to Noyo Cove off CA 1. Follow North Harbor Drive to the end of the parking lot past the CA 1 bridge underpass. Portage your kayak about 50 feet over small rocks to an easy beach launch. Noyo Harbor information (707-964-4719). Near Jug Handle State Reserve (707-964-4630). *(1A)*
Nearest Campsite: Russian Gulch State Park is 2 miles north on CA 1, call Mendocino County Regional State Parks (707-937-5804).
Best Paddle Time/Tide: Morning and early afternoon in beginning low tide or slack; return in ebb.

The Noyo River stretches 4 miles upstream from the harbor. Paddling upriver offers a glimpse of what life in one of California's last working fishing towns is really like. Today it is the most important fishing port in Mendocino County, well known for its sole, Pacific cod, and salmon. Noyo is named after No-you-bida, the Pomo Indian village at the mouth of the river.

The tidally influenced Noyo puts out a moderate current and is a good paddle for beginners and intermediates. The best time to paddle is morning, to avoid the strong winds that often occur in the afternoon. Beware of foggy conditions and fishing boat traffic, and be mindful of the tides so you don't get stranded upstream while you're having lunch.

You won't see as much forest as you do on Big River; the Noyo River environment is mostly village scenery. The harbor, where whales are occasionally spotted, is especially scenic and historic. There are excellent restaurants and smoked salmon houses, and the harbor is a fine place to trade with a fisherman for fresh salmon.

Don't go under the CA 1 overpass; the currents get tricky in the channel. Additionally, this channel is used mainly by large commercial fishing vessels. Paddling through this narrow ship channel past the harbor to open ocean is definitely not recommended. If you want to go to the cove, begin from the beach launch.

Paddling Noyo Cove from the beach launch, Noyo's second public access, is a perfect cove paddle for intermediate kayakers. The headlands standing on each side of the Noyo are less than a quarter mile apart but provide a small and safe area to poke around the cliffs and rocks. The cove is a fantastic whale-watching area, and otters, seals, and kelp beds near the rocks offer views of marine life. Don't paddle close to the river mouth where the rock jetty forms a retaining wall for the dangerous channel—you'll get swept in. Since the beach is so close, it's easy to return for a picnic or delicious lunch in the harbor. Sneaker waves (waves 4 feet high or higher that a paddler doesn't see coming; they are typically unpredictable, can be very dangerous, and are more common in coastal areas that feature shallow shelves) do occasionally enter the cove, so always check behind and all around you as you paddle.

Use and develop your bracing and balancing skills in the wind chop on sunny days here. Be sure to check your safety level at the beginning of your paddle. A good bailout point is adjacent to the boat ramp.

Caspar Creek to Caspar Headlands State Beach and Reserve

Launch site 2, p. 46

Preferred NOAA Chart: 18628, "Elk to Fort Bragg" (subsection of NOAA chart 18626, "Elk to Fort Bragg")

Estimated Paddle Time: 1 hour

Trip Rating: SK 2

Special Hazards: Afternoon winds; stay away from backwash chop near headlands

Launch Site: This bank launch is before the mouth of Caspar Creek. Take CA 1 for 5 miles south of Noyo Bay, turn west on Caspar Creek Road and follow it to the end—at the mouth of Caspar Creek. Roadside parking. Caspar Headlands State Beach and Reserve (707-937-5804).

Nearest Campsite: Russian Gulch State Park is 3 miles south of Caspar Creek, call Mendocino County Regional State Parks (707-937-5804).

Best Paddle Time/Tide: Late summer and fall, before rainfall. Not tide dependent.

This is a 1-mile-long beginner's paddle into a small protected cove. Bank launch from the creek and paddle its southern end. Harbor seals haul out from offshore rocks near the launch area. This quiet cove is a birdlover's paradise, with many migratory shorebirds at close range along the way. Paddle at a distance from the headlands, where there is moderate wave backwash, and return before rounding the headlands at the point.

Big River

Launch site 3, p. 46

Preferred NOAA Chart: 18628, "Elk to Fort Bragg" (subsection of NOAA chart 18626, "Elk to Fort Bragg")

Estimated Paddle Time: 4 hours

Trip Rating: SK 2

Special Hazards: Rolling lumber; strong ebb current in shallow water will hit chop unexpectedly

Launch Sites: There are two launch sites 1 mile south of Mendocino on CA 1:

1. The beach launch site is a big sandy beach on the east side of CA 1 along the north side of Big River. On CA 1, turn east on North Big River Road. Immediately after the turnoff is a parking area and sandbar beach with easy access to the river.

2. Along Big River Road, just 100 feet past the first launch site are "Georgia Pacific" property signs. About 100 feet past the signs is a flat sandy parking lot and easy riverbank launch. Locals often use this launch. Locals say Georgia Pacific has sanctioned kayak use here due to "eminent domain." *(3A)*

Nearest Campsite: Van Damme State Park is 2 miles south of Big River, call Mendocino County Regional State Parks (707-937-5804).

Best Paddle Time/Tide: Mornings and afternoon ending in high tide or slack; return in ebb. Moderately tide dependent.

Plan this beginner's trip to coincide with the tides: Head upstream up to 8 miles with the flood, picnic along the banks while the tides turn, and float back down with the ebb. A lightly traveled road runs parallel to the river, but aside from that you'll feel far from civilization, enjoying solitude and wildlife—river otters, beavers, falcons, hawks, plovers, and whimbrels. Here, you can easily imagine the Tamals and the later fishermen working the river, which is arcaded by large pines and redwoods and cuts through the headland hills.

The river winds along beautifully and is wide and strong enough along the bends to create a small chop, but there are calm areas for practicing wet exits and rescues as well. On a windy day in areas not bordered by open fields, the gusts will whip across the water like a wind tunnel and darken the water surface. If you're between two banks with thickly wooded trees, it will create a stiff chop in shallow areas. The surface water has a fast westward drag; the deeper water will pull you upstream. When these strong gusts occur, paddle along the banks.

On Big River, the abundant woodlands attract bird and animal life typical of the Pacific Northwest. Bald eagles nest in the treetops, beavers play by the Georgia Pacific lumber dikes, and curious and friendly harbor seals poke around your boat at the takeout. You'll see a variety of stilts, plovers, mallards, and mergansers working the feeding areas near their rookeries along the riverbanks. You can also find big clams along these banks. The paddle can be as leisurely or as athletic as you like, with plenty of areas to beach, picnic, rest, catch some sunshine, and paddle again.

After paddling to the takeout, stronger paddlers might consider poking past the CA 1 underpass into the semiprotected ocean cove. It is generally a safe channel mouth to paddle, unlike other channels in this area. Observe the current at the river mouth: If it is running very swiftly, paddling in the channel is not recommended. If it's calm, then paddle to your right along the riverbank, where the water runs less swiftly along the headland bend. Watch for loose branches and trunks floating downriver. The cove is semiprotected by headlands on each side, and a high sandbar across the cove that prevents waves spilling into the beach area. Don't go past or near the sandbar where the waves break—a turbulent area where river meets ocean water. Paddle across from the north to the south headland and back upstream again, under the underpass, to your launch site.

This excursion will give you an exhilarating taste of cove paddling in Mendocino, and it's a great bird-watcher's paddle. Big River estuary, including mudflats and marsh, covers more than 1,500 acres and is one of the largest undisturbed estuaries along the coast. Starry flounder and Dungeness crab inhabit these waters, while silver salmon and steelhead trout spawn upstream. Geese, duck, and bald eagles winter in the river's inland watershed. In the cove, brittle sea stars, sea cucumbers, and sea urchin are found in abundance in the rocky intertidal and subtidal areas.

Van Damme State Park: Rock Gardens and Caves

Launch site 4, p. 46

Preferred NOAA Chart: 18628, "Elk to Fort Bragg" (subsection of NOAA chart 18626, "Elk to Fort Bragg")
Estimated Paddle Time: 5 hours (each trip)
Trip Rating: SK 4
Special Hazards: Sneaker waves; boils; afternoon winds; swells
Launch Site: There is an easy sandy beach put-in at Van Damme State Park, 3 miles south of Mendocino on CA 1, next to the parking lot. The sandy beach has virtually no surf. Van Damme State Park (707-937-5804).
Nearest Campsite: Van Damme State Park is 3.0 miles south of Mendocino on CA 1, call Mendocino County Regional State Parks (707-937-5804).
Best Paddle Time/Tide: Morning to early afternoon in tides specific to trips described below.

If you aren't an expert in poking around Mendocino caves in unpredictable conditions, then taking a tour guided by someone familiar with specific caves, habitat, and conditions is highly recommended (see Part 3 for a list of tour guides in the area). Whether or not you are an expert rock garden and cave prober, the following three trips offer the best cave and intertidal trips in the area. Avoid launching near the river channel, where the tides and current work at cross purposes—especially on the south side of the channel by the headlands. Launch and hug the beach side.

Of all the Northern California coastline, Mendocino's is richest in its variety of headlands, caves, and intertidal zone habitat. River otters, harbor seals, and sea lions frequent the caves, while stellar sea lions bask on the outlying rock gardens. The water in the four major intertidal zones is so clear that you'll see ribbed limpets, rockweed, anemone, snails, purple sea urchins, and many crab species.

Be sure to check the tide, weather, and wind conditions specific to each trip described below.

1. **The Northern Caves:** Paddle to the northern caves from Van Damme with a northwest wind and in low tide only. The caves are 1½ to 2 miles from your launch site. The trip takes 5 hours in good weather and can be considerably longer in wind and chop. You'll paddle through the four major intertidal channels, pass by Spring Ranch, and many tide pools filled with marine life. Paddle through the channels around the headland caves. Explore and enjoy. Paddle back to your launch site with the current flowing south and the winds behind you.

2. **The Intertidal Zone:** Paddle this trip only in low or slack tide with a north or south wind. From Van Damme, paddle ½ to 1 mile out to the headlands on the north end of the beach. The headlands you'll paddle along are those of Spring Ranch. As you reach the rock gardens and tide pools, you'll find yourself in an exquisite ecological puzzle. You can observe a variety of invertebrate organisms, crabs, and abalones in this pristine environment.

3. **The South Caves:** It's best to paddle this route in calm or in a south wind. This is not a tide-dependent trip. Paddle out the south end of the beach and then out to the blow hole (you can't miss it—it spouts a plume of water 100 feet in the air). Of the three major caves to explore, the first is underneath the Little River Cemetery and has an amphitheater back chamber and a trail. The second is a series of triple-chamber caves whose ceilings have fallen out. The three separate amphitheaters are linked by arch rocks, and waves pump you along from chamber to chamber. The third major cave group is very narrow, and you'll need to work your way inside carefully with your paddle down at your side until you see the cave chamber lit from underneath. Follow the arch rocks and you'll paddle through a beautiful waterfall. These caves are more intricate and dangerous than the northern caves.

Albion Flat

Launch site 5, p. 46

Preferred NOAA Chart: 18628, "Elk to Fort Bragg" (subsection of NOAA chart 18626, "Elk to Fort Bragg")
Estimated Paddle Time: 2 hours
Trip Rating: SK 1
Special Hazards: Leisure boaters
Launch Site: There is a concrete/wood boat ramp at Schooner's Landing (707-937-5707). On CA 1 in Albion, turn east on Albion Flat Road, then drive down the north bank of the Albion River and head into Schooner's private dock and camping area. $5 parking fee.
Nearest Campsite: Albion Flat Campground is adjacent to Schooner's Landing on CA 1 (707-937-0606).
Best Paddle Time/Tide: Anytime. Not tide dependent.

Ideally suited to beginners, this 3-mile river paddle launches from an RV campground, where there's a nice picnic area and store. When it's foggy and rainy everywhere else along the coast, Albion Flat is clear, sunny, and hot. Paddle upriver in the morning and float down later in the day, stopping for a picnic or a swim. You'll see river otters, beavers, and seals along the way. On summer weekends, the parking lot fills early with pleasure boaters going out for ocean salmon. To avoid them, arrive very early or skip the summer season altogether.

Paddling out of the harbor to the ocean is not recommended unless you are a strong intermediate paddler.

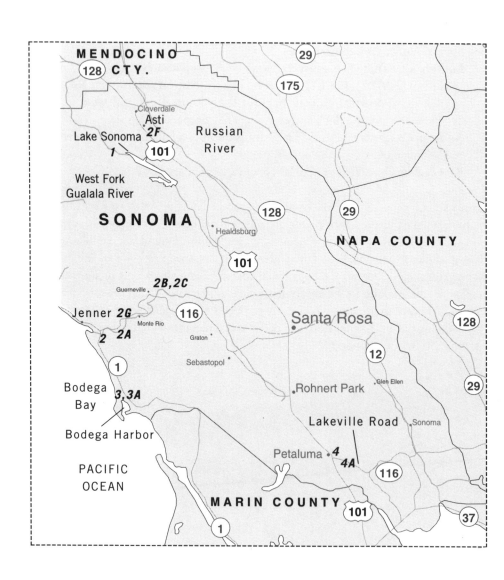

MENDOCINO CTY.

128

29

175

Cloverdale

Asti
2F

Russian
River

Lake Sonoma

1

101

West Fork
Gualala River

SONOMA

Healdsburg

128

29

NAPA COUNTY

101

Guerneville

2B, 2C

Jenner 2G

116

Santa Rosa

128

Monte Rio

2A

Graton

2

12

1

Sebastopol

Bodega
Bay

3, 3A

Rohnert Park

Glen Ellen

29

Bodega Harbor

Lakeville Road

Sonoma

PACIFIC
OCEAN

Petaluma

4

4A

116

MARIN COUNTY

101

37

1

Sonoma County

1. Lake Sonoma

2. Russian River

3. Bodega Harbor

4. Petaluma River and Petaluma Marsh

Lake Sonoma

Launch site 1, p. 54

Estimated Paddle Time: 3 hours
Trip Rating: SK 1
Special Hazards: Submerged trees
Launch Site: Launch from the Yorty Creek boat ramp, which has ample parking. From Santa Rosa, drive 16 miles north on US 101 to the Dry Creek exit in Healdsburg. Turn left and drive about 11 miles northwest to the Lake Sonoma Visitor Center, which you'll see on your right. From the visitor center, follow the road 10 miles northwest to the Yorty Creek boat ramp. Parking and launching are free. However, launching boats with official boat licenses is $2. Picnic areas, swimming, and fishing are available. Managed by the Army Corps of Engineers (707-433-9483).
Nearest Campsite: Lake Sonoma has several campgrounds (707-433-9483).
Best Paddle Time/Tide: Morning and afternoon. Not tide dependent.

A paddle around the northern creeks of Lake Sonoma is a peaceful trip for beginner paddlers; here the lake is limited to canoes and kayaks only. The rest of Lake Sonoma is filled with powerboaters, jet-skiers, water-skiers, and lots of wind. In the northern creeks of this 381,000-acre human-made lake is an abundance of woodlands and birdlife, and along Lake Sonoma's protected northern slough, Yorty Creek, are threatened peregrine falcons, hawks, bald and golden eagles, ospreys, and black-tailed deer. Yorty Creek is well protected from afternoon winds, so you can paddle here with kids and family in either the morning and the afternoon. Also check out the wildlife exhibit at the visitor center and the fish hatchery, which are open daily from 9 to 5. Picnic and camping areas abound, and fishing here is rewarding, with plentiful large- and smallmouth bass, landlocked steelhead, and sunfish.

Russian River

Launch site 2, p. 54

Preferred NOAA Chart: 18640, "San Francisco to Point Arena"
Estimated Paddle Time: 4 hours
Trip Rating: SK 2
Special Hazards: Afternoon winds; rolling lumber or limbs
Launch Site: This river beach launch is 2 miles south of Jenner on Willow Creek Road, off CA 1. Parking is available at the launch. Head to the south end of the CA 1 bridge at Jenner, turn east off the bridge onto Willow Creek Road, and follow this unpaved road about ½ mile. On the

left is a small dirt parking area with a No Camping sign. Park here for an easy carry down to beach.

Nearest Campsite: Bodega Dunes Campground. From Jenner, drive 10 miles south on CA 1. Operated by Sonoma Coast State Beach (707-875-3483).

Best Paddle Time/Tide: Mornings in beginning low or slack tide; return in ebb. During the summer months, the river mouth is often closed off to the ocean, at which times the river is nontidal.

This is a leisurely, beginner's big-river paddle, with gravel beaches for short hikes and picnics. Afternoons get windy, so be sure to return with the ebb tide. Practice rescue and brace skills in the deeper water—this is an ideal spot for it.

The river features several ponds and freshwater marshes, and ospreys nest along the river; you can watch them diving for fish at the river mouth and along the river when you return with the tide. About an hour into the trip, you'll be across from pastures and the small town of Duncan Mills. Soon after, you'll paddle by Casini Ranch, which offers plenty of campsites and picnic tables along the Russian River—and wooded preserves.

The Russian River unfortunately has very little public access and some fussy landowners. Nonetheless, there are a few other launch sites, which I've listed below (with keys to their location on the county map), although most have little or no parking. All are fairly easy paddles under normal conditions.

1. Monte Rio—roadside parking and launch along River Road. *(2A)*
2. Guernewood Park—at intersection of Guerneville Road and River Road, there is a public swimming beach. *(2B)*
3. Johnson's Beach in Guerneville—at Armstrong Woods Road and River Road. *(2C)*
4. Alexander Valley Campground between Healdsburg and Guerneville (also known as Trowbridge Campground)—north of Alexander Valley Bridge on west side of Russian River. Easy bank put-in. *(2D)*
5. W.C. Trowbridge in Healdsburg—20 Healdsburg Avenue in Healdsburg. East bank put-in. *(2E)*
6. Crocker Creek Bridge near Asti—Cook's Hollydale Beach off River Road, Crocker Creek Bridge, and Russian River; 1 mile south of Asti. Easy put-in right next to bridge. *(2F)*
7. Moscow Campground in Moscow—a good place to camp and have dinner nearby at the Jenner's Willow Creek Road launch site. *(2G)*

Bodega Harbor

Launch site 3, p. 54

Preferred NOAA Chart: 18643, "Bodega Bay and Tomales Bay" (subsection of NOAA chart 18640, "San Francisco to Point Arena")

Estimated Paddle Time: 2 hours

Trip Rating: SK 3

Special Hazards: Strong afternoon winds that will push a paddler toward the mouth of the harbor; steep waves; wildlife

Launch Sites: Two public launch sites in Bodega Harbor off CA 1:

1. Adjacent to Westside Regional Park's parking lot on Westside Road in Bodega Harbor. From the town of Bodega Bay, drive north a short distance on CA 1. You'll see a sign for Westside Regional Park and Eastside Road. At the sign, turn southwest onto Bay Flat Road and travel 2 miles, looping around the bay, to the campground parking and launching area.

2. Adjacent to the U.S. Coast Guard station in Bodega Harbor, along Doran Beach Road. From the town of Bodega Bay, take CA 1 south 1 mile to Doran Beach Road and follow it to the U.S. Coast Guard station. The boat launch is 500 feet west of the station, and adjacent to the parking lot. *(3A)*

Nearest Campsite: Sonoma County Parks' Doran Campground and Westside Campground have several campsites in Bodega Bay, adjacent to the harbor (707-875-3540).

Best Paddle Time/Tide: Morning and early afternoon in beginning high tide or slack; return in flood.

This shallow, 800-acre harbor, a popular area for fishing and clamming, contains moderate surf, open water, shallow subtidal channels, freshwater wetlands, tidal mudflats, and salt marshes. Low tides create shallow, swift currents or shoals along the wetlands and mudflats. This diversity makes the trip most suited to intermediate paddlers, but on calm days, this trip is fine for beginners too.

If you start at the north harbor launch, near Westside Regional Park, and head south, you'll kayak through shallow wetlands. Currents can be moderate but not swift, so this is a good place to develop paddling skills. Here you'll see lots of shorebirds, such as oystercatchers and stilts poling the sand for clams. As you paddle farther south toward the mouth of the harbor, the water feels calm, but be prepared for spotty gusts of wind and fog, particularly in the afternoon. Look for the seals, otters, and whales that inhabit this area.

The harbor mouth and out toward the ocean are favorite spots for pleasure boaters and windsurfers, so watch where you're going.

Petaluma River and Petaluma Marsh

Launch site 4, p. 54

Note: See trip 14 in Marin County for Marin trips launching from the Petaluma River.

These easy boat launches provide an excellent opportunity for several beginner and intermediate paddles.

Preferred NOAA Chart: 18654, "San Pablo Bay"

Estimated Paddle Time: 4 hours

Trip Rating: SK 2

Special Hazards: Afternoon gusts, shallow water, and mud

Launch Sites: Three public boat ramps with adjacent parking:

1. Petaluma Marina at 781 Baywood Drive at R Street (707-778-4489). Take US 101 to Petaluma, turn east on CA 37, then north on Lakeville Road to Petaluma Marina, 1 mile south of the Petaluma Turning Basin.
2. Lakeville Marina. From CA 37, turn north on Lakeville Road. Lakeville Marina is just south of the intersection of Lakeville Road and Stage Gulch Road. This is a smaller and less busy boat ramp area. For more information call Petaluma Visitors Center (707-769-0429). *(4A)*
3. Black Point Boat Launch Ramp in Novato on Petaluma River. Take CA 37 east to Black Point Road. At the end of the road is the launch ramp. Operated by Marin County Department of Parks and Recreation (415-499-6387). *(4B)*

Nearest Campsite: Petaluma KOA is 4 miles south of Petaluma on US 101 (707-763-1492).

Best Paddle Time/Tide: Paddling up the Petaluma River is best in the morning with the flood; return in the early afternoon with slack or beginning ebb. If you're going out to San Pablo Bay, paddle in the morning with beginning high tide or slack; return in the early afternoon in flood to avoid strong winds in San Pablo Bay.

A paddle up the slow, flat river offers a scenic patchwork of open marsh, wetlands, and the working Petaluma Harbor, and a first-rate view of historic Petaluma. Along B Street, you'll see the Petaluma feed mill and café row. Public boat docks are on B Street (day-use fee) if you're interested in a lunchtime stroll through the old town. Along C and D Streets, you'll see the Petaluma Foundry, galleries, and more cafés. The North Bay Rowing Club has a small boat dock here on D Street, if you'd like to dock and stroll from here. This is still a working waterfront, so you'll see a few commercial fishing boats as well as the *Petaluma Queen*, the sternwheeler built and still operated by the Barker family. Across from the *Petaluma Queen* is a microbrewery, adjacent to public access docks. The brewery has excellent fresh foods for a lunch or picnic stop.

If you launched from Lakeville Marina or Black Point Boat Launch Ramp, you can return down the river and take in the Petaluma Marsh, operated by the Department of Fish and Game. The Petaluma Marsh is adjacent to both launch sites and is accessible only by water. A short paddle around its shores is worthwhile. You'll see an abundance of nesting stilts, oystercatchers, terns, herons, and egrets. Have a picnic in the marsh area, or lunch at Papa's Taverna, a Greek Restaurant (707-769-8545) at 5688 Lakeville Highway, with a dock 1 mile north of the Petaluma Marsh and 3 miles south of Lakeville Marina.

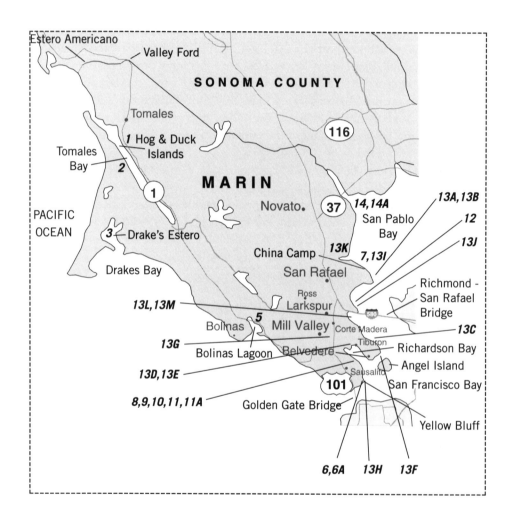

Estero Americano

Valley Ford

SONOMA COUNTY

Tomales

1 Hog & Duck
Islands

Tomales
Bay *2*

116

MARIN

PACIFIC
OCEAN

3 Drake's Estero

1

Novato.

37

14,14A

San Pablo
Bay

13A,13B

12

13J

China Camp

13K

7,13I

Drakes Bay

San Rafael

Ross

Richmond -
San Rafael
Bridge

13L,13M

Larkspur

580

13C

Bolinas

5

Mill Valley

Corte Madera

13G

Tiburon

Richardson Bay

Bolinas Lagoon

Belvedere

13D,13E

Angel Island

San Francisco Bay

8,9,10,11,11A

101

Sausalito

Golden Gate Bridge

Yellow Bluff

6,6A *13H* *13F*

Marin County

1. Tomales Bay State Park Area: Miller Park Launching Facility (Nick's Cove) to Hog Island and the Western Shore

2. Tomales Bay State Park: Heart's Desire Beach

3. Point Reyes National Seashore: Drake's Estero (Northern Slough) to Captain Cook Marker

4. Estero Americano

5. Bolinas Lagoon

6. Horseshoe Bay to Point Bonita

7. China Camp

8. Dunphy Park Easy Paddles

9. Angel Island

10. The Tide Rips at Yellow Bluff

11. Sausalito Harbor in Moonlight

12. Loch Lomond Marina to Marin Islands and East Brother Light Station

13. Other Marin Access Points

14. Petaluma River to San Pablo Bay National Wildlife Area or Novato Creek/Bel Marin Keys

An Introduction to Tomales Bay

The name *Tomales* comes from the Miwok Indian word for *bay*, and the Miwoks lived along Tomales Bay in various shoreline settlements. The bay, which is 13 miles long, 1 mile wide, and very shallow, lies in a drowned rift valley formed by earth movement along the San Andreas Fault. The south end, at Heart's Desire Beach, is less than 10 feet deep. The wide expanses of mudflats are exposed at low tide. Three main streams feed the bay: Keys Creek, Lagunitas Creek, and Olema Creek. Since these creeks are small, there is little freshwater coming into the bay, but both salt- and freshwater marshes are found along its edges.

The fine bottom materials of Tomales Bay host myriad inhabitants, including worms, clams, snails, crabs, herring, jellyfish, and the famous Tomales Bay oysters. Rows of oyster racks are visible at low tide at several points along the eastern shore of the bay, and the oysters are offered for sale along CA 1.

Bird-watchers have identified more than 100 species of birds in the area. Godwits, willets, dunlins, buffleheads, scoters, ducks, great blue herons, and egrets are commonly seen.

The National Oceanographic and Atmospheric Administration and the Audubon Canyon Ranch have been studying the effect of light kayak traffic on seal haulouts in Tomales Bay. Their studies indicate that kayakers flush seals and pups from their island haulout sites, so kayakers are now restricted from paddling in certain areas during the pupping season and must always paddle at least 300 feet from seals.

Tomales Bay State Park Area: Miller Park Launching Facility (Nick's Cove) to Hog Island and the Western Shore

Launch site 1, p. 60

Preferred NOAA Chart: 18643, "Bodega Bay and Tomales Bay" (subsection of NOAA chart 18640, "San Francisco to Point Arena")

Estimated Paddle Time: 2 hours

Trip Rating: SK 2

Special Hazards: The wind comes up strongly and quickly and can produce confused chop at a moment's notice.

Launch Site: Boat ramp and easy bank launch. Take US 101 to Petaluma, and take the off-ramp to Central Petaluma. At the end of the off-ramp, turn west onto East Washington. Follow East Washington and the signs for Tomales-Petaluma Road. Head west on Tomales-Petaluma Road until it ends and turn left onto CA 1 (The sign reads "State Highway 1"). Proceed south on CA 1 for 4 miles. On the right you'll see a restaurant whose white clapboard side is painted "Nick's Cove Restaurant." Turn right into adjoining Miller Park Launching Facility parking lot. $5 day-use parking fee. Managed by Marin County Parks Department (415-499-6387). Nick's Cove Restaurant (415-663-1033). Livermore Marsh and Marshall Marsh are owned by Audubon Canyon Ranch (415-868-9244). Call the Point Reyes National Seashore (415-663-1092) in advance to request permission to go ashore on Hog and Duck Islands. Camping on Hog and Duck Islands is not allowed as of 1998.

Nearest Campsite: Tomales Bay State Park has many campsites (415-669-1140). To get permission to go ashore or camp on Hog and Duck Islands, call the Point Reyes National Seashore (415-663-1092).

Best Paddle Time/Tide: Mornings and calm early afternoons in beginning high tide or slack; return in flood. Strongly tide dependent.

Before launching on this 3-mile beginner's paddle, check out the fog and wind for a few minutes. Tomales has fast tidal changes; a little extra fog or wind can turn a good choppy paddle into a treacherous experience. Head out to Hog Island, which lies in the middle of Tomales Bay near the mouth of Walker Creek. Harbor seals haul out on the shores of the island and its tiny neighbor, Duck Island. Both islands are sanctuaries owned by Point Reyes National Seashore; call ahead to get permission to land on Duck Island if you'd like to tour this marine life sanctuary. Cross from there to the western shore of Tomales, which has numerous small beach cove campsites in which to clam, have a picnic, or just watch the Tule elk along the ridges. Be careful not to get too close to the mouth of Tomales Bay. Large rip currents, sneaker waves, and swell are always active in this constricted area. Cross back to the eastern shore in beginning to mid-flood. You'll experience a moderate chop on your return paddle; if it looks too choppy, you can wait a few minutes until peak high tide, when the water is calmer. Wherever you are in Tomales, the wind and waves can change quickly, so keep a sharp eye and adjust your trip planning to the weather conditions.

After crossing back to the eastern shore of the bay, paddle south from Miller Park and look for the heron rookery in a eucalyptus grove just south of the Miller Park boat ramp. A little farther south of the eucalyptus grove is Livermore Marsh, a fresh- to brackish-water marsh owned by Audubon Canyon Ranch. Insects, pintails, and widgeons inhabit the marsh.

One mile south of Livermore Marsh is Marshall Marsh, a small freshwater willow swamp also owned by Audubon Canyon Ranch. The marsh banks usually have a lot of riprap, and are home for small California amphibians from newts to tree frogs. Adjacent to Marshall Marsh are the town and docks of Marshall. Stop here for a picnic and then head north again to Miller Park. You'll still be paddling in flood along the shore, so expect small chop on your return. Landing along the banks or ramp in Miller Park is easy, since both the banks and the ramp are protected from chop.

Tomales Bay State Park: Heart's Desire Beach

Launch site 2, p. 60

Preferred NOAA Chart: 18643, "Bodega Bay and Tomales Bay" (subsection of NOAA chart 18640, "San Francisco to Point Arena")
Estimated Paddle Time: 4 hours
Trip Rating: SK 2
Special Hazards: Paddling near the mouth; afternoon winds
Launch Site: This easy, sandy beach launch is 2 miles north of Inverness on Sir Francis Drake Boulevard. From Sir Francis Drake Boulevard, turn onto Pierce Point Road at Tomales Bay State Park, which leads you to the Heart's Desire Beach launch. This is a smooth beach launch in no surf, with plenty of adjacent parking and nice rest rooms. Tomales Bay State Park (415-669-1140).
Nearest Campsite: Tomales Bay State Park has many campsites (415-669-1140). To get permission to go ashore or camp at Hog and Duck Islands call the Point Reyes National Seashore (415-663-1092).
Best Paddle Time/Tide: Morning and midafternoon in beginning high tide or slack; return in flood.

Heart's Desire Beach and the Tomales Bay coastline have all the ingredients for a beautiful beginner's paddle. It's best to kayak out with the ebb tide and return with the flood.

Beachcombing is especially pleasant on the pristine, shell-strewn beaches, such as Shell, Indian, and Pebble, alongshore to the north and south of Heart's Desire. Many local beaches are accessible only to paddlers. Miwok relics are as undisturbed as the old Bishop pines and the elk in the park. Picnics and short hikes on local trails are pleasant diversions here.

If you headed north, begin your return paddle when you're parallel with Hog Island. The current gets strong past the island and sweeps quickly to the turbulent wash at the mouth of the bay. The afternoon winds do pick up a bit, but as long as you're along the same side of the bay as Heart's Desire, you'll be safe and have fun in the chop. Landing back at the beach is easy, because it's shallow and sandy.

Tomales Bay State Park, northwest of Inverness and just south of Heart's Desire, includes 2 miles of bay shoreline with four sandy beaches where swimming is possible in sheltered bays. Indian, Pebble, and Shell Beaches are connected along a trail beginning at Heart's Desire. Spotted owls have been sighted in the Bishop pine forest that hugs the shoreline, and Pacific tree frogs are common. There is clamming at Heart's Desire and Pebble Beaches. Inverness has wonderful cafés for lunch or dinner.

Point Reyes National Seashore: Drake's Estero (Northern Slough) to Captain Cook Marker

Launch site 3, p. 60

Preferred NOAA Chart: 18647, "Drakes Bay" (subsection of NOAA chart 18640, "San Francisco to Point Arena")
Estimated Paddle Time: 5 hours
Trip Rating: SK 2
Special Hazards: Strong afternoon winds and strong tidal change make for a muddy landing; afternoon chop.
Launch Site: There is a sandy/muddy beach launch at Johnston's Oyster Farm in Point Reyes National Seashore. Take US 101 to Sir Francis Drake Boulevard and head west for 4.6 miles on Sir Francis Drake to Inverness. Turn left onto Estero Trail, which will take you to Johnston's Oyster Farm, a private working farm that is best accessed during the day on weekends. Please ask for permission to launch when you arrive. The launch area is the beach adjacent to the giant shell mounds; park off the roadside. Call the Audubon Canyon Ranch at 415-383-1644 in advance to make sure that Drake's Estero is open to the public; it is usually closed from June through September to protect the seal pups. The launch and return can get muddy. Be sure to take an extra pair of old sneakers.
Nearest Campsite: Point Reyes National Seashore has many campgrounds (415-663-1092).
Best Paddle Time/Tide: Early mornings to calm early afternoons in mid- to high tide, launching in beginning flood or slack and returning in flood.

Point Reyes National Seashore, the landmass west of the San Andreas rift zone, is famous for the diversity of its ecosystems, nearly 400 bird species, and its marine life. Near the Visitor Center (on Bear Valley Road in Point Reyes, approximately 10 miles southeast of the Heart's Desire launch; also called Bear Valley Visitor Center) is a display of Coast Miwok structures.

A fine paddle for beginner and intermediate kayakers, this slough on Point Reyes is very sensitive to tidal flows. It's particularly important to use a tidal chart for the esteros, because tides shift quickly in these shallow mudflats. Plan your trip so you launch at high ebb and return in mid-/low flood, to avoid fighting the strong tidal currents and the mud at the same time. The winds, usually northwesterly, pick up a good pace in the afternoon.

Begin by paddling along the oyster beds, toward the center of the estero. After a ½ mile, or one hour, of windy paddling as you veer across the estero to the "Captain Cook" marker on the eastern tip of Drake's Estero, you'll come to a sandy beach. Picnics are nice here, because the beach is out of the wind. A five-minute hike through sand leads you to beautiful Point Reyes Beach on the western shore.

Head back during the early part of the low-tide action. A good return route is to paddle north along the shore where you landed; on the way you'll see clear estero tide pools with anemones. Don't paddle into the adjacent slough arms; before reaching the next slough arm, paddle toward the center of the estero and into the longest arm you can see. Look down the arm and you should see the Johnston's farm buildings in the distance. The return paddle is a good beginner's exercise in kayaking against wind. Just allow time—about two hours—for your return. You'll be landing in mud, so be prepared to use your extra pair of sneakers. Paddle as close to the muddy beach as you can before stepping out and hauling your kayak on shore; the mud is more than ankle-deep here.

Drake's Estero is the largest saltwater lagoon in coastal Marin. The shallow estero receives freshwater flow only from minor streams. Broad mudflats are exposed at low tide. For more than 50 years, Johnston's Oyster Farm has leased the tidelands within the estero for oyster farming, and the delicious Pacific oysters are for sale here. You'll paddle past the wooden oyster farm racks beaded with large luminous oysters—please do not disturb! The estero widens to become lush with brush, which attracts migratory birds, yet remains secluded enough to host a resident population of herons, egrets, hawks, and friendly seals.

Invertebrates found in the mudflats include giant geoduck clams, stringworms, Pacific oysters, sea anemones, sea stars, crabs, and harmless rays. There are also harbor seals and leopard sharks. Caspian terns, kites, and Canada geese feed in the shallow estero.

Estero Americano

Launch site 4, p. 60

Preferred NOAA Chart: 18640, "San Francisco to Point Arena"
Estimated Paddle Time: 6 hours
Trip Rating: SK 2
Special Hazards: Strong afternoon winds, tidal current, mud
Launch Site: This is an easy launch on the lagoon bank next to the Valley Ford bridge. Limited parking spaces are available. Take US 101 to the East Washington exit in Petaluma. Go west off the exit onto East Washington Street, which becomes Bodega Avenue in 1 mile. Follow Bodega Avenue for 8 miles, turn right onto Petaluma Valley Ford Road, and follow it for 12 miles. About a ½ mile past the small town of Valley Ford, turn left onto Valley Ford Franklin School Road. You'll see a bridge over Estero Americano after driving a mile. Pass over the bridge and you'll see a dirt launch and parking area immediately on your left. Park and launch here.
Nearest Campsite: Point Reyes National Seashore has many campgrounds (415-663-1092).

Best Paddle Time/Tide: Morning. Launch in beginning high tide or slack; return in flood. Return before ebb turns this shallow area into mud.

If you don't mind a little dust or mud at the launch area, you'll have no problem anticipating this lovely, slow beginner's paddle through rural paradise. Bird-watchers especially will enjoy this trip. You'll view abundant greenery and farm life while sheltered from winds for most of this 8-mile paddle west to the mouth of the estero. You can stop anywhere along the banks and enjoy the views and lunch. Before you get to the mouth, you'll see a wire fence across the entire estero, but there's a large cut in the fencing that allows paddlers to enter the wide mouth area. As you kayak closer to the mouth, you'll begin to see herons, egrets, hawks, stilts, plovers, dowitchers, sandpipers, and migratory birds. If you have a difficult time finding enough water to paddle before reaching the mouth, however, you might as well turn around. Rest assured the water will only get shallower, and the tide will ebb faster than the best tide predictions for this area can forecast.

Bolinas Lagoon

Launch site 5, p. 60

Preferred NOAA Chart: 18680, "Point Sur to San Francisco Bay"
Estimated Paddle Time: 3 hours
Trip Rating: SK 2
Special Hazards: Strong afternoon winds and tidal current at mouth
Launch Site: This is an easy launch on a lagoon bank next to the roadside on CA 1. Take CA 1 four miles west of Stinson Beach to Audubon Canyon Ranch. All along the lagoon side of CA 1 across from the ranch is public access. Launch where there is parking and good (not muddy) access to the lagoon. The most feasible off-road parking and launching access are just across from Audubon Canyon Ranch.
Nearest Campsite: Samuel Taylor State Park is 12 miles north of the Bolinas Lagoon on Sir Francis Drake Boulevard (415-488-9897).
Best Paddle Time/Tide: Morning. Launch in beginning high tide or slack and return in flood by midafternoon, to avoid strong winds.

It's best to take this beginner/intermediate trip at high tide so that when you return, it won't be as muddy.

The 1.5-mile–wide lagoon opens through a small channel to Bolinas Bay and Duxbury Reef. Bolinas Lagoon, a county-owned nature preserve, includes 1,200 acres of sheltered water, salt marsh, and mudflat. In winter, the lagoon becomes an estuary as freshwater runs off into the lagoon. In summer, the lagoon is mostly a saltwater marsh. In the 1800s, logging in the surrounding hills permanently increased siltation and filled the now shallow lagoon.

Along its flatwater perimeter, you'll see a number of shorebirds. Plovers, sandpipers, herons, egrets, ducks, avocets, and Virginia rail are abundant here.

Paddle from Audubon Canyon Ranch across the lagoon to its western shore and then parallel with Olema–Bolinas Road. Circle Kent Island, the small island near the channel opening. This low-lying islet is separated from the Bolinas perimeter at low tide. Landing on the island is not permitted, because it is a seal haulout site. Stay at least 300 feet from the seals. Harmless bat rays and leopard sharks feed along Kent Island. For lunch, land along sandy beach of Bolinas Lagoon Open Space Preserve for a picnic.

While it's still high or slack tide, launch and head west (to your right) out the small channel toward Duxbury Reef. Here you're paddling in a semiprotected cove. If the channel has little to no surf, you can head farther west to the reef, but don't venture out the reef unless you are with someone who can direct you through the narrow channel between the reef rocks. Do not venture beyond Duxbury Point, which is hit by tide rips and rogue waves.

Duxbury Reef is California's largest exposed shale reef. The waves and currents pound the soft shale to continuously changing shapes. Soft shale is a unique habitat for an unusual assemblage of rock-boring clams, barnacles, sea stars, and mussels. Unique to Duxbury Reef is a small burrowing anemone, *Halcampa crypta*. The entire reef is a marine reserve, so marine life cannot be removed.

Returning to Bolinas Lagoon through the channel will take extra effort against beginning ebb tide. You can either paddle through it or portage around it after landing at the beach. Return along the eastern perimeter to your launch site. Shorebirds will be numerous in the channel as the tide begins to ebb.

Stop in Bolinas or Stinson Beach for a great lunch or stroll, and also check out the following: Audubon Canyon Ranch (415-868-9244); Point Reyes Bird Observatory (415-868-1221); Bolinas Lagoon Open Space Preserve, managed by Marine County Open Space Preserve (415-499-6387); Slide Ranch, a nonprofit entity that runs an environmental education center, including education programs on weekends and school education programs during the week (it is owned by the Golden Gate National Recreation Area; call in advance for program information and reservations—415-381-6155); and the Palomarin Trailhead 5 miles north of Bolinas.

Horseshoe Bay to Point Bonita

Launch site 6, p. 60

Preferred NOAA Chart: 18680, "Point Sur to San Francisco Bay"
Estimated Paddle Time: 6 hours
Trip Rating: SK 4

Special Hazards: Strong tidal current; afternoon winds; tanker traffic; whirlpools and rips in channel, especially under Golden Gate Bridge

Launch Site: There are two launch sites:

1. An easy, protected beach launch at Horseshoe Bay (locally known as Horseshoe Cove) in moderate to little surf.

2. A concrete boat ramp at Horseshoe Bay Marina. The Horseshoe Bay Marina ramp is near the Coast Guard station, east of Fort Baker at the northern end of the Golden Gate Bridge. Both launches are on property managed by the Golden Gate National Recreational Area (415-331-1540). Take US 101 to Vista Point, south of Sausalito, to Sommerville Road. Follow Sommerville Road to the marina. Marin Headlands Visitor Center at Fort Baker (415-331-1540). ***(6A)***

Nearest Campsite: Golden Gate National Recreational Area has several campsites (415-331-1540).

Best Paddle Time/Tide: Calm mornings with ending ebb tide or slack; return in flood. Strongly tide dependent.

Be sure to plan this paddle for early morning, in little wind or fog. Along the way, watch for rip currents and large, following seas. Stay inside the tideline eddy so you won't be swept out to sea in strong ebbs. This is a full-day advanced paddle of approximately 6 miles. I highly recommend you paddle with Sea Trek, local tour guides, or a local kayak group.

The scenery is spectacular—the towering green rolling hills of Marin, rocky seashore, and the rolling currents of the Golden Gate. The route takes you under the Golden Gate and along the northern shore of the channel to Point Bonita. This paddle is along semi-exposed ocean coast, but numerous locations along the way offer safe landing spots through small but occasionally hard, dumping surf (1 to 3 feet); other spots are more exposed and require more skill. One of the sheltered spots is Kirby Cove. Wear a helmet for surf landing here. It offers a superb lunch spot and interesting shoreside exploring, such as World War I gun emplacements. There are numerous rock gardens and caves to explore to the southwest, from Point Diablo to Point Bonita. At Point Bonita, you can leave the shelter of the headlands and poke your nose out into the big water of the Pacific.

Paddlers must pay strict attention to the tides in the Golden Gate. Currents are very strong, often reaching 4 to 5 knots. To paddle under the Golden Gate Bridge in an ebb tide, hug the shore until you emerge from under the bridge. Paddle hard for 50 feet past the bridge to hop the eddy flowing back to Horseshoe Bay. If you can't do that safely, land at Kirby Cove instead, and wait for the ebb current to slow down. Plan to ride out the ebb and return in the next slack or flood.

Also check out the Marine Mammal Center (415-289-7325).

China Camp

Launch site 7, p. 60

Preferred NOAA Chart: 18649, "Entrance to San Francisco Bay"
Estimated Paddle Time: 2 hours
Trip Rating: SK 2
Special Hazards: Afternoon winds create strong chop in shallow water.
Launch Site: This is an easy beach launch in little or no surf at China Camp
    State Beach. From US 101 at San Rafael, take the San Pedro Road off-
    ramp. Head east along the bay and follow the signs to China Camp State
    Park. There is a $5 day-use fee.
Nearest Campsite: Marin Park, Inc. is 10 miles northwest of Sausalito on
    US 101 north toward San Rafael (415-461-5199).
Best Paddle Time/Tide: Mornings in beginning high tide or slack; return in
    flood. Moderately tide dependent. Return before midafternoon due to
    strong winds.

This area is sunnier on a foggy day than much of Marin, and the water here is
considerably warmer. Launching at the beach at historic and beautiful China
Camp offers several optional destinations for these intermediate paddles. If you
launch in early to midmorning, and the tide is slack or going out, a trip south
to McNear's Beach County Park is a good option. If you're a skilled paddler, go
around the rocky points and up to San Pablo Bay. If it's midmorning and close
to high tide, a northern destination such as Santa Venetia Marsh Open Space
Preserve is another scenic paddle.

These trips offer views of wildlife, from seals to pelicans, herons, egrets,
godwits, oystercatchers, ducks, and hawks. In either tide direction, be aware that
early to midafternoon winds from the Golden Gate make paddling difficult and
slow. Time your trip to avoid these winds and have a late lunch or stroll during
midafternoon.

To head for Santa Venetia Marsh Open Space Preserve, follow the coastline north along China Camp. Small sandy beaches along here make nice spots
for lunch or a rest. As you proceed along the shore, the next wide strip of beach
area you'll come to is Gallinas Beach. If it's not muddy, bird-watchers should
paddle into the Open Space Preserve along South Fork Creek. Be sure to paddle back by late morning, or make a long, leisurely picnic here to avoid possible
strong afternoon winds.

If you head south to McNear's Beach County Park, follow the coastline for
about 2 miles. You'll see a small peninsula; paddle around it and enter the cove.
Visit the beach here at McNear's Beach County Park. This is a good trip, especially for early mornings—you'll be one of the lucky paddlers to return without fighting the afternoon wind.

China Camp itself offers wonderful opportunities for a fascinating tour of the region's natural and cultural history. Many Chinese came to California with the Gold Rush, but as the mines played out, many turned to commercial fishing. Chinese fishing camps flourished along the northern coast, including 30 camps on San Francisco Bay. These new immigrants were so successful in the San Francisco Bay shrimp trade that other fishermen pressured the government into passing anti-Chinese fishing laws, which virtually destroyed the nascent immigrant communities. But Frank Quong's shrimp and bait shop still flourishes at his family's fishing camp in China Camp, the only surviving community from the era. Frank still goes out almost every day to fish, but his shrimp catch is now very small. Shrimp were once abundant in the bay, but pollution and a reduction in freshwater flows due to dams have greatly reduced the population.

China Camp State Park and its wonderfully preserved family cabins and shrimp shelling buildings are open daily; take a ranger-led tour. Frank's Café in China Camp or the numerous picnic areas along the beach are ideal for lunch.

Dunphy Park Easy Paddles

Launch site 8, p. 60

Preferred NOAA Chart: 18649, "Entrance to San Francisco Bay"
Estimated Paddle Time: 2 hours
Trip Rating: SK 2
Special Hazards: Afternoon winds create strong chop in shallow water.
Launch Site: This is a beach launch in little or no surf. Take US 101 to the Sausalito exit. Take Bridgeway and follow the signs to Sausalito. Turn left on Napa Street, the first street after the light at the intersection of Bridgeway and Easterby Street. Parking is limited but free for 24 hours, so get there early. Managed by Marin County Parks Department (415-499-6387).
Nearest Campsite: Marin Park, Inc. is 10 miles northwest of Sausalito on US 101, and just south of San Rafael (415-461-5199).
Best Paddle Time/Tide: Morning. Launch in slack and return in flood.

Dunphy Park is a great launch site for all Strawberry Point/Richardson Bay/Bothin Marsh trips. It is an easy beach launch with no surf and it doesn't get muddy with tidal exchange. Parking overnight is permitted. Just offshore is a narrow gravel bar used by egrets and other shorebirds. Its land navigation point is a large white gazebo you can see from well offshore.

The Sausalito waterfront is just a short distance away, 2 miles east from your launch site. Along the way you will find spectacular views of the entire bay, luxurious estates, and funky houseboat communities.

The short (4 miles northwest of Dunphy Park), relaxing paddle from Dunphy to Strawberry Cove is always fun. Strawberry Cove is a marsh featuring a large expanse of cordgrass, which grows in shallow areas subject to strong tidal changes. Next to Strawberry is De Silva Island, where great blue herons nest. Directly across Strawberry Cove, Richardson Bay's northwest cove, is Strawberry Point and Brickyard Park. This is a pretty area, not overused, and good for a stop.

If the tide is high, another good stop is northwest under the bridge, at the bird and wildlife preserve of Bothin Marsh, a 112-acre nature preserve with several sloughs. There's a small boat ramp nearby at Mill Valley's Bayfront Park, but it's too muddy to use at low tide. Four small bridges rise over creeks and the channel and are perfect places from which to observe bird and marine life. Paddle through the sloughs and you'll see egrets, buffleheads, grebes, avocets, willets, and many other migratory birds that stop at this preserve along the Pacific Flyway.

Follow the coast back to your launch site. There is little or no swell, and while afternoons can be a bit breezy, the wind is usually not too bad. This area can get muddy, but that shouldn't stop you from using rest points that aren't muddy or from enjoying the birdlife and quiet away from congested Marin traffic.

Richardson Bay is an ideal area for a beginner to practice trip paddling and rescue skills. From Sausalito's small sheltered bay, paddle northeast to Richardson Bay Linear Park, the single rocky and green stretch of land northwest of Tiburon and Belvedere Peninsula. The journey there may take an hour, and paddling this stretch will help you develop continuity and rhythm. Near the park you can practice rescue skills. The bay adjacent to Richardson Bay Linear Park is relatively shallow and typically a little warmer. If the wind takes you, you'll be blown safely to the shoreline park and not out to the open bay. This trip is essential if you are fresh out of an introductory class and your goal is, perhaps, to paddle to the open bay. Since nature is unforgiving of those who visit unprepared, you should practice rescue skills and learn not to panic when you're dumped out of your boat. Here you can also learn to evaluate wind and weather conditions and practice basic land range navigation. Richardson Bay is also an ideal area for parents to take kids in a double.

At 55-acre Richardson Bay Park—a long, narrow, grass wetland—and Richardson Bay Wildlife Sanctuary, owned by the Audubon Society (415-388-2524), you can observe more than 80 species of birds as well as harbor seals, brown pelicans, and egrets. The park and sanctuary are on Tiburon Boulevard (CA 131) in Tiburon, 2 miles east of Mill Valley. Respect the seasonally posted wildlife refuge signs along Strawberry Point, which prohibit kayaks and all other boat traffic when seals are pupping.

Angel Island

Launch site 9, p. 60

Preferred NOAA Chart: 18649, "Entrance to San Francisco Bay"
Estimated Paddle Time: 6 hours

Trip Rating: SK 4

Special Hazards: Rips. Strong current with opposing strong afternoon winds can make steep waves.

Launch Site: Launch from the beach at Dunphy Park (see "Dunphy Park Easy Paddles," p. 71).

Nearest Campsite: See "Dunphy Park Easy Paddles," p. 71.

Best Paddle Time/Tide: Morning. Launch in ending flood.

This is a full-day, advanced paddle that is best undertaken with a group of paddlers or a local tour guide. (Sea Trek and other local guides are excellent.)

From Sausalito's Dunphy Park, start this trip early in the morning at ending flood. Head northeast toward Peninsula Point, the tip of Belvedere—a fairly smooth paddle. At Peninsula Point you'll encounter swift currents due to a cliff-like drop in depth. Here you'll use your strong forward stroke and bracing skills. Raccoon Strait is narrow, and parts of it are deep—some of the deepest water in the bay. Taking advantage of the ending ebb current will speed your paddle, as you cross to the northern end of Angel Island. You'll need a combination of bracing and rudder skills to control your course and speed. Your destination can be Ayala Cove (3 miles from Dunphy), north along the beach to Campbell Point (3½ miles from Dunphy), or south to West Garrison (2½ miles from Dunphy).

Whatever your destination, check the wind conditions, weather, and surge of waves along the beaches at Angel Island before you cross Raccoon Strait. It may be that you'll decide to modify your plan and head to another beach. Depending on the conditions, you may want to eddy-hop up the shore to Ayala Cove and practice bracing in tide rips and eddies. Hopping up to Ayala Cove is a great experience in learning how to read water.

Allow the early afternoon to start your return to Dunphy Park. Plan an angle that uses the flood tide to get to Peninsula Point. Raccoon Strait currents also vary daily. As you paddle, modify your direction based on the swiftness and direction of currents in the strait and the wind conditions. Hug the coast as you go around Peninsula Point and stay inside the eddy. Head north and west toward the white gazebo at Dunphy Park.

Angel Island was formerly called Wood Island; the trees that covered it were logged off for shipbuilding long ago. At various times, the island, the largest in San Francisco Bay, has served as a seafarer's anchorage, a Mexican rancho, a wartime Japanese internment camp, a Civil War garrison, and a quarantine station for Chinese immigrants. The poetry on the walls above the bunk beds of the interned Chinese is both beautiful and troubling. Authorities treated these people cruelly. Today, Angel Island is a temporary rest stop for thousands of herons, egrets, and migratory waterfowl along the Pacific Flyway. Ayala Cove was named after Captain Ayala, the first explorer to find the opening of San Francisco Bay from the sea. He spent several weeks in Ayala and Horseshoe Coves.

For more information on Angel Island State Park, call 415-435-1915.

The Tide Rips at Yellow Bluff

Launch site 10, p. 60

Preferred NOAA Chart: 18649, "Entrance to San Francisco Bay"
Estimated Paddle Time: 3 hours
Trip Rating: SK 2
Special Hazards: Steep waves; rips; eddies bigger on ebb tides
Launch Site: Launch from the beach at Dunphy Park (see "Dunphy Park Easy Paddles," p. 71).
Nearest Campsite: See "Dunphy Park Easy Paddles, p. 71.
Best Paddle Time/Tide: Mornings. Launch in slack and return in flood.

Yellow Bluff, southeast of Dunphy Park, is an ideal area for a group of intermediate paddlers who want to improve bracing, rescue, and paddling skills in eddies and tide rips. Put in on the beach at Dunphy Park; paddle southeast, following the shore, for 1½ miles around Sausalito Point to Yellow Bluff; and tuck in before Point Cavallo, the next large headland southeast of Dunphy, past Sausalito Harbor. The tide rips around Yellow Bluff kick butt, and you can paddle from rip to rip to get a lesson in bracing. The force of the eddy breaks and tide rips changes continually, so it's best to kayak with a group that has paddled here before. Check in with the Coast Guard Station Golden Gate (415-331-8247) before venturing out.

Sausalito Harbor in Moonlight

Launch site 11, p. 60

Preferred NOAA Chart: 18649, "Entrance to San Francisco Bay"
Estimated Paddle Time: 3 hours
Trip Rating: SK 2
Special Hazards: Unlighted boat traffic
Launch Sites:
1. Schoonmaker Beach in Sausalito. Easy, protected launch along public beach. Be careful to park in designated public parking spots or, with permission, at the adjacent Bay Model parking lot. There are rest rooms and telephones at the beach. Take US 101 to Sausalito and get off at the Sausalito exit. You'll be on Bridgeway as you follow the signs to Sausalito. Go south on Bridgeway until you see the Bay Model signs, which are a few feet north of the intersection of Easterby (a street that ends on the west side of Bridgeway) and Bridgeway. Follow the unmarked steep road down (which is called Liberty Ship Way on maps) and head straight to the beach. For more information on directions, call Schoonmaker Point Marina, 85 Liberty Ship Way (415-331-5550). For rental and equipment

information, call Sea Trek (open on weekends and other times per Sea Trek schedule) at its Schoonmaker Point location (415-332-4465).

2. Sausalito's Margaritaville Restaurant is adjacent to a small boat ramp, on the left as you face the restaurant. You can park there, launch or land, and catch a meal or drink at Margaritaville. Margaritaville Restaurant is at 1200 Bridgeway Avenue near Turney Street. To make reservations at Margaritaville, call 415-331-3226. *(11A)*

Nearest Campsite: See "Dunphy Park Easy Paddles," p. 71.

Best Paddle Time/Tide: Summer and early fall. Launch around 6 P.M. and return after full moon rise around 10 P.M. Early evening winds and fog can be strong in the summer.

Harbor paddles in Sausalito are a feast of fun and architectural wonder. Paddle north from Schoonmaker Point along the harbor and you'll encounter interesting houseboats (but please respect the owners' privacy). Along the way you'll see herons hunting for food on the banks and seals basking on the docks.

Full moon paddles are enchanting and easy, if you know your course. Local paddling groups and guides do splendid full moon and sunset paddle trips for beginners and the whole family. These trips offer kayakers the magical experience of paddling when the colors of shore and skyline change and meld from San Francisco to Sausalito. If you paddle these trips on your own, you should be an intermediate paddler. Bring a good light, reflective equipment, and excellent self-rescue skills.

From your launch in Sausalito, paddle north along the harbor toward Strawberry Cove (1½ miles from Dunphy Park). Return along the shore for fine views of the Sausalito and San Francisco shorelines. Margaritaville Restaurant is a great place to get a bite or a drink after a trip, or to meet paddling friends prior to launch.

Loch Lomond Marina to Marin Islands and East Brother Light Station

Launch site 12, p. 60

Preferred NOAA Chart: 18649, "Entrance to San Francisco Bay"

Estimated Paddle Time: 4 hours

Trip Rating: SK 4

Special Hazards: Strong currents with opposing strong wind will create steep waves; large-vessel traffic

Launch Site: Launch ramp at Loch Lomond Marina, 110 Loch Lomond Drive in San Rafael (415-454-7228). Take US 101 to the Central San Rafael exit and turn right onto 2nd Street, which later becomes Point San Pedro Road. Proceed 2 miles and turn right onto Loch Lomond Drive. Launch fee is $5 per kayak. Adequate parking and nearby food stores.

Nearest Campsite: Marin Park, Inc. is 10 miles northwest of Sausalito on US 101, and just south of San Rafael (415-461-5199).

Best Paddle Time/Tide: Calm mornings. Launch in slack and return in beginning ebb.

Like any open-bay paddle, this advanced, 6-mile excursion requires planning: Use your tide tables and check the day's weather forecast. The first 2 miles, heading eastward to East Brother Light Station (in Contra Costa County), will be in shallow slack water. In the first half hour, you'll pass the Marin Islands, one of which is privately owned; the other is a national wildlife refuge. These islands host a large population of nesting egrets. Head due east from the Marin Islands for 2 miles, correcting for the day's tidal current, to East Brother Light Station. This lighthouse, the oldest in the Bay Area, is now a privately owned inn on East Brother Island. East and West Brother Islands (The Brothers) serve as navigational entrances from eastern San Francisco Bay into San Pablo Bay.

Halfway across to East Brother Light Station, you'll paddle into San Pablo Strait, the main channel north from the Golden Gate to San Pablo Bay. Timing your crossing through main deep-water channels is important; you'll be paddling in slack to beginning ebb, which presents only a slight current, helpful on your return to the Loch Lomond Marina.

The innkeepers of the East Brother Light Station prefer that you not land on this rocky area of East Brother Island. If you need to land, do so in the nearby private Point San Pablo Yacht Harbor ½ mile south of East Brother Light Station.

I recommend you begin your return trip before late morning to take advantage of slack or ebbing tide. Watch for sea lions on the rocks and islands and a variety of birds as you return.

Other Marin Access Points

There are numerous launch sites along the public shoreline in Marin (refer to any Marin County map). Unfortunately, most of them are very tide dependent and provide no adjacent parking. Note that some of the additional launch sites listed here have limited parking, semirestricted public access, tidal access, or strong afternoon winds.

Launch Sites:

1. Remillard Park in San Quentin. From US 101, go 2 miles east on Sir Francis Drake Boulevard toward San Quentin. The launch site is on the beach, 100 yards west of San Quentin State Prison on Sir Francis Drake Boulevard. Easy bank launch to many San Pablo and San Francisco Bay points. Parking (unlimited time) adjacent to launch site. Morning use only, since strong afternoon winds make this a popular windsurfer site. Look for the huge metal statue of Sir Francis Drake (some believe he landed here). Across the street is Remillard

Brickyard, a State Historic Landmark. For more information call Marin County Parks Department (415-499-6387). *(13A)*

2. San Quentin's beach launch. From US 101, go 2 miles east on Sir Francis Drake Boulevard to the city of San Quentin. Turn right off Main Street, under the south end of the Richmond–San Rafael Bridge. Parking on street only. Mornings only due to strong afternoon winds; popular with windsurfers. *(13B)*

3. Paradise Beach County Park. From US 101, take the Tiburon Boulevard (CA 131) exit east to Tiburon. Proceed 5 miles and turn north on Trestle Glen and then east on Paradise Drive. Proceed 3 miles to the park entrance. Day-use fees ($5 to $7); closes at sunset; a moderately difficult 100-yard carry down to easy beach launch. Managed by Marin County Parks Department (415-499-6387). Day use strictly observed. Good site for San Pablo Bay trips. Not fun to return here, since you have to lug your kayak up a steep hill. *(13C)*

4. Blackie's Pasture and Richardson Bay Linear Park in Tiburon. Mid- to high-tide launch/return sites only. *To Blackie's Pasture:* From US 101, go east 2 miles on Tiburon Boulevard (CA 131) and turn south onto Blackie's Pasture Road—a dirt road at the beginning of Richardson Linear Park. Blackie's Pasture has an easy beach launch and adequate adjacent parking. *To Richardson Bay Linear Park:* From US 101, go east a half mile toward Tiburon on Tiburon Boulevard (CA 131). Along the shore you'll see a narrow parking area and a small sandy beach. Both launch areas are good for Richardson Bay and San Pablo Bay sites, and both are within the Richardson Bay Bird Sanctuary. Their public access is managed by Richardson Bay's Audubon Sanctuary (415-388-2524). Call in advance because these access areas are sometimes closed seasonally (from October to March) due to seal pupping or bird migration. *(13D)*

5. Strawberry Landing Day Use (unincorporated between Tiburon and Mill Valley). Mid- to high-tide launch/takeout site only. From US 101, go west on Seminary Drive and proceed 1 mile until it becomes Great Circle Drive. Park and launch along the banks where it's not muddy. Good launch site for trips to Strawberry Cove, Richardson Bay, and San Pablo Bay. For information, call Marin County Parks Department (415-499-6387). *(13E)*

6. Sam's Anchor Café at Tiburon docks. 25-27 Main Street in Tiburon (415-435-4527). From US 101, go east 5 miles on Tiburon Boulevard (CA 131) to Tiburon. Turn south onto Main Street. These are private docks, but you can launch or land if you purchase a meal or drink. Limited parking. *(13F)*

7. Mill Valley Bayfront Park. Small boat ramp adjacent to parking lot. From US 101, go west on East Blithdale Avenue 1 mile, turn south onto Camino Alto Road, and proceed ½ mile to Sycamore Avenue. Turn east onto Sycamore and follow the signs to Bayfront Park. Managed by Mill Valley Parks Department (415-383-1370). Mid- to high-tide launch/return site only. Launch for trips along Strawberry Cove, to Richardson Bay, and out to San Pablo Bay. *(13G)*

8. Horseshoe Cove near Fort Baker. Boat ramp and beach launch by the U.S. Coast Guard Station Golden Gate. Take US 101 to Vista Point south of Sausalito

to Sommerville Road. Follow Sommerville Road to Marina. Safe harbor launch near Golden Gate Bridge. Good put-in site for advanced open-coast trips. Advanced paddlers can launch and play in ebb, ride the eddy out, and ride the ebb back. A superb launch for advanced paddlers for Angel Island trips in flood tide. Don't paddle outside the harbor if you're not ready for rough water. A strong ebb current can suck you out into big rips. If this happens to you, just ride the tide to the beach at Kirby Cove and wait for slack tide. For more information, call the U.S. Coast Guard Station Golden Gate (415-331-8247). *(13H)*

9. San Rafael's McNear's Beach. Easy beach launch. From US 101, go east on 2nd Street, which becomes Point San Pedro Road for 2 miles. Turn onto Cantera Way and proceed ¼ mile to the park entrance. Day-use fee ($7 on weekends). Managed by Marin County Parks Department (415-499-6387). Launch to sites along San Pablo Bay. *(13I)*

10. San Rafael Beach Park. From US 101, go east on 2nd Street and turn onto Francisco Boulevard in San Rafael. Follow Francisco Boulevard to the end. Public park is adjacent to guest moorage in private yacht club. Moorage for "shopping" only. Park is operated by City of San Rafael Park and Recreation Department (415-485-3333). Restricted hours for parking. *(13J)*

11. San Rafael's McInnis Park. Small boat launch. From US 101, go east on Smith Ranch Road ½ mile until it ends at McInnis Park. Managed by Marin County Parks Department (415-499-6387). Good launch sites for Gallinas Creek to Santa Venetia Marsh Open Space and sites along San Pablo Bay. *(13K)*

12. Larkspur's Creekside Park on Bon Air Road. Easy bank launch and dock. From US 101, go west ½ mile on Sir Francis Drake Boulevard and turn south onto Bon Air Road. Follow signs on Bon Air Road to Creekside Park. The parking area is adjacent to the launch sites. The Marin Rowing Association maintains a facility and dock here (415-461-1431). *(13L)*

13. Larkspur's Corte Madera Creek. Small public-access pier. From US 101, go west on Lucky Drive and follow it ¼ mile to its intersection with Doherty Drive. Mid- to high tide only. There is limited public parking adjacent to the pier, but a high school parking lot is across the street. Managed by the Marin County Parks Department (415-499-6387). *(13M)*

14. Sausalito is working on a water-steps small-boat landing on Bridgeway. Call the Visitor Center for information (415-332-0505). (Note: This launch site is not on the county map, because it is still under construction.)

Petaluma River to San Pablo Bay National Wildlife Area or Novato Creek/Bel Marin Keys

Launch site 14, p. 60

Preferred NOAA Chart: 18654, "San Pablo Bay"
Estimated Paddle Time: 5 hours

Trip Rating: SK 3

Special Hazards: Afternoon wind, strong 2- to 3-foot chop by the river mouth

Launch Sites: There are two public boat ramps:

1. Public boat ramps on either side of the CA 37 bridge over the Petaluma River. Off US 101, head east on CA 37 to Harbor Drive. Follow Harbor Drive to boat ramps and parking at Port Sonoma–Marin (707-778-8055). For refuge information, contact the San Pablo Bay National Wildlife Refuge (510-792-0222).

2. Black Point Boat Launch Ramp in Novato on the Petaluma River. Take CA 37 east to Black Point Road. At the end of the road is the launch ramp, operated by the Marin County Department of Parks and Recreation (415-499-6387). *(14A)*

Nearest Campsite: Petaluma KOA is on US 101, 12 miles north of the Port Sonoma–Marin and Black Point boat ramps (707-763-1492).

Best Paddle Time/Tide: Morning and early afternoon in slack or beginning high tide; return with flood.

Launching from these public boat ramps near the mouth of the Petaluma River offers easy access northeast to the San Pablo Bay Wildlife Refuge and south to Novato Creek and the Bel Marin Keys. Plan this intermediate paddle so that you return with the wind behind you. Be sure not to paddle in low tide here, since you can get stuck in the mud.

Paddle along the east side of the river mouth, along the San Pablo Bay coastline. The preserved Sonoma Baylands Tidal Marsh Area extends along the bay banks to the Mare Island Naval Shipyard. Open bay waters, tidal wetlands, and mudflats from the Petaluma River mouth to Mare Island have been preserved as the 13,000-acre San Pablo Bay National Wildlife Refuge. If you paddle out the mouth for 2 miles (about an hour), you'll pass through this refuge, which together with the Sonoma Baylands links the wetland ecosystem. These tidelands and marsh provide habitat for the endangered salt marsh harvest mouse, ducks, scaups, and migrating shorebirds. Along the way you'll also see harbor seals in the countless muddy shoals.

The most accessible portion of this area is the refuge at Lower Tubbs Island, 3 miles from the Petaluma River mouth. Around the island, you'll see jack rabbits and pheasants. You can circle back across the Petaluma River mouth to the Novato Creek and the Bel Marin Keys sloughs. A short paddle up Navato Creek, flanked at the mouth by two tall radio towers, will give you a different perspective of the bay—views of houses and overdevelopment in a wetlands area.

Contra Costa County

1. Pinole Bayfront Park along Point Pinole Regional Shoreline Cove or to Pinole Marina

2. Pinole Bayfront Park to Rodeo Marina

3. Port Costa along Martinez Regional Shoreline

4. Port Costa to Martinez Harbor

5. Point Molate Beach to Castro Rock and Red Rock

6. Keller Beach to Red Rock or to Brooks Island

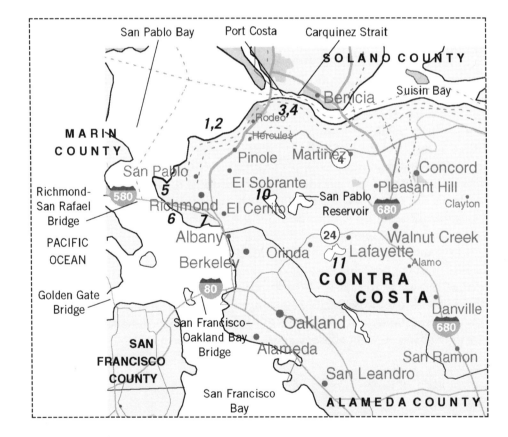

7. Richmond Marina Bay Harbor to Brooks Island

8. Franks Tract State Recreation Area to Little Franks Tract

9. Franks Tract State Recreation Area to Brannan Island

10. San Pablo Reservoir

11. Lafayette Reservoir

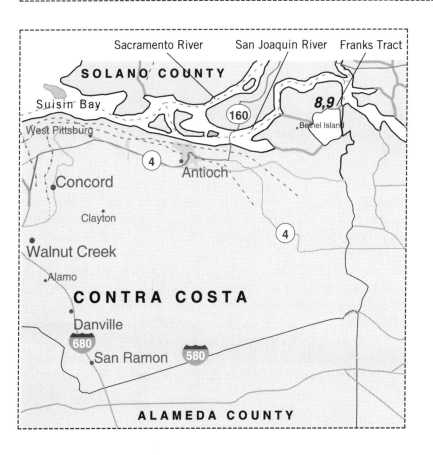

Pinole Bayfront Park along Point Pinole Regional Shoreline Cove or to Pinole Marina

Launch site 1, p. 80

Preferred NOAA Chart: 18656, "Suisun Bay"

Estimated Paddle Time: 3 hours

Trip Rating: SK 3

Special Hazards: Strong afternoon winds and current can create steep chop.

Launch Site: A small dirt boat ramp in Bayfront Park. On Interstate 80 to Pinole, take the San Pablo Road exit. Head west to Pinole. Turn west on Tennant Avenue and proceed until you see the Bayfront Park sign directly across the railroad tracks. Turn right at the entrance of Bayfront Park and proceed along 500 feet of smooth dirt road. The boat launch is next to the white footbridge, on the northeast side of the water treatment plant on the shore of Pinole Creek. Use the parking lot near the park entrance. A picnic area, phones, and rest rooms are available. Managed by East Bay Regional Park District (510-562-PARK).

Nearest Campsite: Skyline National Trail Camp is off Interstate 80 in Berkeley, 14 miles south of Pinole. Managed by East Bay Regional Park District (510-562-CAMP).

Best Paddle Time/Tide: Midmorning at end of high tide, and return by midafternoon in low tide.

As you paddle 50 feet out the quiet creek mouth to the semiprotected cove, be aware of the winds. The tides are not a strong factor for the launch or return on this intermediate paddle, but the afternoon winds are very gusty. It's best to be on the water in the morning or early afternoon.

Not all paddles offer pristine glimpses at preserved areas. This paddle provides a dramatic dichotomy of preserved shoreline to the south and the effects of industrial overuse to the north. If you head south out of the creek mouth, you'll paddle along the newly preserved Point Pinole Regional Shoreline, which offers narrow, linear access to the bay. Here you'll observe graywacke and Franciscan formations along the banks. The shore is green with brush, and you'll see some shorebirds. To the north of Pinole Creek mouth, you can poke around the industrial banks and see old iron pilings. Currently, there is no public access to parts of the coast. In the future, the area north of the creek mouth will be linked for public access to the shoreline park to the south.

Please note that landing at the East Brother Light Station, just to the south of this area, is not recommended due to the extreme danger of launching and docking.

Pinole Bayfront Park to Rodeo Marina

Launch site 2, p. 80

Preferred NOAA Chart: 18656, "Suisun Bay"
Estimated Paddle Time: 4 hours
Trip Rating: SK 3
Special Hazards: Very strong afternoon winds combined with strong currents and large-boat traffic
Launch Site: Launch from Pinole Bayfront Park (see launch description on p. 82). Rodeo Marina and harbormaster: 13 Pacific Avenue in Rodeo (510-799-4436).
Nearest Campsite: Anthony Chabot Regional Park in Oakland is 25 miles southeast of Pinole, off Interstate 580. East Bay Regional Park District (510-562-CAMP).
Best Paddle Time/Tide: Midmorning at end of high tide, and return by midafternoon in low tide.

This intermediate trip, which launches from the Pinole Creek mouth, is 4 four miles long each way. It's best to paddle with the end of high tide or slack tide, then paddle back with the beginning of low tide. Linger for lunch at Rodeo Marina.

Paddle north along the San Pablo Bay shoreline from Pinole Creek, and you'll observe the increasing effects and views of an immense oil refinery industry. Next to the group of UNOCAL oil tanks south of Lone Tree Point is a submerged ship off the beach. Paddle near shore but far enough away so that you don't get caught in the shoals made by currents in the shallow beach areas. As you round Lone Tree Point after 3 miles of your launch site, look for a single large eucalyptus tree on the grassy bluff. From this marker, it's only a quarter of a mile to the Rodeo Marina.

This aged marina has a public access dock for landing and features a fun restaurant. When you approach the marina, you'll see the old wooden dock below the wide parking lot. All the other areas have fences—those are private parking lots for private docks, so stay away. The old public access wooden dock is directly behind the marina, next to the public (not fenced in) parking lot. Don't be surprised if you see a family of peacocks run down the docks to welcome you.

After landing your kayak on the dock, go for a short stroll around the harbor and check in at the harbormaster's office. You can picnic in the general public parking area or at the public dock or stop in at the local restaurant.

Rodeo got its name from the raucous rodeos said to have taken place here during roundups. After California became a state, the roundups and cattle shipment ceased. The late 1800s saw the birth of the immense oil industry, and the lovely working towns that grew along the San Pablo shoreline. While its marina has seen better days, Rodeo is fine example of the bay's industrial landscape.

Although Rodeo owes its rebirth to oil, oil continues to be a major polluter of Contra Costa County's shoreline as well as all of San Francisco Bay. Petroleum and chemicals used in processing enter the water through refinery waste discharges (what you've been paddling through) and accidental spills. Selenium from these shoreline refineries damages bay ecosystems and may be hazardous to people who eat fresh local fish. Additionally, motorists who dump used auto oil in the gutter or on the ground contribute significantly to this pollution. When it rains, as is has done more heavily in recent years, this oil washes down storm drains and creeks and into the bay.

Port Costa along Martinez Regional Shoreline

Launch site 3, p. 80

Preferred NOAA Chart: 18656, "Suisun Bay"

Estimated Paddle Time: 3 hours

Trip Rating: SK 2

Special Hazards: Afternoon winds; strong chop

Launch Site: A beach launch from a protected cove with a carry down a small bank. Take Interstate 80 east in Oakland and proceed 40 miles to Crockett. Turn east on Carquinez Scenic Drive and proceed for 3 miles, following the signs to Port Costa. In Port Costa, turn onto Canyon Lake Drive and follow it to the end. Once in the parking lot, turn left to the end of the fence bordering the railroad tracks. Park here and carry over across the railroad tracks to a 50-foot carry down the bank. For an easier carry down, cross the tracks where the fence ends, turn right, and walk along the bank for 20 feet. A small trail and 4-foot bank ledge is at the east tip of this small sandy beach. Nearest harbormaster information: Martinez harbormaster (510-313-0942). The Martinez Marina is managed by the East Bay Regional Park District (510-562-PARK).

Nearest Campsite: Anthony Chabot Regional Park in Oakland is 35 miles south of Port Costa, off Interstate 580. Call East Bay Regional Park District (510-562-CAMP).

Best Paddle Time/Tide: Morning in slack; return in beginning ebb.

Once you scout the easiest place to carry down your kayak, the launch will be very easy in this semiprotected cove of Carquinez Strait. Although a few more public access launch sites are located along the strait, they are in dangerous currents and therefore not recommended.

It's best to make this trip during the end of high tide, so you have either slack or low tide pushing you back to Port Costa. On this easy intermediate paddle of 6 miles you can just poke along the lovely, hilly shoreline. The next trip is more challenging and takes you 6 miles one way to Martinez Harbor.

Port Costa to Martinez Harbor

Launch site 4, p. 80

Preferred NOAA Chart: 18656, "Suisun Bay"
Estimated Paddle Time: 3 hours (one way)
Trip Rating: SK 2
Special Hazards: Afternoon winds; strong chop
Launch Site: Launch from Port Costa (see launch description on p. 84).
Nearest Campsite: Anthony Chabot Regional Park in Oakland is 35 miles south of Port Costa, off Interstate 580. Call East Bay Regional Park District (510-562-CAMP).
Best Paddle Time/Tide: Early morning in little or no wind, at the beginning of high tide.

This paddle is for strong intermediate kayakers. It's essential to make this 6-mile, one-way shuttle trip at the beginning of high tide, preferably in the morning with little or no wind. Martinez Harbor has plenty of parking and some fun diners.

For roughly the first half of the trip, you'll be kayaking along Carquinez Strait Shoreline Park. The strait can be swift, even at the beginning of high tide, so hugging the coast all along the way to Martinez Harbor is recommended to keep out of the wind and the stronger currents. The winds around the strait bends can be unpredictably strong, even if you started out with little or no wind. There are several small sandy and muddy banks where you can bail out and return later in ebb tide if necessary. Paddle close to the shoreline to see stilts, egrets, and herons. Harbor seals play around the strait.

Martinez Harbor is next to the bridge pilings. As you enter this charming spot, look for the small-craft dock by the restaurant.

Point Molate Beach to Castro Rock and Red Rock

Launch site 5, p. 80

Preferred NOAA Chart: 18649, "Entrance to San Francisco Bay"
Estimated Paddle Time: 3 hours
Trip Rating: SK 2
Special Hazards: Afternoon winds; chop
Launch Site: This is a mid- to high-tide beach launch in little to no surf. Heading west on Interstate 580, turn off onto Western Drive, the last exit off the interstate before the Richmond–San Rafael Bridge. Follow Western Drive and the POINT MOLATE signs. There is street parking near the beach launch site, as well as a playground and picnic sites. Note that this area has street crime. For information, call Richmond Parks (510-

231-3004). The large sign warning HIGH EXPLOSIVE MATERIAL IN ADJACENT AREA refers to the navy's fuel depot.

Nearest Campsite: Anthony Chabot Regional Park in Oakland is 25 miles southeast of Point Molate, off Interstate 580. Call the East Bay Regional Park District (510-562-CAMP).

Best Paddle Time/Tide: Mid- to high-tide launch. Check tide table to launch in slack and return in flood tide. Morning to early afternoon before midafternoon winds.

For a fun 3½-mile intermediate paddle, launch in the morning from the beach in no surf and head south 1¾ miles to Red Rock, just 170 feet south of the Richmond–San Rafael Bridge. An abundance of iron oxides gives this rock its brick red color. To the Spanish, it was *moleta*, named for the grinding stone. Just after you launch you'll paddle past Castro Rocks, a well-established seal haulout. Red Rock and Castro Rocks support dense colonies of egrets and herons; migratory birds also use these rocks as resting areas. Please paddle at least 50 yards from the rocks to avoid disturbing the resident wildlife.

Keller Beach to Red Rock or to Brooks Island

Launch site 6, p. 80

Preferred NOAA Chart: 18649, "Entrance to San Francisco Bay"
Estimated Paddle Time: 3 hours
Trip Rating: SK 2
Special Hazards: Afternoon winds; chop
Launch Site: This is a sandy beach launch in no surf. In Richmond, follow Garrard south to Western. Turn right onto Western and drive until you see the small beach, identified by a sign as Keller Beach, at the end of the fenced shoreline. Operated by East Bay Regional Park District (510-562-PARK).

Nearest Campsite: Skyline National Trail Camp is off Interstate 80 in Berkeley, 20 miles east of Keller Beach. Managed by the East Bay Regional Park District (510-562-CAMP).

Best Paddle Time/Tide: Morning in slack; return in flood. Check tide table and avoid midafternoon winds.

The trips out to Red Rock or Brooks Island are an easy 3½ miles. Paddling to Red Rock, you'll encounter mostly chop and a few clearly visible navigational points along the way: follow the shore north ¼ mile along Western Avenue to Cypress Point. Continue north another mile to the long wharf (officially called Chevron Long Wharf, where 26 million metric tons of oil were shipped out in 1997) and then 3 miles northwest to Red Rock.

To reach Brooks Island, follow Keller Beach south to the protected lagoon along Ferry Point. The lagoon attracts egrets, herons, and resident Canada geese. You'll see riprap along the shore here. From Ferry Point, swing wide to avoid the backwash of 3- to 5-foot swells around the point. Follow the shore eastward to Richmond Harbor Channel. Cross south to the tip of Brooks Island and land along the shell beach before you see the fence. Behind the fence is a prohibited area of sensitive bird habitat. For more information on Brooks Island, see "Richmond Marina Bay Harbor to Brooks Island," below.

Richmond Marina Bay Harbor to Brooks Island

Launch site 7, p. 80

Preferred NOAA Chart: 18649, "Entrance to San Francisco Bay"
Estimated Paddle Time: 2 hours
Trip Rating: SK 2
Special Hazards: Afternoon winds and shallow water create mild chop.
Launch Site: There is a concrete boat ramp at Richmond Marina Bay Municipal Harbor, 1340 Marina Way in Richmond (510-236-1013). From Interstate 580, go west on 23rd Street/Marina Bay Parkway in Richmond, then south on Regatta Boulevard. Turn onto Marina Way South and proceed 1½ miles until you see a small MARINA sign, and turn left onto Hull Street. Proceed to the Richmond Marina Bay Municipal Harbor. To tour the island, make reservations through East Bay Regional Park District (510-562-CAMP). A minimum of five people are required for each reservation, with a flat fee of $25 per reservation and an additional $6 transaction fee per reservation. You must make reservations to get a tour of the island.
Nearest Campsite: Anthony Chabot Regional Park in Oakland is 20 miles east of Richmond, off Interstate 580. Call East Bay Regional Park District (510-562-CAMP).
Best Paddle Time/Tide: Mornings with little wind, return in midafternoon in (at most) moderate wind. Launch in ebb and return in flood.

Brooks Island is a kayaker's paradise, and no one can reach Brooks more easily than a kayaker. An added bonus: This trip is fine for beginners. Located ¼ mile outside Richmond's Harbor Marina, this hilly island, which narrows to a long sandy spit, is ideal for wave surfing on the bay side and superb for paddle touring on the harbor side. The island's Ohlone Indian archaeological sites, raucous nesting bird colonies, and native meadows are formidably protected by tidal mudflats, occasionally tricky afternoon winds, and challenging shoals. Pick up a free tidal schedule at the Richmond Marina before you set out.

The launch ramp at the modern Richmond Marina Pier is one of the most convenient in the Bay Area. You can easily park in the harbor lot and change in their tidy public rest rooms. Then pick up a tide schedule at the harbormaster's office and check the forecast. Launch directly from the wooden pier, where the water is shallow. Just slide your boat over the pier and hop in.

It's best to launch either before 11 A.M. or after 6 P.M. The shallow channel and the strong afternoon winds combine to make a challenging paddle if you start late in the afternoon. By 6 P.M., the channel will have calmed down a bit, and with late-summer light you can easily go for a two-hour paddle. Plan to land on the island's sandspit on the western tip, along the northern shore and just west of the wooden fence.

Along the harbor are several interesting historical landmarks. The Liberty shipyards and the Richmond Ford Plant helped shape Bay Area industry. As you paddle out to the island, the view is breathtaking. The whole bay glimmers before you, with Angel Island just 5 miles away.

As you leave the calm harbor mouth, crosswinds will slap at you, and you'll encounter fast currents in a shoal. Your boat might spin a bit hitting cross waves, but with some modest paddle bracing you can smoothly maintain your balance and your course. Remember that tidal flows in shallow waters can be tricky.

Straight ahead of you is the hilly part of the island. As you get closer, you'll see a series of broken pier posts peeking out of the water. This is a dangerous spot, and signs alert you that entering this area is strictly forbidden. The mudflats here are not to be reckoned with, since they act like quicksand. The far safer landing, as mentioned earlier, is the legal one, just past the wooden fence along the spit. This landing also protects the wildlife refuge bordering the fence.

The long human-made sandspit is composed of two endangered ecosystems: salt marsh and coastal strand meadow. Along the sandy beach gather nesting colonies of Caspian tern, black skimmers, oystercatchers, snowy egrets, black-crowned night herons, kites, and avocets. As you pass these colonies near the tip of the spit, you can see the wooden fence. Ideally, you should dock near the fence, resting your kayak on the ice plants. The smooth sand and soft mud make landing quite easy. Don't dock far from the fence; the afternoon tide will separate that area from the rest of the island.

The bay side of the island offers glimpses of Angel Island, Red Rock, and Bird Rock. Bird is a small, rocky island 50 feet from the southwestern side of Brooks Island. Red Rock is southwest of Castro Point, to the south of the Richmond–San Rafael Bridge. Bird Rock is used by seals as a haulout area, and Red Rock—indicated on NOAA charts for the area—is a nesting area for local and migratory birds. It gets its name from its abundance of iron oxide.

If you plan to kayak surf, this is the place. Be sure to wear a helmet. Land by the fence and portage your kayak a few feet across the ice plants to the other side of the island. The portage will save you a very difficult paddle around the horn of the spit. The waves on this side of the island take a long time to peak. You get some nice runs and then brace as they crash near the beach. This side of the island is a safe place to develop bracing skills, as you'll have plenty of time between sets. Turning over isn't a worry, either; there are no rocks to hit your head on as you pull off your spray skirt and land along the sand. Pay special attention to the wind generated on the bay side. International sail competitors love this spot, so if it's especially windy or if there's a race, you might want to do some beach wave play rather than ride the waves.

As in all shallow, narrow straits, the winds are challenging. A fall storm can bring treacherous south winds. There can be a stiff wind chop beside the Ford Plant, accelerating to the Golden Gate. This can create funnel waves, which only very capable wave surfers should engage. Since winds are always present, here's a quick rule of thumb for maximum velocities: Don't go out if west winds exceed 30 knots, north winds exceed 25 knots, or the more tricky south winds exceed 15 knots. Most commonly, west winds join the south wind, so on your return trip you will be paddling in a following sea. East winds rolling down the East Bay hills are very rare, but they can gust up to hurricane force.

Aided by those following seas, allow an hour for your return trip to the harbor. If the cross waves pound your boat and you feel you're losing your course, just keep paddling parallel to the bay waves and head toward the old fishing pier between the island and the harbor. This area has a rocky breakwater that stops the intense afternoon waves. Then turn your kayak toward the harbor, and you can smoothly paddle straight in. But if you're ready to paddle in a following sea, go for it!

Real estate investors and the federal government tried their best to develop Brooks Island. Thanks to bureaucratic bungling, however, the island has survived and flourished without development. During World War I, the navy set out to dredge the harbor channel. They planned to level the island and build a massive breakwater from Point Isabel near Albany to Castro Rocks near Richmond. They had hopes of building dreadnought battleships and launching them into the deepened channel. The plans also called for a chapel, a hospital, and an airport where the harbor now sits. But plans were scrapped when dredging could not be completed before war's end. In the 1920s, the City of Richmond started massive sluice dredging and built a breakwater to protect the harbor. The 10,000-foot-long breakwater churned up thousands of fossilizing clams. The sluice dredging, now too expensive to complete, allowed the clams and sediment to make a spit. These 20,000-year-old bottleneck clams lie profusely along the beach, in various stages of fossilization. By the 1950s, thanks to the failed dredging attempt, two coastal ecosystems—coastal strand and salt marsh—established themselves on the island. Flora and fauna soon colonized the spit, including native plants rarefied by continued local urbanization.

The island was again threatened in the early 1960s when a developer, who had obtained all the permits but could not afford a costly drawbridge required by the harbormaster, attempted to build condominiums. Peace finally came to the island in the late 1960s, when the upset developer sold the island to East

Bay Regional Parks. Recently birds have discovered the island is a highly suitable breeding ground.

In the 1970s, the East Bay Regional Park District conducted a research project on Brooks Island. Fred McCollum, a graduate student working on his thesis, was sent to Brooks Island to study rodents. That was 20 years ago, and until 1997 McCollum was the resident tour guide and island keeper. You must call the East Bay Regional Park District in advance for an island nature tour; touring the island is otherwise prohibited. If you get a reservation through East Bay Regional Park District, they will conduct the tour. From the meadows on top of the hill, you'll see coyote brush, blue hyacinth, and wyethia. According to journals kept by Spanish sailors, Ohlone Indians living here used these plants to make delicious pinole cakes. You'll also see the soap plant. McCollum once told me the Ohlones used the soap plant not only for its medicinal value, but also as a successful fishing lure.

If you walk along the island trail past the fence, you'll immediately be scolded by hundreds of migratory birds nesting in hierarchies along the pond. So keep a brisk pace along the beach and be careful not to venture off the trail and closer to the nesting boundaries—they are off-limits to everyone.

From the beach, you'll view the high clay bluffs, which erode a few feet every year. The hill's rock layers were once part of a quarry mined by a railroad company and the source of the rocks used in the building of San Quentin. You can still see the rail system that transported the rocks from a quarry to the shore. Before the quarry was mined in the 1800s, the island was farmed by a Yugoslavian family. Remnants of the foundation of their farmhouse, as well as the water pipe, cistern, and cattle's well spring, are still visible. But the well spring is now contaminated by bacterial growth.

This is also a nice area from which to view Bird Rock, a whitened rock composed of graywacke and igneous extrusions. Oystercatchers, as well as harbor seals, breed around it. The flowers along here are plentiful. As you keep walking, you'll see the quarry, now a punctured aquifer, which the Ohlones used for their freshwater. San Francisco's renowned Trader Vic and his pal Bing Crosby used the quarry area for wild picnics from the 1960s to the 1980s.

Whether your plans call for wave surfing or coastal paddling, Brooks Island is most definitely an extraordinary scenic area and a fun paddling adventure.

The Sacramento Delta

Bird-watchers will prize this area of Northern California in particular. Paddling is best between October and March, when the ever numerous jet-skiers and water-skiers find the waters too cold. The Sacramento River and the San Joaquin River (also called Gallaher Slough on some maps) north of Franks Tract are extremely windy—nationally recognized windsurfers favor this area. Strong easterly winds pervade the Delta as a whole, which can make misplanned trips treacherous on your return if you have to paddle against the tide and wind. Tidal activity strongly influences the Delta, so plan your trip carefully. Excellent maps for the Delta are available at any fishing or bait store.

Although public marinas are abundant in the Delta, powerboaters often overuse them, even in the off-season. The following are trips chosen to minimize your paddle in possibly congested areas, while making sure you have a great nature paddle in California's richest ecological diner: the Sacramento Delta.

Franks Tract State Recreation Area to Little Franks Tract

Launch site 8, p. 81

Preferred NOAA Chart: 18661, "Sacramento and San Joaquin River"
Estimated Paddle Time: 3 hours
Trip Rating: SK 2
Special Hazards: Winds; chop; jet-skiers; water-skiers
Launch Site: Public boat ramp. Take CA 4 about 5 miles north of the town of Brentwood, toward Bethel Island. Off CA 4, go east onto Cypress Road for a mile and then north on Bethel Island Road. Drive 2 miles on Bethel Island Road, and then go east on Gateway Road. The ramp is at the end of Gateway Road.
Nearest Campsite: Delta Resort on Bethel Island, 6777 River View Road, on the San Joaquin River (510-684-9351). Or Brannan Island State Recreation Area, 17645 Highway 160 (916-777-6671).
Best Paddle Time/Tide: October through March, launch before 10 A.M. in ending flood; return before 3 P.M. in ebb tide.

Ducks, geese, an occasional eagle, herons, and egrets are permanent residents of this area, known as Franks Tract. Launching into Piper Slough, follow the Bethel Island shore northwest a mile and observe several coves and small sloughs. The only large channel you'll encounter will be on your left; this is the opening of the False River—about 1½ miles into your paddle. Head about a quarter mile into this slough. Natives call this area Little Franks Tract because it is quiet and uncluttered by powerboaters and fishing enthusiasts, and it is rich in birdlife. Exit the False River, cross Piper Slough, and head northeast along the shore of Webb Tract. Paddle a mile in the narrow channel along the Webb Tract shore and the marsh spits. Here is another protected area for a good look at birdlife. If you go farther than a mile along the shore of Webb Tract, turn around before you reach the second mile, where Old River Flats—a fast channel known for many powerboats—enters. Start your return along the shore of Webb Tract as you paddle west. Cross the False River to Piper Slough, and be aware of increasing winds. Return along the shore of Bethel Island.

Franks Tract State Recreation Area to Brannan Island

Launch site 9, p. 81

Preferred NOAA Chart: 18661, "Sacramento and San Joaquin River"
Estimated Paddle Time: 6 hours (one way)
Trip Rating: SK 2
Special Hazards: Afternoon wind; leisure-boat traffic; chop
Launch Site: Public boat ramp. Take CA 4 about 5 miles north of the town
   of Brentwood, toward Bethel Island. Off CA 4, go east onto Cypress
   Road for 1 mile and then go north on Bethel Island Road. Drive 2 miles
   on Bethel Island Road, and then go east on Gateway Road. The ramp is
   at the end of Gateway Road.
Nearest Campsite: Brannan Island State Recreation Area at 17645, Highway 160 (916-777-6671). The San Joaquin River is the dividing county
   line between Contra Costa and Sacramento Counties. Brannan Island,
   on the northern shore of the San Joaquin River, is in Sacramento County.
Best Paddle Time/Tide: October through March, launch before 9 A.M. in
   beginning flood and land on Brannan Island before 3 P.M. to avoid late
   afternoon winds.

From the water, the landing ramp at Brannan Island Recreation Area is 100
yards south of the intersection of Sevenmile Slough and Threemile Slough,
which opens to the Sacramento River. You will see a marina and boat ramp at
the landing area on your left along the shore of Brannan Island.

This intermediate, 12-mile (one way) paddle can be done as a shuttle, or
you can camp overnight at Brannan Island Recreation Area and return the next
day to Franks Tract. The conditions vary dramatically here, and the summer and
fall are very popular seasons for powerboaters and jet-skiers. Given the narrow
channel of Threemile Slough, which may have some steep shoals because it is
so shallow, and the number of powerboaters and windsurfers who frequent the
San Joaquin River (this is one of the busiest rivers in the country for these
sports), it's well worth taking the shorter trip listed prior to this one (p. 91) as
an exploratory paddle, to be sure this longer trip is right for you. In the late fall,
winter, or early spring, the Delta is almost peaceful.

As with the previous trip, launch in Piper Slough. Follow the Bethel Island
shore northwest a mile and observe several coves and small sloughs. Ducks,
geese, an occasional eagle, herons, and egrets are permanent residents of Franks
Tract. The first large channel you'll encounter will be on your left. This is the
opening of the False River, about 1½ miles from the launch. Paddle 1 mile along
the north shore of this slough, called Little Franks Tract by the natives because
it is quiet and uncluttered by powerboaters and fishing enthusiasts, and it is rich
in birdlife. One mile up the False River, there is a narrow slough on the right
called Fisherman's Cut. It's a narrow, shallow, protected channel around the

east side of Bradford Island and will take you to the Stockton Deep Water Channel. Paddle up Fisherman's Cut about 2 miles. Exit Fisherman's Cut and cross the Stockton Deep Water Channel to the south shore of Twitchell Island. Beware of winds and boat traffic here. Paddle another mile along the Twitchell Island shore in the Stockton Deep Water Channel, and then head directly north. Round the point of Twitchell Island and then follow its shoreline. Now you're on the western shore of Twitchell Island, in Threemile Slough. Continue north along this western shore for a mile up Threemile Slough. The channel widens when a branch of the Sacramento River enters from the southwest. Continue to follow the shore of Twitchell Island, which ends when you cross a small channel near a big beach and swimming area. When you cross this small channel, you'll be paddling west along the next leg of land—the tip of Brannan Island. Land at the ramp on the northeast shore of Brannan Island, about ½ mile from the end of Twitchell Island.

San Pablo Reservoir

Launch site 10, p. 80

Estimated Paddle Time: 3 hours
Trip Rating: SK 1
Special Hazards: Afternoon winds
Launch Site: There is a public launch ramp at the San Pablo Reservoir. Take Interstate 80 north of Berkeley and exit east to San Pablo Dam Road. Follow San Pablo Dam Road to the main entrance of the San Pablo Reservoir. Follow the signs to the launch ramp. There is a $5 launch fee and a $5 day-use parking fee. San Pablo Reservoir (510-223-1661).
Nearest Campsite: Anthony Chabot Regional Park is 30 miles southeast of El Sobrante, off Interstate 580 in Castro Valley. The park has several campsites and is managed by the East Bay Regional Park District. For reservations, call 510-562-CAMP.
Best Paddle Time/Tide: Morning to early afternoon. Not tide or current dependent.

You don't have to do the entire 7-mile circumnavigation of the lake to enjoy its lovely surroundings and picnic areas. This is a beginner's trip. The lake is a smooth-water paddle before midafternoon, but winds do pick up later in the day. Fishing boats abound on summer weekends.

Paddle directly from the launch ramp across the lake to San Pablo Preserve on the north shore. You can poke along the banks or into the coves for a glimpse into one of California's richest trout habitats. There are two easily identifiable picnic areas along this side of the lake, if you'd like to land and replenish yourself. Paddle for 3½ miles, and you'll see the marina on the other side. As you cross the lake to the marina, beware of fishing boats (no powerboats or jet-skis allowed). Paddle along the south shore and return to the boat launch.

Lafayette Reservoir

Launch site 11, p. 81

Estimated Paddle Time: 2 hours

Trip Rating: SK 1

Special Hazards: Afternoon winds

Launch Site: There is a public launch ramp at Lafayette Reservoir. From Walnut Creek, drive west on CA 24 and take the Acalanes exit, which loops around and ends up at Mount Diablo Boulevard. Turn left onto Mount Diablo Boulevard and drive ¾ mile to the signed entrance to the park on the right. Follow the toll gate road less than ¼ mile to the launch ramp. Parking is $5 and launching is $3. There is adequate parking near the ramp. Lafayette Reservoir is owned and operated by the East Bay Municipal Utility District, which stipulates that boats must be at least 10 feet long and 23½ inches wide and that all paddlers must wear life jackets; for more information, call them at 510-284-9669.

Nearest Campsite: Anthony Chabot Regional Park is 40 miles south of Lafayette off Interstate 580 in Castro Valley. The park has several camp-sites and is managed by the East Bay Regional Park District. For reserva-tions, call 510-562-CAMP.

Best Paddle Time/Tide: Morning to early afternoon. Not tide or current de-pendent.

Lafayette Reservoir is fairly warm, which makes it a good place to practice rescue skills and paddle techniques in a group. The wind picks up in the midafternoon. A paddle from one end of the reservoir to the other is less than ½ mile, so this is a suitable beginner's trip. You'll be paddling in the brush hills of the East Bay.

The reservoir has several picnic areas and hiking trails. A full day spent hik-ing, picnicking, and kayaking at this park is a day well spent.

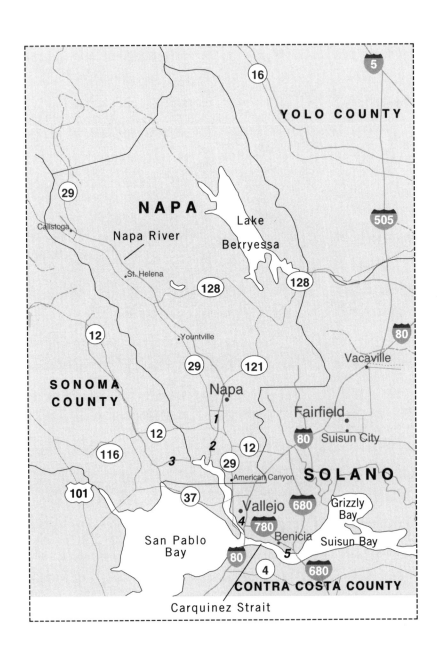

Napa County and Solano County

1. John F. Kennedy Memorial Park to Cuttings Wharf

2. Cuttings Wharf to Napa Marsh Wildlife Area

3. Hudeman Slough to the Napa Sloughs

4. Brinkman's Marine to Dutchman Slough (Solano County)

5. Benecia's Mothball Fleet (Solano County)

John F. Kennedy Memorial Park to Cuttings Wharf

Launch site 1, p. 96

Preferred NOAA Chart: 18654, "San Pablo Bay"
Estimated Paddle Time: 4 hours
Trip Rating: SK 2
Special Hazards: Afternoon winds
Launch Site: There is a small boat ramp in John F. Kennedy Memorial Park, a Napa municipal park on the west side of CA 121, one intersection south of Napa Valley College. Off CA 121, follow the signs into the park, to the parking lot and adjacent launching facility. Picnic areas and washrooms are available. For information, call the Napa Valley Marina (707-252-8011). Moore's Resort at Cuttings Wharf (707-253-2439).
Nearest Campsite: Pleasure Cove Resort at Lake Berryessa is 16 miles northeast of Napa on CA 121 (707-966-2172).
Best Paddle Time/Tide: Morning and afternoon. Not tide dependent.

Paddling out of this launch area south along the Napa River to Cuttings Wharf is a pleasurable, leisurely, beginner's half-day trip through picturesque rolling hills and marshlands. It can get hot here, since it's a dry area, and the wind can be breezy. If you want to be warm and enjoy a quiet river paddle to a wharf/café, this is the paddle for you. Along the way you'll see ducks and herons.

After about two hours of paddling, on the right you'll see Moore's Resort, the privately owned small-craft ramp at Cuttings Wharf. You can dock there for free and have lunch at the café. Start your return at or before 1 P.M. so you don't caught in the strong Napa Valley winds.

Cuttings Wharf to Napa Marsh Wildlife Area

Launch site 2, p. 96

Preferred NOAA Chart: 18654, "San Pablo Bay"
Estimated Paddle Time: 3 hours
Trip Rating: SK 2
Special Hazards: Afternoon winds; opposing strong current create strong chop in shallow water.
Launch Site: There is a small-craft ramp at Napa Sea Ranch Marina, at the end of Cuttings Wharf Road. In Napa, take CA 12 west and get off at the Cuttings Wharf exit. Follow Cuttings Wharf Road south to the marina. Napa Sea Ranch is at 3333 Cuttings Wharf. Adequate parking is adjacent to the ramp. There is a $1 small-boat launch fee. Napa Sea Ranch (707-252-2799).

Nearest Campsite: Pleasure Cove Resort at Lake Berryessa is 16 miles northeast of Napa on CA 121 (707-966-2172).

Best Paddle Time/Tide: Early morning in little or no wind in ebb tide and return in early afternoon in flood.

This is an 8-mile-long intermediate paddle. Since this area comprises the narrow portion of the Napa River, paddling in the afternoon will present higher winds in narrow straits, which causes continuous chop. Paddling in continuous chop is great exercise, but it does diminish the enjoyment. This section of the Napa offers plenty of quiet and solitude, even though Cuttings Wharf is near the county airport. You'll paddle about 3½ miles south down the gently winding river to Napa Slough, the uppermost slough channel of Napa Marsh Wildlife Area.

Along the way, you'll encounter some undisturbed wetland areas mixed with considerable commercial and residential development. As you get closer to the slough, the land is consequently more marshy and less developed, and hosts an abundance of egrets, herons, and other birdlife. The slough mouth is the first large open channel you'll see on your right, around a gently rounded point. Once you're in the slough, the Napa Marsh Wildlife Area is on your left. Don't poke so far into the slough that you wind up grounded in mud. Paddle in safely for up to ¾ mile, to just after the pronounced bend in the slough.

The slough is a quiet, pristine area for bird-watching. Have a picnic on the banks, where you can set your boat up far enough so the incoming tide won't wash it away. Be prepared to do a mud walk after landing and putting your kayak up on safe ground.

Return to Cuttings Wharf with high tide in late morning or early afternoon and visit the café at Napa Sea Ranch.

Hudeman Slough to the Napa Sloughs

Launch site 3, p. 96

Preferred NOAA Chart: 18654, "San Pablo Bay"

Estimated Paddle Time: 3 hours

Trip Rating: SK 2

Special Hazards: Afternoon winds; some chop

Launch Site: There is a launch ramp at the end of Skaggs Island Road. From Sonoma, head south on CA 12, and go east on CA 121. Turn right on Ramal Road, proceed for a few miles, then turn right onto Skaggs Island Road. Follow Skaggs Island Road to the Hudeman Slough boat ramp. Parking is adjacent to the ramp. Operated by County of Sonoma, Regional Parks Department (707-539-8092).

Nearest Campsite: Pleasure Cove Resort at Lake Berryessa is 16 miles northeast of Napa on CA 121 (707-966-2172).

Best Paddle Time/Tide: Morning and early afternoon. Not tide dependent.

Paddling 2 miles southwest down Second Napa Slough will take a lovely, quiet hour. This is a good beginner's trip. The views are of unparalleled wetlands bordered by Wildcat Mountain on your left. Ducks and herons are plentiful here. After the first mile, you'll cross Third Napa Street Slough on your right. Continue to paddle down Second Napa Slough and return when the slough turns south, at its crossing with Sonoma Creek. Watch for the wind to pick up in midafternoon. Hug the banks to avoid having the wind against you, and use your paddle in a semiraised position, to catch the wind; it acts as a sail when the wind is with you. Return to the Hudeman Slough boat ramp.

Brinkman's Marine to Dutchman Slough (Solano County)

Launch site 4, p. 96

Preferred NOAA Chart: 18654, "San Pablo Bay"

Estimated Paddle Time: 3 hours

Trip Rating: SK 3

Special Hazards: Strong current; strong afternoon winds; commercial boat traffic

Launch Site: There are public launch ramps adjacent to Brinkman's Marine on 1 Curtola Parkway at Harbor Way in Vallejo (707-642-7521). From Interstate 80, go west on Curtola Parkway to its end at Harbor Way in Vallejo. Vallejo harbormaster (707-648-4370). The launch ramp is maintained by the City of Vallejo. Parking is adjacent to the ramps.

Nearest Campsite: Pleasure Cove Resort at Lake Berryessa is 26 miles northeast of Vallejo on CA 121 (707-966-2172).

Best Paddle Time/Tide: Morning and early afternoon. Launch in slack; return with beginning ebb.

For this 5-mile-long intermediate paddle, be sure to start in slack and return in slack or beginning ebb. Look ahead and plot the trip. In the Napa River here and in Dutchman Slough, currents can get fast, and fighting them is hard work. The river has unusual shoals due to its shallow depth, which ranges from 4 to 9 feet. Also be aware of your paddling lane; many fishing boats use the narrow river channel. Paddling upstream 2½ miles brings you past the Vallejo Municipal Dock, the Vallejo Yacht Club, and the beautiful Vallejo Marina and harbormaster's office.

From the northern part of the marina, you can cross over to hug the shore of Mare Island, where you'll see lots of ships and cargo. Mare Island Naval Shipyards services several nuclear submarines. But don't land here—the navy doesn't want anyone to disturb their shipyard. From here, paddle north a few minutes and head west into the mouth of Dutchman Slough. Be aware of fishing boats here.

Now you can look forward to a retreat from the shipyard and urban development. Dutchman opens up before you within an hour of your paddle. Poke inside its winding bends and you'll chance upon some avocets nesting and perhaps a few seals lounging around on the banks. Along the banks on your left is the Napa Marsh Wildlife Area, which encompasses two marine sloughs—Dutchman and South Sloughs. Watch for egrets and herons here.

This is a good bailout point if the winds are stronger than you expected, if you get there much later than mid-high tide, or if you would like a shorter paddle. Paddling in a slough is mysterious and invigorating. You'll encounter fast winds blowing across your bow in these flat marshes where there's nothing to stop them. Dutchman is particularly nice, because, if you catch the wind just right, you can bring up your paddle as a sail and let it glide you up the slough. Of course, then there's the problem of paddling back against the wind. On your return, the easiest solution is to hug the bank that breaks the wind direction and keep paddling. If you get tired, remember low tide is coming soon if you started in mid-high tide. Stop and have lunch on the quiet banks of the slough.

Remember that the tide changes from high to low every six hours, making sloughs a very extreme paddling area. You can be stuck in mud quickly. As soon as you can paddle in weakening high tide or in the beginning of low tide, go for it. On your return to the ramp, hug the marsh banks and cross the river after the bridge.

If you decide instead to paddle another 2 miles upriver from the mouth of Dutchman Slough, you'll find yourself at South Slough. A longer, wider slough that winds deep into the marsh, South Slough is home to seals, stilts, avocets, egrets, and herons. Winds can be quite rough in this wide, open slough.

Return with the low tide and paddle along the marsh banks to avoid the increasing afternoon winds. On your return, be aware of shoals and boat traffic. You can cut across to the Vallejo Marina and hug the banks until you get to Brinkman's if the shoals are too confused. Numerous picnic areas and cafés make the Vallejo Marina and Brinkman's a good place to stop.

If you want to find out more about the Mare Island Naval Shipyard, visit the Vallejo Naval and Historical Museum at the corner of Marin and Capital Streets in Vallejo.

Benecia's Mothball Fleet (Solano County)

Launch site 5, p. 96

Preferred NOAA Chart: 18654, "San Pablo Bay"
Estimated Paddle Time: 5 hours
Trip Rating: SK 4
Special Hazards: Strong currents and opposing wind; steep waves; large, commercial boat traffic
Launch Site: The public ramp at Benecia Marina is at the end of West 9th Street; operated by the City of Benecia (707-746-4285). From Interstate 80, turn east on Interstate 780 and proceed 4½ miles to Benecia. Turn south on East 2nd Street and proceed ½ mile to West 9th Street. Turn west on West 9th Street and follow the signs to Benecia Marina.
Best Paddle Time/Tide: Morning. Return by early afternoon due to high winds. Launch in slack; return in beginning ebb.
Nearest Campsite: Pleasure Cove Resort at Lake Berryessa is 31 miles northeast of Benecia on CA 121 (707-966-2172).

Pay careful attention to the tide tables so you can have the late morning/ early afternoon ebb tide with you on your way back from this 9-mile-long intermediate paddle.

The Mothball fleet is 4½ miles northeast of Benecia. You'll be paddling close to shore for most of the trip. When exiting Benecia Marina, watch for boat traffic and breaking waves on the western side of the marina. Head out along the industrial shore of Benecia to the Port of Benecia Wharf, a long wharf at an angle to the shore. Swing wide around the wharf to avoid the confusing water surrounding it. Swing back closer to the shore and watch for small eddies and whirlpools under the Benecia–Martinez Bridge. The bridge will have the fastest water and shoal action. You'll then enter shallow Suisun Bay, with a slower current.

Continue to paddle close to shore until you reach The Mothball Fleet—a dozen military ships. The fleet will come into view several miles before you reach it. Stop next to the fleet and have lunch in your boat.

After World War II, more than 300 military ships were anchored here in neat rows. Today, nearly all have been scrapped, and only a few ships have been maintained in case of a military emergency.

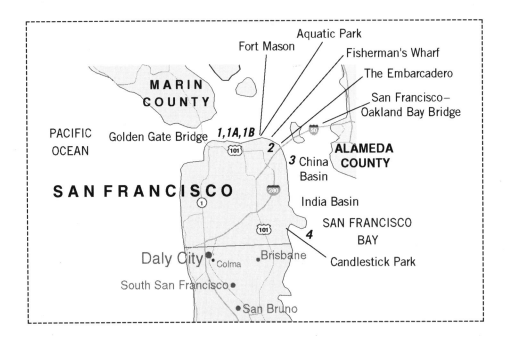

Aquatic Park

Fort Mason

Fisherman's Wharf

The Embarcadero

MARIN
COUNTY

San Francisco–
Oakland Bay Bridge

PACIFIC
OCEAN

Golden Gate Bridge

1,1A,1B

2

ALAMEDA
COUNTY

3 China
Basin

SAN FRANCISCO

India Basin

SAN FRANCISCO
BAY

4

Daly City
Colma
Brisbane

Candlestick Park

South San Francisco

San Bruno

City and County of San Francisco

1. San Francisco Waterfront Tour

2. Embarcadero Water Stairs to Pier 54

3. Pier 54 to Hunters Point

4. Candlestick Point State Recreation Area to the Brisbane Shoreline

San Francisco Waterfront Tour

Launch site 1, p. 104

Preferred NOAA Chart: 18649, "Entrance to San Francisco Bay"
Estimated Paddle Time: 3 hours (one way)
Trip Rating: SK 4
Special Hazards: Strong afternoon winds, strong opposing current, steep waves under the Bay Bridge
Launch Sites: There are three public access launch sites for the San Francisco waterfront:

1. To Crissy Field. The advantages of this beach launch are that it has plenty of parking and you launch in small surf. Managed by the Golden Gate Recreational Area (GGNRA) (415-556-0560). Take US 101 toward the Marina District in San Francisco. Go to the western end of Marina Boulevard and head straight into the Presidio. Turn right onto Zankowitz Road in the Presidio and park nearest the beach. *Note:* Crissy Field is undergoing massive renovations as of this writing. These efforts will restore the historic marshland, add a promenade and picnic tables, and connect Crissy with Marina Green. If Zankowitz Road is closed due to this restoration, the other small roads just a few yards to either side of Zankowitz also provide direct access to the beach launch and adjacent parking.

2. To the narrow public park along the breakwater of City Yachts. Take US 101 toward the Marina District in San Francisco. Go to the western end of Marina Boulevard and turn north at the end of Marina Green, before entering the Presidio. Drive 500 yards and park in the public parking area nearest the breakwater to launch (don't park in the San Francisco Marina parking spaces). This is a very protected beach launch. Public rest rooms and telephone are available. For more information on directions to City Yachts, call the marina (415-567-8880). *(1A)*

3. To Aquatic Park. Take US 101 to the Fisherman's Wharf area in San Francisco. Turn onto Bay Street, heading west. At the end of Bay and Hyde Streets there are limited parking spaces next to the beach. This is a well-protected beach launch near the scenic Hyde Street Pier, which features historic ships of the San Francisco Maritime National Historical Park. For historic ship tours and information in Aquatic Park, call The National Maritime Museum (415-556-3002). *(1B)*

Nearest Campsite: Candlestick State Park, off US 101 at the 3Com/3rd Street exit (415-822-2299).
Best Paddle Time/Tide: Morning, in little or no wind, in flood tide. If you make this a round trip, wait for the tide to ebb before beginning your return—preferably in late morning to early afternoon, to avoid strong midafternoon winds.

For this one-way shuttle, use the shuttle site at the ramp and dock at public Pier 54, located at 489 Terry A. Francois Boulevard (also known as China Basin Street). Turn right onto China Basin Street, just north of the intersection of 3rd and 16th Streets. Pier 54 is the small-craft concrete ramp and wooden dock near the bright yellow Bay View Yacht Club. Be sure to make note of obvious landmarks around the ramp/dock area (specifically, the large boats under repair nearby) before you launch, because it's tricky to locate the entry ramp otherwise when you return. Plans are under way to improve public access with a new, wider boat ramp and pier.

It's safest to make this trip with a group of experienced paddlers. The best time to start is 9 A.M., with a flood tide. If you start later, you'll be hit by chop and wind from at least two sides. As you scan the shore, pick out the area where the flux of fast current meets the slower current. Stay clear of there, or be prepared to use hip movements to steady yourself as you paddle. Launch out in little to no surf. From Crissy Field east to Fort Mason (1 mile) expect some moderate to strong chop, changing wind, and wave action. Don't be surprised if you have to use hip movements to balance you as you face wind, an oncoming wave chop, and chop along your starboard side (due to rebounding splash from the retaining walls). Keep a watchful eye for heavy traffic, including beginner windsurfers, sailboats, tour boats, and tankers. You'll be outside San Francisco Yacht Harbor, so be aware of speeding sailboats. Turn your head often, to observe waves and traffic from all sides. And be sure to paddle into any harbor along the way if the chop gets too confused and turbulent. Be especially watchful of the waves that splash around the retaining wall along the point at Fort Mason. While wind conditions vary throughout this trip, generally the most windy area is from your launch site to Fort Mason. Boat traffic is also heaviest in this area as well.

At Fort Mason, head into the historic ship marina known as the National Maritime Museum's Hyde Street Pier at Aquatic Park. You can edge right up to the three-masted ship, the *Balclutha;* the sidewheel ferry *Eppleton Hall;* and the *Eureka*—all nestled in port. This area offers a unique view of nineteenth-century ships set against the sleek skyline.

Follow the coast east to the San Francisco Yacht Harbor and check out the sailboats. As you round Fort Mason to Aquatic Park, you'll see diminishing wind chop and small swell. Currents are flat and calm along Fisherman's Wharf to the Embarcadero. Be sure not to hug too close to the shore here; the currents will take you back to Fisherman's Wharf. In the new section of the Embarcadero, directly south of the Ferry Building, if you paddle near enough along the Waterfront Promenade, you'll see the water stairs. This is a great launch or bailout point, depending on the tide level and chop. You can land your kayak here and go for a short stroll, or picnic along the sidewalk stairs. Keep paddling near the shoreline but beware of the Bay Bridge pilings—the next area of swift currents where the bridge towers create a small whirlpool action. After the bridge pilings, you'll continue south toward the industrial area parallel to 3rd Street, the most underused and calmest section of the trip. Public Pier 54 is next to a small bright yellow yacht harbor.

Embarcadero Water Stairs to Pier 54

Launch site 2, p. 104

Preferred NOAA Chart: 18649, "Entrance to San Francisco Bay"
Estimated Paddle Time: 1 hour
Trip Rating: SK 3
Special Hazards: Strong winds, confused chop, nearby large-vessel traffic channel
Launch Site: There is a 20-foot carryover to this wet-stairs launch site. In San Francisco, take Embarcadero east to the intersection with Folsom Street. The wet stairs (you can use them to walk down into the water), are along the Waterfront Promenade where the narrow concrete stairway enters the bay. Drop off your kayak along the launch site and park in nearby fee parking lots. San Francisco harbormaster (415-292-2013). Historic ship information; National Maritime Museum (415-561-6662).
Nearest Campsite: Candlestick State Park, off US 101 at the 3Com/3rd Street exit (415-822-2299).
Best Paddle Time/Tide: Morning. Launch in beginning high tide and paddle in flood (shuttle trip).

For those less interested in the previous three-hour trip, I recommend this lovely, calm, one-hour intermediate shuttle trip along the Embarcadero to Pier 54. This paddle is best done in flood tide, so you're paddling with the current. Although you won't experience the spectacular north-bay scenery and historic gold-rush ships, you will get a glimpse of other historic ships and a breathtaking view of the south bay as well as the industrial areas and history of San Francisco Harbor.

Before launching, spend 15 minutes reading the black-and-white-striped landmarks along the seawall sidewalk, Waterfront Promenade. The development of San Francisco Harbor—as you'll discover from the stunning landmark photos, poems, and journal excerpts of the workers who built the harbor and the ships—originated with the extraordinary cultural diversity of its strong labor movement. Near the end of Waterfront Promenade is Pier 41, where the World War II submarine USS *Pampanito* is berthed. This pier is quickly becoming a historic-ship and cultural center of its own, and you'll find a paddle around it worthwhile.

From this point south along the industrial piers, the trip is calm and offers glimpses of the south bay and the industrial ships. It's roughly an hour's paddle from Pier 41 to Pier 54. Dock and enjoy a picnic or one of the nearby restaurants along 3rd Street.

Pier 54 to Hunters Point

Launch site 3, p. 104

Preferred NOAA Chart: 18649, "Entrance to San Francisco Bay"
Estimated Paddle Time: 3 hours
Trip Rating: SK 3
Special Hazards: Afternoon winds, chop, commercial shipping traffic
Launch Site: The launch site is at the ramp and dock at public Pier 54 on Terry A. Francois Boulevard, also known as China Basin Street. Turn right onto China Basin Street, just north of the intersection of 3rd and 16th Streets. Pier 54 is a small-craft concrete ramp and wooden dock adjacent to 489 China Basin Street, the home of the bright yellow Bay View Yacht Club. Be sure to make note of what the ramp/dock area looks like before you launch; it can be tricky to locate when you return. San Francisco harbormaster (415-292-2013). Plans are under way to improve public access with a new, wider boat ramp and pier.
Nearest Campsite: Candlestick State Park, off US 101 at the 3Com/3rd Street exit (415-822-2299).
Best Paddle Time/Tide: Morning to midafternoon. Launch in slack; return in beginning ebb.

Note that this is a beginner's paddle through an industrial area. From the launch, paddle south past the tugs and docks through the old wooden piers and broken-down railroad tracks. The first small dock area is The Ramp Resort. Adjacent to this is another guest-use dock area, the Ramp restaurant. The next half-hour will bring you to the Hunters Point Naval Shipyard. This is an industrial paddle through a toxic wasteland. (Environmentally active paddlers monitor further toxic waste dumping in these areas.) Interestingly enough, the ducks seems to like it here. Beware of submerged broken pier pilings and waste material—and don't land in the Hunters Point area.

Candlestick Point State Recreation Area to the Brisbane Shoreline

Launch site 4, p. 104

Preferred NOAA Chart: 18649, "Entrance to San Francisco Bay"
Estimated Paddle Time: 3 hours
Trip Rating: SK 2
Special Hazards: Strong afternoon winds
Launch Site: You can launch in little to no surf on most days on the south beach of Candlestick Point. The beach is near the windsurfing launch piers. From San Francisco, take US 101 south and exit at Candlestick Park. Follow the signs to the Candlestick Park entrance. Do not turn into the stadium parking lots; continue to follow the road as it leads around the perimeter of the bay to Candlestick Point Recreation Area (415-557-4069). A day-use fee is charged if you park inside the recreation area, but there's good roadside parking. (Note: Candlestick Point is the border between the City and County of San Francisco and San Mateo County.)
Nearest Campsite: Candlestick State Park, off US 101 at the 3Com/3rd Street exit (415-822-2299).
Best Paddle Time/Tide: Early morning to early afternoon, in slack to high tide only.

This is a nice launching spot for beginners in slack to high tide to explore the bay south of Candlestick Park. Check the tide table and the day's weather conditions before you leave. Winds are strong here in the afternoon, making Candlestick Park a favorite windsurfing site. Be sure to return by early afternoon. This paddle takes you by some office parks, but along the Brisbane shoreline you can watch herons and egrets ply the muddy rocks and marsh. Fishing boats ply the waters here, which are home to smooth hound sharks, perch, and sculpin.

Candlestick Park beaches are good slack- to high-tide launch/return sites for trips to Oyster Point, Coyote Point, and points southward for intermediate paddlers. If you continue, be sure to check the tide table and the day's conditions for returning. You don't want to get stuck in mud or face strong midafternoon winds.

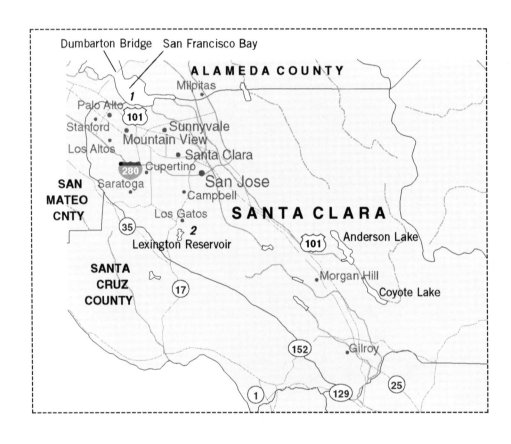

Santa Clara County

1. Palo Alto Baylands to Dumbarton Bridge

2. Lexington Reservoir

Palo Alto Baylands to Dumbarton Bridge

Launch site 1, p. 112

Preferred NOAA Chart: 18651, "San Francisco Bay (Southern Part)"
Estimated Paddle Time: 4 hours
Trip Rating: SK 3
Special Hazards: Strong afternoon winds and chop; mud at launch site and in channel during low tide
Launch Site: There are low and high tide launch piers made for kayaks and windsurfers. Parking is adjacent to the launch site. Take US 101 to Palo Alto and take the Embarcadero Road exit. Follow Embarcadero Road east to its end at the Palo Alto Nature Reserve. Follow the dirt road leading to the reserve, then park in the Palo Alto Sailing Station parking area. San Francisco Bay National Wildlife Refuge (510-792-0222).
Nearest Campsite: Memorial County Park in La Honda is 20 miles southwest of Palo Alto on Pescadero Road (650-879-0212).
Best Paddle Time/Tide: Early morning in little or no wind in mid-high tide; return in high tide by late morning to avoid strong winds.

This trip can be easily customized for beginners and intermediate paddlers. The launch site and nearby area provide a splendid array of routes and learning areas for various skill levels, scenic vistas, and bird and marine life. In short, this is the ultimate launch area for the south San Francisco Bay wetlands. There are no motorboats, and few surfers and kayaks. Check the tide book before you plan your trip. The ocean pumps 400 million gallons of water in and out of the bay every 12 hours.

This area is a shallow, muddy mix of pristine marsh and mudflats. At least, it's as pristine as it gets—it's part of the last 5 percent remaining freshwater marsh not yet developed. Nearly every inch of privately held San Francisco Bay marshlands have development plans stamped all over them. So this wetland is what western North America's largest bay once really looked like.

After you slide into your kayak from the easy launch, spend a few minutes on the water near the dock and just watch the tidal flow and the wind. The morning is a great time to follow the marsh banks to Dumbarton Bridge, to the left and north of you. There's lots of mud, and the currents and wind pick up predictably as the day grows longer. Here you can really learn how to plan for wind, currents, and chop. You're in a slower, shallower part of the bay and can easily assess your comfort level in increasing chop, and return to calmer waters if necessary.

As the bay opens before you, you'll observe several dozen birds feasting on a mud buffet—the roving display of diatom and crustaceans swimming in the nutrient-rich mud. Avocets, stilts, whimbrels, plovers, sandpipers, and the endangered clapper rail all feed here. If the chop or the currents get too strong while you're enjoying the wildlife, just paddle through the smaller sloughs across from the dock. These hidden sloughs connect overland on a wooden footbridge that serves as a trail.

Take this trip often to practice and develop your skills in current and chop while enjoying the varied birdlife.

Lexington Reservoir

Launch site 2, p. 112

Estimated Paddle Time: 2 hours

Trip Rating: SK 1

Special Hazards: Submerged tree limbs, modest afternoon winds

Launch Site: There is a launch ramp at Lexington Reservoir. Take CA 17 east toward Santa Cruz. Turn off at Alma Bridge Road, less than a mile east of Los Gatos. Follow Alma Bridge Road to Lexington Reservoir, and follow signs to the ramp. Operated by Santa Clara County Parks and Recreation (408-358-3741). There is a $3 launch fee, and adequate parking and picnic areas.

Nearest Campsite: Henry Cowell Redwoods State Park is 10 miles south of Lexington Reservoir on CA 9 (408-335-4598).

Best Paddle Time/Tide: Morning, before late afternoon, when winds pick up or fog rolls into the valleys. Not tide dependent.

Lexington Reservoir is the largest of three nearby reservoirs, and yet motors are not allowed on the lake. Three miles long and bordered by redwoods and hills, it is suitable for beginner and intermediate paddlers, family trips and picnics, and practice sessions for rescue skills. Birds and fish are abundant in the quieter areas of the reservoir.

Lexington's center is used often by windsurfers, so paddling along the banks and the arms of the reservoir is more scenic and avoids possible collisions with beginning windsurfers. The water is warmer here than in the bay, and mornings are great for a long beginner's paddle to develop your endurance and paddle stroke. A good 5-mile excursion takes you from the ramp south along the eastern shore and into the various arms till you reach the end of the reservoir and then returns along the opposite shore. Cross back to the launch ramp ¼ mile before the dam.

If you're a beginner, paddle with a group; there are no resources in the nearby area to call on for emergencies.

San Francisco Bay

San Mateo–Hayward Bridge

Daly City

South San Francisco

Pacifica   San Bruno

3

Millbrae   Burlingame

4,7,8   Foster City

Montara

San Mateo   *5,5A,6,9,10*

Belmont

Princeton

San Carlos

92

11

Redwood City   East Palo Alto

Half Moon Bay

1,2,2A

Menlo Park

1

PACIFIC
OCEAN

Portola Valley

San Gregorio

12

Pescadero

**SAN
MATEO**

Pescadero Creek

**ALAMEDA
COUNTY**

84

Dumbarton Bridge

82   *101*

**SANTA CLARA
COUNTY**

280

35

1

**SANTA CRUZ
COUNTY**

35

San Mateo County

1. Princeton Harbor to James Fitzgerald Marine Reserve

2. Princeton Harbor Tour

3. Pacifica to Half Moon Bay (Open Coast)

4. Coyote Point Marina to Anza Lagoon

5. Bayside Joinville Tidelands Park to the Bay

6. Bayside Joinville Park to Marina Lagoon

7. Parkside Aquatic Park

8. Lakeshore Park

9. Foster City Lagoon: Boat Park

10. Belmont Slough: Sea Cloud Park

11. Redwood City Marina to Corkscrew Slough

12. Pescadero Slough and Marsh

Princeton Harbor to James Fitzgerald Marine Reserve

Launch site 1, p. 116

Preferred NOAA Chart: 18682, "Half Moon Bay"
Estimated Paddle Time: 4 hours
Trip Rating: SK 4
Special Hazards: Strong winds, steep waves, strong currents, and wave backwash near headlands
Launch Site: This is a beach launch in a protected harbor along the beach next to California Canoe and Kayak in Princeton (650-728-1803). From CA 1 at Princeton, turn west onto Harbor Drive. Turn onto Princeton Avenue (there is only one way to turn). Follow the signs to California Canoe and Kayak at 214 Princeton Avenue, at its intersection with Vassar Street. California Canoe and Kayak shares the building with the Half Moon Bay Yacht Club.
Nearest Campsite: Half Moon Bay State Beach is 5 miles south of Princeton (650-726-8820).
Best Paddle Time/Tide: Morning to early afternoon. Launch in slack; return in beginning flood. Windy in midafternoon.

Check in at California Canoe and Kayak prior to your paddle for an update on conditions and to let them know your itinerary. This is an advanced trip.

The harbor is both calm and scenic. On your right, you'll see a sparsely used quaint fishing dock, and as you paddle along that side of the harbor mouth, there's a nice picnic area near the rock jetty and a fine place to portage your kayak directly to the surfside launch at James Fitzgerald Marine Reserve. I like to paddle along the rock jetty lining the two main traffic lanes inside the harbor. This gives me time to get acclimated to the conditions, which can change quickly here, since this is a short open-coast paddle. I also enjoy a close view of the exquisite great blue herons and egrets that wade along the county water district raft. Near the jetties that separate the traffic lanes, scores of pelicans and egrets create a cacophony that is wonderful to hear.

If the wind feels light from the west, and the swells look under 6 feet at the harbor mouth where the crab fishermen stand on the rock jetties at the lighthouse, I'm comfortable exiting the harbor mouth. Be careful to enter the bay along the outside lane of the rock jetty, since fishing boats tend to speed around the border of the lighthouse to their docks. Paddle south to the beach, and turn your boat around to get a good look at the wave conditions, speed, and swell. If it looks comfortable to you, then go for it! Surf the waves out to at least 15 yards from the rock jetty to avoid the backsplash of waves off the jetty. Paddle along the breakwater to the quiet kelp beds near Pillar Point Rocks (Snail Rock on the nautical chart). Note that the waves can roll in very quietly and quickly in kelp beds, so turn your head to see what's coming up from behind. An amazing variety of shore- and surf birds, and otters and seals, gather here. They'll sometimes follow you. Nonetheless, stay at least 300 feet from all mammals.

When you paddle past the kelp beds before Pillar Point Rocks, you'll be entering a surf zone. This area is particularly dangerous, even for skilled surf kayakers. Beware of going near, around, or past Pillar Point Rocks north to Moss Beach. This dangerous area is strictly an ultimate international surfer area, called Mavericks, where surfers have lost their lives. The rocky landing about 50 yards north of the beach offers great clamming, but stay aware of the shifts in tide. Also, don't get too near the caves in the Marine Reserve; you could easily be swept in or cornered in a dangerous situation.

From here, if you feel comfortable with the wave sets, poke past the kelp beds and get into larger waves, or head closer to the beach and get the wave sets there. The best time to paddle here is the morning, and since you've spent a bit of time around the kelp beds or surfing in, just portage your boat along the sand beach by the rock jetty and have a picnic before launching on the other side into the calm harbor for the return to the launch site.

Princeton Harbor Tour

Launch site 2, p. 116

Preferred NOAA Chart: 18682, "Half Moon Bay"
Estimated Paddle Time: 2 hours
Trip Rating: SK 1
Special Hazards: None
Launch Sites:
1. There is an easy beach put-in off CA 1 at Princeton. On CA 1, 1 mile south of Pillar Point Harbor, are signs for Half Moon Bay State Beach. Follow the signs to the beach, and park along the wide CA 1 shoulder.
2. From CA 1, turn west onto Harbor Drive and then onto Princeton Avenue (there's only one way to turn). Follow Princeton until you see the sign for California Canoe and Kayak at 214 Princeton Avenue, at its intersection with Vassar Street (650-728-1803). Park along the dirt road adjacent to California Canoe and Kayak, and put in along the sandy beach. *(2A)*
Nearest Campsite: Half Moon Bay State Beach is 5 miles south of Princeton (650-726-8820).
Best Paddle Time/Tide: Morning and afternoon. A protected harbor paddle. Can be windy in the late afternoon.

Paddling around the harbor, beginners will feel safe and can improve paddle strokes, perhaps poke near the harbor mouth, and even improve self-rescue skills.

Paddle toward the working fishing pier on its tall beams to the west of you, and you'll pass by what could soon be a relic of the small fishing industry. Have a picnic on the sand beach in little wind, and a hike along the rock jetty for a view of the Mavericks breaking big waves. Paddle along the rock jetty near the harbor mouth, and you'll get into very small waves entering the harbor. You'll be able to judge, but not yet practice, how to enter the ocean from the harbor mouth.

The county raft (on the western end of Princeton Harbor) is a perching site for great blue herons and egrets. Paddle south toward the beach. While still inside the harbor, look for the two main boat lanes separated by two rock jetties. As you enter the first one, near where you launched, you'll see myriad pelicans and other sea birds lining the rocks. As you paddle into the second lane, head for the beach. This is a safe area to practice rescue skills: one-person rescues, T-rescues, and other assisted rescues. The water is shallow and the floor sandy. There's no boat traffic along this part of the harbor beach. This area is protected from waves, so you'll be able to increase your agility and lose your fear of capsize in remarkably calm but nonetheless cold waters.

The harbor does offer a surprising view of marine life. On a recent paddle back into the harbor, I was in the middle of a run of thousands of sardines being chased by seals. Inside the harbor, you'll see a few seals, jellyfish, crabs crawling the rocks, and an occasional otter.

Pacifica to Half Moon Bay (Open Coast)

Launch site 3, p. 116

Preferred NOAA Chart: 18682, "Half Moon Bay"
Estimated Paddle Time: 4 hours (one way)
Trip Rating: SK 5
Special Hazards: Strong wind, steep waves, backwash against headlands, rip currents
Launch Site: Linda Mar Beach in Pacifica is on CA 1. This is an easy beach launch. Parking is available at Pacifica State Beach, managed by the City of Pacifica Department of Parks, Beaches, and Recreation (650-738-7381).
Nearest Campsite: Half Moon Bay State Beach is 4 miles south of Linda Mar Beach (650-726-8820). Shuttle parking is easily available here.
Best Paddle Time/Tide: Morning, on days with low to moderate tides.

This 10-mile one-way shuttle paddle is for advanced kayakers with open-coast skills. The surf is variable, but you can almost always launch from the southern corner of Linda Mar Beach. Paddle south out and around San Pedro Rock, which is both exposed and awesome. If the tide and swell are low enough, there is a passage through the rocks. Then paddle by the massive, impressive cliffs of Devil's Slide. Montara State Beach and James Fitzgerald Marine Reserve are interesting stops, but have potentially dangerous surf and big consistent rip currents. Round Pillar Point and enter Half Moon Bay through the breakwater. The big cliffs and scenery along the way make this a spectacular trip.

Coyote Point Marina to Anza Lagoon

Launch site 4, p. 116

Preferred NOAA Chart: 18651, "San Francisco Bay (Southern Part)"
Estimated Paddle Time: 3 hours
Trip Rating: SK 1
Special Hazards: Moderate afternoon winds
Launch Site: This is a guest launch ramp at a marina. Between Burlingame and San Mateo on US 101, turn east on Coyote Point Drive and follow signs to Coyote Point Marina at 1900 Coyote Point Drive, in San Mateo (650-573-2594). Coyote Point County Recreational Area charges $4 admission. Launching from the Coyote Point Marina inside Coyote Point Recreational Area is free if you don't have a trailer attached to your car. Otherwise, there is an additional $3 charge to park your car and trailer.
Nearest Campsite: Half Moon Bay State Beach is 35 miles west of Burlingame on CA 1 (650-726-8820).
Best Paddle Time/Tide: Early morning. Return by early afternoon due to heavy afternoon winds. Launch in slack; return in flood.

Be sure to get an early-morning start for this 6-mile paddle. Strong winds generate strong chop by midafternoon. This is also a tidally affected paddle, because the wetlands and mudflats get very muddy in extreme low tide. Check your tide table. This is a beginner's paddle because it is in shallow, relative flatwater. There are bailout points along the way, and although the banks of Coyote Point up to Anza Lagoon are partially covered by rocks, when you just want to get off the water, it's viable. A nearby trail along the banks won't leave you too far from some resources.

Paddling out of the marina, you'll encounter chop and traffic; this should be the most challenging part of the trip. As you head 2½ miles northwest along the Coyote Point Park shoreline, you'll see Fisherman's Park, which offers fishing and parking facilities. Fisherman's Park juts out to form the ¼-mile-long protected Anza Lagoon. Try to avoid the narrow channel between Fisherman's Park and Anza Lagoon: This is the channel that lets you inside the Burlingame Recreation Lagoon, which sits right off the noisy highway. A few hundred yards past the Burlingame Recreation Lagoon, you enter horseshoe-shaped

Anza Lagoon. Here you can poke around and also view shorebird habitat.

Return along the same course, following the shoreline back to Coyote Point, which is discernible from a distance because it has several narrow launch ramp sites, and a hundred yards south of the point is the only sandy beach on this trip that also has a launch ramp. Afternoon winds are a windsurfer's heaven here—you want to be off the water by midafternoon.

Bayside Joinville Tidelands Park to the Bay

Launch site 5, p. 116

Preferred NOAA Chart: 18651, "San Francisco Bay (Southern Part)"
Estimated Paddle Time: 3 hours
Trip Rating: SK 3
Special Hazards: Strong afternoon winds, chop
Launch Sites: The concrete launch ramps along Bayfront Shoreline Park are in the following places:
1. A ramp is across from the radio tower on East 3rd Avenue, 200 yards south of the intersection with Foster City Boulevard. There is a dirt lot with a single black bench by the roadside. The dirt lot is across from 3420 East 3rd Avenue, Invision Technologies.
2. There are launch ramps at the park, 200 yards north of intersection of East 3rd Avenue and Marsh Drive. Before this intersection, turn right at the stop sign into an unmarked, narrow dirt road. This is the Bayside Joinville Tidelands Park windsurfer parking lot and launch ramps. There are three launch ramps here, with an adequate central parking lot. Launch ramps are a bit tricky; be sure you can easily get down to the water. Some of the ramps terminate with small rocks that won't be kind to your kayak; other ramps end directly in the water without the hazard. Operated by City of San Mateo Parks (650-377-4640). *(5A)*
Nearest Campsite: Half Moon Bay State Beach is 35 miles west of Burlingame on CA 1 (650-726-8820).
Best Paddle Time/Tide: Mornings without wind. Launch in slack; return in flood. Land before strong midafternoon winds on the bay.

The access ramps of the 2-mile-long park are spaced approximately every 500 yards in this area. While these ramps are built mainly for windsurfers, morning paddles along the bay shoreline are good for beginners. The view is spectacular. Behind you is the San Mateo–Hayward Bridge, while ahead of you is a mildly rocky shoreline where egrets and herons hunt. The current is slight, the waves are small, and the water is shallow—especially over the sandbars. Plan to begin your trip by 1 P.M. to avoid the strong afternoon winds as you paddle north. The best route is parallel to the Bayfront Shoreline Trail.

Bayside Joinville Park to Marina Lagoon

Launch site 6, p. 116

Estimated Paddle Time: 2 hours

Trip Rating: SK 1

Special Hazards: Moderate afternoon winds

Launch Site: There are concrete boat ramps in the park. The park entrance is at East 3rd Avenue and Mariner's Island Boulevard in Foster City. From US 101, take CA 92 east to Mariner's Island Boulevard. Head north to East 3rd Avenue for 1 mile until you see the park signs and parking lot adjacent to the launch sites. Unload your kayak along the launch ramp and then drive your car back out to Mariner's Island Boulevard, where there is street parking. Operated by City of San Mateo Parks (650-377-4640).

Nearest Campsite: Half Moon Bay State Beach is 35 miles west of Foster City on CA 1 (650-726-8820).

Best Paddle Time/Tide: Morning and afternoon. Enclosed slough not open to the bay. Not tide dependent.

This beginner's paddle is appropriate for the whole family. Winds can get high in the afternoon, which can make paddling a little more difficult on the return. This is a warm, sunny, protected suburban paddle around the slough. There are picnic sites along the way on park property.

Parkside Aquatic Park

Launch site 7, p. 116

Estimated Paddle Time: 2 hours

Trip Rating: SK 1

Special Hazards: Moderate afternoon winds

Launch Site: There are concrete launch ramps in the park, which is on Seal Street in San Mateo. From US 101, head east on CA 92, then north on South Norfolk Street. Turn right onto Roberta Drive, then right onto Seal Street and head into Parkside Aquatic Park. Operated by City of San Mateo Parks (650-377-4640). For further information, call Spinnaker Sailing (650-570-7331).

Nearest Campsite: Half Moon Bay State Beach is 35 miles west of Foster City on CA 1 (650-726-8820).

Best Paddle Time/Tide: Morning and afternoon. Enclosed slough not open to bay. Not tide dependent.

This is an alternative launch site for a beginner's paddle in sunny, warm, enclosed Marina Lagoon. As in Marina Lagoon, on the previous trip, the wind usually picks up in the afternoon on the return paddle, but it's not too strenuous. Great picnic park, parking, and rest rooms. Lovely moonlight paddle area.

Lakeshore Park

Launch site 8, p. 116

Estimated Paddle Time: 2 hours
Trip Rating: SK 1
Special Hazards: Moderate afternoon winds
Launch Site: This is a sandy beach launch at Lakeshore Park in San Mateo. From US 101, take CA 92 east to South Norfolk Street. Head South on South Norfolk Street, turn left onto Day Avenue, and left onto Marina Court. Follow Marina Court to the park. Operated by City of San Mateo Parks (650-377-4640).
Nearest Campsite: Half Moon Bay State Beach is 35 miles west of Foster City on CA 1 (650-726-8820).
Best Paddle Time/Tide: Morning and afternoon. Enclosed slough not open to bay. Not tide dependent.

This pretty city park has picnic tables and recreation facilities. Winds can be challenging in the afternoon, but not strenuous, on this beginner's paddle in Marina Lagoon. Good for the family.

Foster City Lagoon: Boat Park

Launch site 9, p. 116

Estimated Paddle Time: 2 hours
Trip Rating: SK 1
Special Hazards: Moderate afternoon winds
Launch Site: There is a concrete launch ramp in the park. From US 101, go east on CA 92 and south on Foster City Boulevard. The Boat Park is on the west side of Foster City Boulevard, directly before the little bridge. Park in the parking lot and use the launch ramp. Operated by City of Foster City Parks Department (650-345-5731).
Nearest Campsite: Half Moon Bay State Beach is 35 miles west of Foster City on CA 1 (650-726-8820).
Best Paddle Time/Tide: Morning and afternoon. Enclosed lagoon—not tide dependent.

Beginners can paddle along the lagoon and develop their skills, particularly in midafternoon winds. Picnic areas and places to rest are readily available. This is a sunny, warm, protected paddle. The views are of a scenic suburban housing development. Good for the family.

Belmont Slough: Sea Cloud Park

Launch site 10, p. 116

Preferred NOAA Chart: 18651, "San Francisco Bay (Southern Part)"
Estimated Paddle Time: 4 hours
Trip Rating: SK 3
Special Hazards: Afternoon winds, tidal currents
Launch Site: There is a long carryover to launch at this beach in San Mateo. From US 101, go east on CA 92, south on Edgewater Boulevard, and left onto Pitcairn Lane, which takes you into Sea Cloud Park. Operated by City of San Mateo Parks (650-377-4640).
Nearest Campsite: Half Moon Bay State Beach is 35 miles west of San Mateo on CA 1 (650-726-8820).
Best Paddle Time/Tide: Morning to early afternoon. Launch in slack; return in flood. The launch is tide dependent.

You'll have to look for a good place to launch on the beach, and the return can be muddy if you wait until ebb to come back. If this is too tricky a launch, go to the Port Royal Park launch site, just southwest of Sea Cloud. Belmont Slough is open to the bay, so it offers both some wildlife viewing and mostly protected paddling with some currents, but generally flood and ebb are not strong. Get off the water by midafternoon to avoid gusty afternoon winds. Wind in sloughs is like wind in an alley—there is a funnel effect that can give it a boost.

The most interesting option is to paddle north to the bay and then southeast around the point and into Steinberger Slough. The mouth of Steinberger is ½ mile south of the mouth of Belmont Slough. This is a 7-mile excursion that requires paddling in shoal waters in the open bay for 2 miles and returning in flood currents. It's a good, short open-bay trip. Seals, kites, herons, egrets, and white pelicans work the rich marsh grasses from Belmont Slough into Steinberger Slough.

Redwood City Marina to Corkscrew Slough

Launch site 11, p. 116

Preferred NOAA Chart: 18651, "San Francisco Bay (Southern Part)"
Estimated Paddle Time: 6 hours
Trip Rating: SK 3
Special Hazards: Strong afternoon winds; strong chop
Launch Site: There is a launch ramp and low pier at the Redwood City

Launching Facility on Chesapeake Street; operated by Port of Redwood City Yacht Harbor (650-306-4150), 675 Seaport Boulevard in Redwood City. From US 101, go east on Seaport Boulevard, then left onto Chesapeake Boulevard. Drive to the end, where the Redwood City Launching Facility has a launch ramp and a large parking lot. The parking lot is directly across the street from the launch ramp, which has a $3.50 day-use fee. A hose and washroom are available. Take US 101 to Redwood City, turn left on Veterans Boulevard, right on Seaport Boulevard, and left on Chesapeake Street. Proceed to the end of Chesapeake Street, where the launch ramp and pier are on the right, and the parking lot is on the left.

Nearest Campsite: Half Moon Bay State Beach is 35 miles west of Redwood City on CA 1 (650-726-8820).

Best Paddle Time/Tide: Early morning launch in slack; return with flood. Get off the water before 3 P.M., when winds increase. Strongly tide dependent.

This is a 10-mile intermediate paddle with beautiful scenery, plentiful wildlife, and interesting paddling problems. After an easy launch near the industrial harbor and millworks of Redwood City, you'll paddle north about 45 minutes in the warm, relatively calm water of Redwood Creek, to the open bay. It's a good place to see egrets and herons eyeing their prey in the water. Along the way you'll see several narrow slough mouths, bypassing Corkscrew Slough among them. You'll paddle back to Redwood Creek through Corkscrew from Steinberger.

When you reach the mouth of the bay, sailboats may be racing around Redwood Point to the northwest, a cue to hug the shore somewhat to protect yourself from wind. Head north toward the Dumbarton Bridge, trying not to hug the shore too closely—there are rocks and rough currents. Stay about 100 to 200 feet offshore, where the open bay shoals and the wind is brisk but not too strong. Even in slack, the bay current will be against you, and you'll paddle north and west for at least two hours through shoals to Steinberger Slough. This trip is a test of paddling endurance, but the rewards are plentiful. Terns dive into the water near your boat and triumphantly retrieve their catch, while the winds and warm water spray your boat.

Steinberger Slough is located at the tip of Bair Island on your left. Paddle between the second island and the slough mouth, then head south into the slough. Within a few hundred feet, you'll be paddling in more protected waters. Picnic along the left bank—it's not as muddy as the right. Be careful to pull your kayak well up into the ice plants; otherwise, the flood tide may float your boat off without you.

Steinberger is large and open to some wind. The tall power towers you'll paddle near are homes for hundreds of egrets, living condo-style on the platforms. Paddle south about an hour and a half along Steinberger Slough to the mouth of Corkscrew Slough, which has a much smaller mouth than Steinberger but is easy to find—it's the first mouth on the left.

Corkscrew is the place to use your paddle as a sail now and then. The water is calm here, and when the wind is coming from behind you, you can angle your paddle to catch it. It's a kick. Along other parts of the slough, you'll be paddling close along the banks to protect yourself from strong winds.

Wildlife in Corkscrew Slough is abundant and diverse. Seals from Mowry Slough, to the east, hang out here in the early afternoon. Birdlife is particularly plentiful—egrets, herons, kites, pelicans, and great blue herons live in this pristine environment.

The island you're paddling around is Bair Island, saved by local kayakers and environmental groups from development as a hotel. Both the illegal construction and the attempt to block public access were halted. It took more than 10 years and 14 million federal dollars to purchase this piece of land originally sold for a dollar to a developer.

As Corkscrew Slough widens and straightens toward the ship channel, Redwood Creek, you'll be paddling in shallower waters and encounter 2- to 3-foot following seas—nothing too serious, just fun. When you enter the channel mouth, be prepared for afternoon chop and big wind. Hug the banks as you paddle south along the western shore to the entrance of the marina, and then cut across to the ramp when you reach the millworks. If you paddle through the middle of the channel, you'll be working a difficult chop and clawing through wind. You can expect to paddle 45 minutes from the Corkscrew Slough mouth to the takeout.

Pescadero Slough and Marsh

Launch site 12, p. 116

Preferred NOAA Chart: 18680, "Point Sur to San Francisco Bay"
Estimated Paddle Time: 3 hours
Trip Rating: SK 1
Special Hazards: Muddy tidal flats
Launch Site: There is a short carry down to the sandy bank launch at the south end of the Pescadero Lagoon bridge on west side of CA 1. Park in the adjacent Pescadero State Beach parking lot. Pescadero Marsh Nature Preserve is 14 miles south of Half Moon Bay on both east and west sides of CA 1. Pescadero Marsh Nature Preserve (650-879-2170). Call in advance to confirm slough water table.
Nearest Campsite: Butano State Park has many campsites and is 5 miles east of Pescadero on CA 1 (650-879-2040).
Best Paddle Time/Tide: September through February. Closed March through August for seal pupping and bird nesting. Call in advance to verify water level, which changes with rainfall and the extent to which the slough is open to the ocean. Not tide dependent.

Note that Pescadero Slough is identified as Pescadero Creek on some maps. When Pescadero Slough is flowing to the ocean, the water level lowers considerably, so it is highly recommended to call the Pescadero Marsh Nature Preserve in advance to check the water level. If the mouth is closed, paddling up the entire slough is possible. If the mouth is open at the ocean, paddling up the slough a few miles or so may be all you can do before it gets too muddy to continue. It's a 4-mile trip all the way up the slough, taking roughly three hours, but you can go at your own pace. This is a flatwater paddle, so you can return at any time.

The slough is wide in most places, and unlike at Elkhorn, you won't be in the awkward position of paddling up a finger in the slough, getting lost, and carrying your boat out through the mud.

Pescadero Marsh is the largest coastal marsh between San Francisco Bay and Elkhorn Slough (south along the coast in Monterey County), providing an impressive habitat for a variety of wildlife.

Pescadero Slough runs through Pescadero Marsh, a preserved marshland set away from the highway. Its banks occasionally flood in winter. The result is a nutrient-rich smorgasbord of fresh- and saltwater organisms that keep migratory wildlife well fed. Ospreys, white pelicans, stilts, and eagles have been observed here in the late fall, and the marsh is an important stop along on the Pacific Flyway. It provides sanctuary for a wide variety of other birds, including migratory loons, grebes, shovelers, and scaups. Its year-round residents include great blue herons, snowy and great egrets, coots, kites, kestrels, and hawks. More than 180 species of birds have been officially documented here by the California Department of Fish and Game, along with 50 kinds of mammals, 33 amphibians, and more than 380 plant species. Seal and anadromous fish are abundant when the slough mouth is open to the ocean after heavy rainfall.

SAN MATEO COUNTY

SANTA CLARA COUNTY

SANTA CRUZ

PACIFIC OCEAN

Loch Lomond Reservoir

Boulder Creek

Ben Lomond

Felton

Scotts Valley

Davenport

Santa Cruz

Soquel

Capitola

Aptos

Rio Del Mar

Opal Cliffs

Santa Cruz Small Crafts Harbor

2

1,6,7,8,9

3

4,5

Monterey Bay

Watsonville

1

35

9

17

101

152

129

1

Santa Cruz County

1. Santa Cruz Small Crafts Harbor to Soquel Point

2. Cowell Beach Surf Skills

3. Loch Lomond Reservoir

4. Rio Del Mar Beach to Capitola Wharf (Hooper Beach)

5. Wave Play: Hooper Beach (Capitola Wharf) to Soquel Point

6. Santa Cruz Small Crafts Harbor to Natural Bridges State Beach (Return at Cowell Beach)

7. Sunset and Full Moon Paddle from Santa Cruz Small Crafts Harbor

8. Santa Cruz Small Crafts Harbor to Moss Landing (Open Coast)

9. Santa Cruz Small Crafts Harbor to Del Monte Beach (Open Coast)

Santa Cruz Small Crafts Harbor to Soquel Point

Launch site 1, p. 130

Preferred NOAA Chart: 18685, "Monterey Bay"
Estimated Paddle Time: 3 hours
Trip Rating: SK 4
Special Hazards: Strong afternoon winds; steep waves; chop
Launch Site: There is a small boat ramp at the Santa Cruz Small Crafts Harbor. From CA 1, head west on Soquel Avenue, then south on 7th Avenue to its end at East Cliff Drive. Turn right onto East Cliff Drive and then right onto Lake Street. Follow the signs to the Santa Cruz Small Crafts Harbor boat ramp. There is a $5 launch fee. Harbormaster's office (408-475-6161).
Nearest Campsite: New Brighton State Beach is 4 miles south of Santa Cruz on CA 1 (831-464-6330). ´
Best Paddle Time/Tide: Mornings up to calm early afternoons. Check your tide table to make sure that your trip is not on an extreme-low- or extreme-high-tide day. Beware of south winds in the harbor mouth, which can make entering or exiting very dangerous.

This 3-mile paddle for beginners can quickly become an intermediate trip if the northwest winds pick up. Keep in mind that local guides offer to lead this trip. If you paddle in the morning, you'll paddle with the shore winds.

Santa Cruz Harbor is much less a tourist harbor than Monterey Bay. Consequently, paddling in Santa Cruz is a bit easier because the boat lanes aren't as traveled. Be aware of the wave break to your right along the jetty as you exit the harbor. If the waves are breaking on the right side of the harbor mouth, cross over to the left and exit the harbor. The reefs along Santa Cruz cover a wide offshore area. Keep an eye out for waves breaking along them. These reefs are spectacular areas from which to view marine life. Otters, seals, shearwaters, and pelicans frequent these calm waters, which feature beautiful kelp beds. As you paddle south out of the harbor, be aware of possible sudden wave breaks, especially along the reefs between Twin Lakes State Beach and Black Point.

After you paddle out the Small Crafts Harbor southeast toward Soquel Point, you'll encounter your first small patch of kelp beds. Twin Lakes State Beach will be the first beach south, which has lots of riprap. Stay in the kelp beds. Bonita Lagoon, just south of Twin Lakes, has smoother wave sets coming to shore. It is also a small freshwater lagoon that gets its water through a culvert at its north end. Both Lincoln Beach and Sunny Cove have rocky intertidal areas with waves breaking along the reefs. Corcoran Lagoon has a small protected beach, and is often a good area to paddle along the shore. Corcoran is a coastal lagoon with an influx of salt- and freshwater.

The water gets confused along the shore of Soquel Point, where cliffs and waves create backwash; paddle farther from waves along here. Your return to the harbor will require paddling with moderate wind in your face.

Cowell Beach Surf Skills

Launch site 2, p. 130

Preferred NOAA Chart: 18685, "Monterey Bay"
Estimated Paddle Time: 3 hours
Trip Rating: SK 2
Special Hazards: Occasional large wave sets and dumping surf
Launch Site: Beach launch in moderate 2- to 4-foot waves. From CA 1, head south on Bay Street to Cowell Beach. Park in front of the beach, next to the Dream Inn. Launch at the northern end of the beach, away from swimmers and the Dream Inn. For surf classes, call Kayak Connection at 408-479-1121 and ESKAPE! Sea Kayaking at 408-427-2247.
Nearest Campsite: New Brighton State Beach is 4 miles south of Santa Cruz on CA 1 (831-464-6330).
Best Paddle Time/Tide: Morning to early afternoon with mid-high- and mid-low-tide conditions. Don't go out in north winds.

Take a surf class before you venture out for this beginning to intermediate paddle. Spending a morning to develop your bracing skills (and have fun doing it) is essential if you want to pursue open-coast trips or even if you want to paddle when sudden strong winds come up in bays. The most accessible area that will ensure gradual wave development is Cowell Beach, which is often crowded with aggressive board surfers.

The northern part of the beach is sheltered by Point Santa Cruz and Santa Cruz Reef and is a good place to launch. Check the tide table, also. If it's too low a tide, the beach turns completely to tide pools and sand, and there are no waves. You'll want to start in 3- to 5-foot waves, then gradually build up, both in height and spacing. It's relatively sheltered, so the wave speeds won't mount too quickly. Remember to stay out of the way of surfers.

Bracing skills are essential to your development as a kayaker. The chance of a forced wet exit or an Eskimo roll is greatly reduced if you can quickly use an effective bracing paddle. Improve your brace skills routinely. After a few sessions, you'll be ready for the open coast.

Loch Lomond Reservoir

Launch site 3, p. 130

Estimated Paddle Time: 3 hours

Trip Rating: SK 1

Special Hazards: Moderate afternoon winds

Launch Site: There is a boat ramp at the reservoir. From CA 1, take CA 17 north and proceed onto CA 17 Business north, 3 miles south of Scotts Valley. From CA 17 Business, turn right onto East Zayante Road, left onto Lompico Road, right onto West Drive, and then right onto Sequoia Avenue and follow it to its end. The launch ramp is adjacent to the parking area near the end of the road. During the day, there is a $2 launch fee, but after 4 P.M. launching is free. Operated by City of Santa Cruz Parks and Recreation at Loch Lomond Reservoir (408-335-7424). Open only during summer. Park closes one hour before sunset.

Nearest Campsite: Loch Lomond Reservoir has many campsites (408-335-7424).

Best Paddle Time/Tide: Morning and afternoon before winds blow into the valleys.

Along the lush Big Trees Nature Trail, you can paddle north from the launch ramp and follow the forested shoreline for 2 miles until you see the forks at the end of the reservoir. Motorized boats are prohibited here. Conditions are not windy in the mornings, but there may be slight chop in the late afternoons. Be aware that fog rolls in quickly in the valleys here, another reason to return before late afternoon. The trip is suited to beginners and is 6 miles long.

Rio Del Mar Beach to Capitola Wharf (Hooper Beach)

Launch site 4, p. 130

Preferred NOAA Chart: 18685, "Monterey Bay"

Estimated Paddle Time: 4 hours (one way)

Trip Rating: SK 4

Special Hazards: Strong afternoon winds; steep waves; chop

Launch Site: This is a beach launch. From CA 1 to Capitola, turn east onto Rio Del Mar Boulevard. Follow Rio Del Mar to its end. Rio Del Mar Beach is at the southern end of Seacliff State Beach. The parking lot is next to the beach. Launch here anytime except in summer, when launching kayaks is not permitted and the area is state patrolled. For more information, call Seacliff State Beach at 831-685-6442.

To leave a car at Capitola Wharf, park along a side street near the wharf. From CA 1 to Capitola, take 41st Avenue south, then take a left onto Portola Drive. Follow the signs to the park, adjacent to Hooper Beach, on the north side of Capitola Wharf. For more information, call Capitola Boat and Bait shop (408-462-2208).

Nearest Campsite: New Brighton State Beach is 1 mile north of Rio Del Mar Beach (831-464-6330).

Best Paddle Time/Tide: Morning to early afternoon to avoid winds. Get off the water by 3 P.M. This launch site not usable in summer.

The launch information bears repeating: Be forewarned—the launch site is closed in summer, and you will be ticketed by the state police if you try to launch. This is an intermediate, 6-mile (one way) shuttle trip. Paddlers who want to work on their surf skills can seek out the good waves along Rio Del Mar Beach. There is a rich variety of wildlife along this trip, notably seals, sea lions, dolphins, otters, and shorebirds.

Launch in small to moderate surf and paddle through it to head north along Soquel Cove. The destination is Capitola Wharf at the northern end of Soquel Cove. The mouth of Aptos Creek cuts Rio Del Mar Beach where you launch. Seacliff Beach will be the first beach site you paddle across, and it may have some long wave sets. Seacliff has nearly 2 miles of ocean frontage below steep sandstone cliffs.

At the first ½ mile, you'll pass the famous 500-foot-long concrete supply boat, the *Palo Alto*. Built in 1918 for use during World War I, the ship was unused until 1929, when it was bought by the Cal-Nevada Stock Company. They towed it to Seacliff, flooded its holds so it would sink, remodeled it, and operated it for two years as an amusement center with a dance floor. The *Palo Alto* is now a prime fishing spot, a roosting site for a variety of seabirds and shorebirds, and a seal haulout. Stay 300 feet from the ship to avoid disturbing the wildlife.

After you pass the *Palo Alto*, continue west to New Brighton State Beach. New Brighton has some tossed wave action against the cliffs, so paddle at a distance. From the beach it's a ¾-mile paddle to the eroding Capitola Bluffs, which have discharged rocks that lie submerged in layers under the water. Beware of these submerged rocks and wave breaks off the reefs. Capitola Bluffs is an important paleontological resource, and a wealth of prehistoric shells are visible in the cliff at low tide.

For the next ½ mile you'll be paddling along the quieter coastline to Capitola. Round the Capitola Wharf to Hooper Beach, where you can land in little or no surf. Hooper is a privately owned sandy beach, leased to the City of Capitola for public access. End your trip here with a shuttle back to Rio Del Mar Beach.

If you opt to make this a round trip, begin the return leg before 1 P.M. to avoid offshore midafternoon winds. If you start by 1 P.M., the winds will be with you on your return.

Wave Play: Hooper Beach (Capitola Wharf) to Soquel Point

Launch site 5, p. 130

Preferred NOAA Chart: 18685, "Monterey Bay"
Estimated Paddle Time: 2 hours
Trip Rating: SK 4
Special Hazards: Strong afternoon winds; steep waves; submerged rocks
Launch Site: This is a sheltered beach launch at Hooper Beach. From CA 1 to Capitola, take 41st Avenue south, then take a left onto Portola Drive. Follow the signs to the park, adjacent to Hooper Beach, on the north side of Capitola Wharf. Park along a side street near Capitola Wharf. For more information, call Capitola Boat and Bait shop (408-462-2208).
Nearest Campsite: New Brighton State Beach is 1 mile south of Capitola on CA 1 (831-464-6330).
Best Paddle Time/Tide: Midmorning at mid- to high tide.

The Hooper Beach area is the perfect place for intermediate paddlers to hone their surf skills. Local kayaking schools conduct surf zone classes here. The surf breaks are small to moderate, with even sets, but the sets get bigger toward Soquel (Pleasure) Point. Beware of submerged rocks at low tide toward the point, and stay clear of board surfers. Find some wave sets in the semiprotected bays along this area and develop wave-set perception and wave setup skills. Brace, ride 'em in, and have lots of fun. Get off the water by 3 P.M. to avoid strong offshore winds.

You can also paddle in the kelp beds along the point. You may see sea otters rafting with you. Harbor seals also thrive in the kelp.

In 1856, the first Capitola Wharf was built as a commercial pier on Soquel Cove. Once railroad service from Watsonville to Santa Cruz began, commercial use of the wharf dropped off. The wharf is now mainly used to launch fishing boats.

Santa Cruz Small Crafts Harbor to Natural Bridges State Beach (Return at Cowell Beach)

Launch site 6, p. 130

Preferred NOAA Chart: 18685, "Monterey Bay"
Estimated Paddle Time: 5 hours (one way)
Trip Rating: SK 4
Special Hazards: Strong winds; steep waves; backwash at headlands
Launch Site: There is a boat ramp at the Santa Cruz Small Crafts Harbor. From CA 1, head west on Soquel Avenue, turn south onto 7th Avenue, and drive to its end at East Cliff Drive. Turn right onto East Cliff Drive,

then right onto Lake Street. Follow the signs to the Santa Cruz Small Crafts Harbor boat ramp. There is a $5 launch fee. Harbormaster's office (408-475-6161).

For the shuttle, leave your car at Cowell Beach. From CA 1, head south on Bay Street to Cowell Beach. Park in front of the beach, next to the Dream Inn.

Nearest Campsite: New Brighton State Beach is 4 miles south of Santa Cruz on CA 1 (831-464-6330).

Best Paddle Time/Tide: Early morning to midafternoon; not tidal dependent. Launch by 10 A.M. and return by 3 P.M. to avoid strong offshore winds.

This is 4-mile, one-way paddle for intermediate paddlers with a shuttle landing at Cowell Beach. The shuttle allows you to avoid the midafternoon winds on return to Santa Cruz Small Crafts Harbor.

Be careful of boat traffic in the harbor after launching from the boat ramp, and watch for wave backwash on the right side of the jetty inside the harbor. Head west and paddle in the middle of the kelp beds from the harbor to the Santa Cruz municipal pier a mile away. This will keep you from the open exchange of water in the San Lorenzo River mouth and from heading too close to the waves and rocks along Santa Cruz Beach.

Paddle near the municipal pier and poke around to Cowell Beach, whose landmark is the large hotel complex, the Dream Inn. Cowell Beach has little or no surf, so landing is easy. Beware of occasional south winds at the harbor mouth and at Cowell Beach. If you wish, paddle from Cowell Beach ½ mile south to Steamer Lane, a world-class and very popular surfing area. Be sure to keep away from the large wave sets around Steamer Lane, and respect surfers who sometimes paddle far out.

From Steamer Lane rounding Point Santa Cruz, another mile, watch for submerged rocks and sharp wave breaks off the cliffs at the point and along the reefs. Be especially careful of reflected waves outside Point Santa Cruz and Seal Rock, a few hundred yards west of the point. There is usually a small swell and no wave break from reefs in the channel between Seal Rock and Point Santa Cruz, and this is a good paddling area.

Generally, there is a wide area of kelp from Point Santa Cruz to Natural Bridges. Paddle in the kelp beds to avoid the intertidal zones of Natural Bridges and its submerged rock shelves. There is no landing of kayaks on Natural Bridges except on the extreme west end of the beach, but I don't recommend landing even there, because the area is often congested with windsurfers. The wave break at Natural Bridges is worth a look. Natural Bridges is a pocket beach, and the waves arrive in long, smooth sets.

Return to Cowell Beach in little to no surf, and land on the north end of the beach only—landing elsewhere at Cowell is prohibited.

In 1958, Woods Lagoon was dredged and reshaped to form a harbor. Two years later, the harbor was expanded into Arana Gulch. Santa Cruz Harbor sits along Arana Marsh, where dominant plant species include pickleweed and cattails, pines, and cypress. Plovers, sandpipers, turnstones, and waterfowl frequent this marsh for food and rest.

Sunset and Full Moon Paddle from Santa Cruz Small Crafts Harbor

Launch site 7, p. 130

Preferred NOAA Chart: 18685, "Monterey Bay"
Estimated Paddle Time: 3 hours
Trip Rating: SK 3
Special Hazards: Strong gusty winds; unlighted boats
Launch Site: There is a boat ramp at the Santa Cruz Small Crafts Harbor. From CA 1, head west on Soquel Avenue, turn south onto 7th Avenue, and drive to its end at East Cliff Drive. Turn right onto East Cliff Drive, then right onto Lake Street. Follow the signs to the Santa Cruz Small Crafts Harbor boat ramp (408-475-6161). There is a $5 launch fee.
Nearest Campsite: New Brighton State Beach is 4 miles south of Santa Cruz on CA 1 (831-464-6330).
Best Paddle Time/Tide: Start one hour before sunset on full moon nights in summer, and paddle only on evenings with little or no wind. Check the tide table for full moon conditions. Beware of infrequent, dangerous south winds in the harbor mouth.

Local guides offer a variety of beginning and intermediate group sunset and full moon paddles (see the listings in Part 3 of this book). As with any open-coast paddle, particularly a night trip, have all the appropriate equipment with you, including night paddle sticks, a flashlight, and an emergency call system—both to your fellow paddlers and to local emergency resources.

From the harbor, head east to Soquel Point. This area is a favorite among otters on moonlit nights in winter. Poke along the shoreline in a tranquil sea and witness the magical play of moonlight on the water.

Santa Cruz Small Crafts Harbor to Moss Landing (Open Coast)

Launch site 8, p. 130

Preferred NOAA Chart: 18685, "Monterey Bay"
Estimated Paddle Time: 5 hours (one way)
Trip Rating: SK 4
Special Hazards: Strong winds; large swells

Meeting Place/Launch Site: Meet at Monterey Bay Kayaks on Del Monte Beach, off CA 1, at 693 Del Monte Avenue for this Monterey Bay Kayaks guided tour. Park at Del Monte Beach, adjacent to Monterey Bay Kayaks (408-373-KELP or 800-649-KELP). You'll be shuttled with the group to the launch site at the boat ramp in Santa Cruz Small Craft Harbor.

Should you need directions to the Small Crafts Harbor, they are: From CA 1, head west on Soquel Avenue, turn south onto 7th Avenue, and drive to its end at East Cliff Drive. Turn right onto East Cliff Drive, then right onto Lake Street. Follow the signs to the Santa Cruz Small Crafts Harbor boat ramp (408-475-6161). There is normally a $5 launch fee.

Nearest Campsite: Veterans Memorial Park is near downtown Monterey (408-646-3865). This is the nearest campsite to the Del Monte Beach meeting place.

This advanced trip is sponsored by Monterey Bay Kayaks. Consult their current schedule and requirements before registering. As of this writing, their requirements are that you have taken Monterey Bay Kayak's basic skills kayaking and surf-zone courses. Their Stroke Clinic is recommended. This guided trip gives advanced paddlers open-coast experience in a well-trained group setting. Along the way you'll perhaps see some shearwater and other open-water birds, dolphins, and other marine life. The group, preferably composed of double kayaks, paddles at an efficient rate of 2 to 3 knots per hour.

Santa Cruz Small Crafts Harbor to Del Monte Beach (Open Coast)

Launch site 9, p. 130

Preferred NOAA Chart: 18685, "Monterey Bay"
Estimated Paddle Time: 8 hours (one way)
Trip Rating: SK 5
Special Hazards: Strong winds; large swells; large breaking waves
Meeting Place/Launch Site: Meet at Monterey Bay Kayaks on Del Monte Beach, off CA 1, at 693 Del Monte Avenue for this Monterey Bay Kayaks guided tour. Park at Del Monte Beach, adjacent to Monterey Bay Kayaks (408-373-KELP or 800-649-KELP). You'll be shuttled with the group to the launch site at the boat ramp in Santa Cruz Small Crafts Harbor.

Should you need directions to the Small Crafts Harbor, they are: From CA 1, head west on Soquel Avenue, turn south onto 7th Avenue, and drive to its end at East Cliff Drive. Turn right onto East Cliff Drive, then right onto Lake Street. Follow the signs to the Santa Cruz Small Crafts Harbor boat ramp (408-475-6161). There is normally a $5 launch fee.

Nearest Campsite: Veterans Memorial Park is near downtown Monterey (408-646-3865). This is the nearest campsite to the Del Monte Beach meeting place.

This advanced trip is guided by Monterey Bay Kayaks. Consult their current schedule and requirements before registering. As of this writing, they require you to have participated in their Santa Cruz Small Crafts Harbor to Moss Landing Open Coast Paddle (see previous trip), and their basic skills and surf-zone courses. Their Stroke Clinic is recommended. This guided trip gives advanced paddlers extreme open-coast experience in a well-trained group setting. Along the way, perhaps you'll see some shearwater and other open-water birds and dolphins, and you'll have a good chance of seeing whales, including blue whales, minkes, and California gray whales, as well as other marine life.

This paddle tests the limits of endurance, since the group—preferably composed of double kayaks—will be paddling at 4 knots per hour. There is a good chance that you will be paddling in winds over 20 knots, and in surf and breaking waves higher than 4 feet at any given place along the trip.

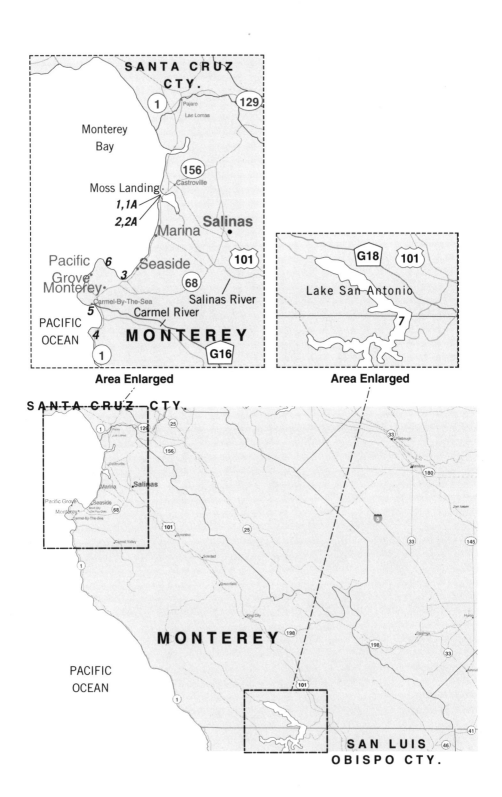

Area Enlarged

Area Enlarged

Monterey County

1. Elkhorn Slough

2. Bird-watching at Elkhorn Slough

3. Del Monte Beach to the Monterey Bay Aquarium:
   Touring the Monterey Bay National Marine Sanctuary

4. Point Lobos to Whalers Cove (Open Coast)

5. Stillwater Cove

6. Lover's Point to Point Pinos (Open Coast)

7. Lake San Antonio

Elkhorn Slough

Launch site 1, p. 142

Preferred NOAA Chart: 18685, "Monterey Bay"
Estimated Paddle Time: 5 hours
Trip Rating: SK 2
Special Hazards: Fast tidal current; strong afternoon winds; mudflats
Launch Sites:
1. There is a launch ramp a few hundred feet north of the entrance to Elkhorn Slough. From CA 1, go west along an unidentified road behind the Little Baja Pottery Shop on the west side of CA 1 in Moss Landing. The turn is ½ mile south of Jetty Road in Moss Landing. The ramp, behind the pottery shop, is inside the entrance of Moss Landing Harbor District.
2. There is the public boat launch at Kirby Park. Kirby has a bank launch and boat ramp off CA 1 west on Dolan Drive, which is ¼ mile south of Elkhorn Slough. Follow Dolan Drive to Kirby Park. Parking and rest rooms are available. *(1A)*

   Your choice will be dictated by the tide; see below. For marine and birdlife information, call the Elkhorn Slough Foundation (408-728-5939). Elkhorn Slough Nature Conservancy (408-633-5555). Elkhorn Slough National Estuarine Research Reserve Visitor Center, 1700 Elkhorn Slough (408-728-2822).

   Both Kayak Connection (408-479-1121) and Monterey Bay Kayaks (408-373-KELP or 800-649-KELP) offer a launch site, and boat and equipment rental for Elkhorn Slough. For great guided kayak tours, call Monterey Bay Kayaks.

Nearest Campsite: Sunset State Beach is 7 miles north of Elkhorn Slough on CA 1 (831-763-7063).
Best Paddle Time/Tide: Morning to early afternoon; check your tide table to make sure you launch in flood and return in ebb. Very tide dependent. You need at least 2 feet of water at Kirby Park. Be aware that a few minutes could make the difference in paddling out in ebb tide and getting stuck in the mud. Afternoon northwest winds at 10 to 20 knots will help you if you return in the afternoon; otherwise, paddling against this wind is extremely difficult.

The paddle up Elkhorn Slough is a lovely and educational tour of one of California's best-preserved wetlands. Elkhorn is a tidal slough managed by the Elkhorn Slough National Estuarine Research Reserve. Its 1,400 acres of wetland and upland are home to some 267 species of resident and migratory birds. Other animals living here include otters, harbor seals, and harmless sharks (leopards and smooth hounds—both bottom feeders). Although this is a public launching area, guided tours are recommended. With the help of a guide, you'll learn much more about the ecology of this fragile marsh—and without a guide, novices have routinely paddled into muddy dead ends here!

By timing your paddle with the tidal current you will avoid paddling against a strong flow at the CA 1 bridge. If low tide is in the morning and high in the afternoon, then launching is best from the public boat ramp in the Moss Landing Harbor District. Take the wider fork in Elkhorn Slough, which is the northern fork, to Rubis Creek. Go as far as you can before it gets too shallow, and paddle back during slack or at beginning high tide. If the high tide is in the morning, and low tide in the afternoon, then plan on paddling up Rubis Creek and spending a long lunch by the dock to wait out the tide change. A word of caution: Stay on the dock and avoid trampling the fragile pickleweed, and do not haul your boat out of the water. To avoid the strong winds, be sure to return before midafternoon. Dock and wait out the tide change.

The launch for this trip is easy, but you have to paddle continuously and strongly while under the CA 1 overpass. Peak currents of 3 knots can tunnel under the bridge, creating areas of obviously rough water that are tough to paddle against. Spend a few minutes judging the calmest water through this area. Many fishing boats and pleasure craft also use this harbor entrance. Always observe the rules of the road and turn your boat into the wake of a larger boat. This is where the slough waters open as a channel to the ocean, so the outgoing current gets a little swift.

To your left you'll see harbor seals in Moss Landing Wildlife Area. Stay at least 50 feet away. There are also many small bottom-feeding sharks here.

Your real mission on this trip is to observe the wetland details as your guide takes you through the lacework of slough waters from Gap Flats Haulout to Pelican Flats to Rubis Creek. On the way you'll pass a few remaining dairy farms in the distance. Rubis Creek is newly remodeled for kayakers and features a small wooden dock where landing is easy. There is a trail (adjacent to an outhouse) from the access uphill to a commanding view of the slough, farms, railroad, and wetland.

Your return should be with the outgoing tide. In the afternoon, the wind does get strong; near the underpass you will be continuously paddling—against the wind but with the tide.

Bird-watching at Elkhorn Slough

Launch site 2, p. 142

Preferred NOAA Charts: 18685, "Monterey Bay"
Estimated Paddle Time: 5 hours
Trip Rating: SK 2
Special Hazards: Fast tidal current; strong afternoon winds; mudflats

Launch Sites: Launch at Elkhorn Slough (see launch description on p. 144). *(2) (2A)*

Nearest Campsite: Sunset State Beach is 7 miles north of Elkhorn Slough on CA 1 (831-763-7063).

Best Paddle Time/Tide: Check tide table for both full moon and sunset paddles and local resources for other calm-weather conditions.

While in the past you may have paddled the slough from a different perspective, witnessing its transformation during the fall migration in October and November as the birds descend to fatten up on its banks is a spectacular experience. Add to the migrating populations the shorebirds that are year-round inhabitants, such as sandpipers, dowitchers, and stilts, and a guided tour with an expert during these months will be well worth your while. The four-hour tours are scheduled for low tide to better view the birds while they are feeding. During migration, tours are available in the morning and evening.

Del Monte Beach to the Monterey Bay Aquarium: Touring the Monterey Bay National Marine Sanctuary

Launch site 3, p. 142

Preferred NOAA Charts: 18685, "Monterey Bay"

Estimated Paddle Time: 4 hours

Trip Rating: SK 2

Special Hazards: Strong afternoon winds; sneaker waves in the kelp beds; steep waves; chop; busy channel

Launch Site: This is an easy, protected beach launch next to Monterey Bay Kayaks, off CA 1 at 693 Del Monte Avenue. Park at Del Monte Beach adjacent to Monterey Bay Kayaks (408-373-KELP or 800-649-KELP).

Nearest Campsite: Veterans Memorial Park is near downtown Monterey (408-646-3865).

Paddling the Monterey Bay National Marine Sanctuary, which extends the length of this paddle, is a kayaker's marine-life paradise. It is home to 80 percent of all North American marine mammal species and contains one of the world's largest giant kelp forests. The underwater Monterey Canyon is deeper than the Grand Canyon and covers some 4,024 square nautical miles. It is a fan canyon—a delta trough at the base of a continental slope—like a similar feature at Big Sur. Monterey Canyon is unique in that it is unusually deep and yet not near a present-day river. It may have been the main drainage for the Great Valley of California during the Miocene epoch.

As you paddle through the kelp forest of Monterey Bay, you'll pass sea otters nursing their young; sea lions and harbor seals barking along the rock jetty; and loons, cormorants, pelicans, and gulls hunting for food. And if you're lucky, you'll even see pods of dolphins or a few whales and their calves. Paddling here is breathtaking.

This trip is for beginning and intermediate paddlers. Confirm the weather, wind, and wave conditions with Monterey Bay Kayaks at Del Monte Beach before your launch. Del Monte Beach is a fairly protected area with generally very light surf. It is best to launch by midmorning, before the wind comes up. The easiest launch is directly down from the picnic tables at the beach. The currents off the beach are light and generally flow north toward Santa Cruz.

With a few strokes you're near an old navy platform that cormorants have claimed as a perch. As you paddle to your left, south toward magnificent Cannery Row, watch the boat traffic in Monterey Harbor and take note of the traffic lanes. Paddle parallel to the pier until you see the open harbor mouth. This boat channel is fairly busy, so cross it quickly to avoid interfering with normal boat traffic. Head for the rock jetty, with its inevitable crowd of harbor seals and sea lions. Be sure to stay at least 50 feet from the seals and the jetty. And this is a prime diving area; don't paddle too close to scuba diving boats or diving flags.

As you paddle down Cannery Row, you'll move into the kelp. Large, luminescent jellyfish are common here. Between the kelp beds and the rocks leading to the Monterey Bay Aquarium, you'll observe otters and seals. Again, stay 50 feet away to protect their habitat and so you don't violate the Marine Mammal Protection Act.

Soon, spectacular Monterey Bay Aquarium will come into view. On very calm days, you can paddle to the harbor seal protection area a few hundred yards south of the aquarium. This sanctuary has submerged rocks and usually gets very turbulent, with moderate to large waves. Don't paddle here. The rocks to the northwest of the Monterey Bay Aquarium are part of the Hopkins Marine Life Refuge, which is operated by Hopkins Marine Station. Stay clear of this area, too, because of the marine mammals and strong wave action.

Allow double time to return because the wind and currents will be against you. Take out at Del Monte Beach.

Point Lobos to Whalers Cove (Open Coast)

Launch site 4, p. 142

Preferred NOAA Charts: 18685, "Monterey Bay"
Estimated Paddle Time: 4 hours
Trip Rating: SK 4
Special Hazards: Steep waves; waves colliding against headlands and rocks; long kelp stretches; very strong afternoon winds
Launch Site: There is a boat ramp in Whalers Cove. Access is limited to 10 divers and 6 kayakers per day. Take CA 1 to Point Lobos State

Reserve, 3 miles south of Carmel. Turn onto Point Lobos Reserve Road, on the west side of CA 1, and at the reserve entrance gate request permission to launch your kayak. There is adequate parking adjacent to the ramp. Picnic areas and rest rooms are available. Landing your kayak in the reserve is not allowed. Point State Lobos Reserve (408-624-4909).

Nearest Campsite: Saddle Mountain Recreation Park is 15 miles east of Point Lobos off Carmel Valley Road (408-624-1617).

Best Paddle Time/Tide: Check the tide table for at least 2- to 3-foot tide days; check weather conditions.

Launching from the protected bay of Point Lobos at Whalers Cove makes this 6-mile, four-hour, advanced paddle much easier, but wear a helmet anyway. This open-coast trip, while short, is nonetheless tricky because of possibly quickly changing offshore weather and swell conditions and the lack of bailout points between Point Lobos and Whalers Cove. At high tide, the beaches in this area are submerged, and sometimes there is violent, dumping surf. Swells can range from 5 to 20 feet and generally appear in calm, large, and rounded sets.

Head south to Blue Fish Cove, the other main cove in Point Lobos. Swing wide around Blue Fish—swells converge here—and avoid the rocks along the cove. On the mile-long paddle from Blue Fish Cove to the Carmel Highlands, the wind can be strong. Venture into the coves along here, not only to protect yourself from the wind but also to investigate the rich marine and other wildlife of Point Lobos.

From the Carmel Highlands, paddle to Yankee Point, discernible by its irregular broken face and the many detached rocks around it. Watch for wave breaks alongshore at the point. You'll notice a bailout spot or picnic area on the beach next to Yankee Point. If you paddle between the wave breaks, which look like upside down Vs on the beach, you'll land smoothly on the beach.

On your return, paddle into the prevailing wind and waves. In winter, the swells are dramatically larger. If they aren't too large and the weather conditions permit, check out the caves, tubes, and arches along China Cove, at the southern tip of Point Lobos State Reserve. Five islands mark the outskirts of the cove; the largest is Bird Island. Because of the cove's unique protected waters formed by this necklace of islands, it's an easy vantage point for whale watching.

Blue whales and minkes are often seen in the area. Harbor seals haul out here and sea otters forage in the kelp beds all along your route. These beds provide habitat for abalones, rockfish, lingcod, and many other species.

Please do not land anywhere in the Point Lobos State Reserve, and stay at least 50 feet from the seals. All marine life within the Point Lobos State Reserve is protected. In 1960, the first underwater reserve in the United States was established here. The reserve features one of two native stands of Monterey cypress in the world.

Stillwater Cove

Launch site 5, p. 142

Preferred NOAA Charts: 18685, "Monterey Bay"
Estimated Paddle Time: 3 hours
Trip Rating: SK 3
Special Hazards: Submerged rocks and tidal reefs
Launch Site: This is a beach launch at Stillwater Cove in little to no surf. There is off-road public parking past The Lodge at Pebble Beach, at the end of Cypress Drive off CA 1 in the Del Monte Forest. Additional public parking is available along the 17th fairway off CA 1, adjacent to the beach. Check conditions in advance with the Monterey harbormaster at Monterey Marina (408-646-3950).
Nearest Campsite: Saddle Mountain Recreation Park is 15 miles east of Point Lobos off Carmel Valley Road (408-624-1617).
Best Paddle Time/Tide: Check tide table for neap tide days; check weather conditions.

Intermediate kayakers will enjoy this cove paddle, which is about 2 miles. Stillwater Cove supports giant kelp sponges, sunflower stars, and a major seal haulout offshore on Pescadero Rocks. It is protected from northwest swells by Pescadero Point. Significant reflected surf hits its rocky substrate and low reefs. Paddle far enough from reflected surf along the rocks and reefs, yet still within the cove, before Pescadero Rocks. Be on the lookout for large diver bubbles on the surface; this is a well-used access point for divers.

Lover's Point to Point Pinos (Open Coast)

Launch site 6, p. 142

Preferred NOAA Chart: 18685, "Monterey Bay"
Estimated Paddle Time: 6 hours
Trip Rating: SK 4
Special Hazards: Very strong afternoon winds; steep swell and waves
Launch Site: This is a long carry down a stairway to a beach launch in 3- to 5-foot surf. From CA 1, take CA 68 to Pacific Grove, turn north onto Forest Avenue, left onto Lighthouse Avenue, and then right onto 17th Avenue. Proceed to the end of the road, to the Lover's Point parking area. Monterey County Parks Department (831-647-7795).

Nearest Campsite: Saddle Mountain Recreation Park 15 miles east of Point Lobos off Carmel Valley Road (408-624-1617).

Best Paddle Time/Tide: Check the tide table to ensure there is no spring tide on the day of the trip. Check the weather conditions with local resources. Be off the water by midafternoon due to offshore fog and winds.

Only advanced kayakers should undertake this 3-mile paddle along open coast. There are no bailout points and no opportunities to land on the rocks along the beach at Point Pinos. The launch is only partly protected from larger waves breaking on the beach, and you may have to launch in 2- to 5-foot swells. It's best to leave from the southern end of the beach, where the waves are generally smaller.

As you paddle north, swing wide around Point Pinos—the next point—to avoid breaking surf. Point Pinos is discernible by its low-lying face and a high lighthouse at its peak. The buoy off Point Pinos is a good destination and turn-around point. This route avoids the huge surf at the point, where the conditions are challenging due to a mix of incoming and rebounding waves. Swing wide around the buoy and return before midafternoon winds increase.

Point Pinos has the oldest continuously operating lighthouse on the West Coast. Built in 1855, today it features a small Coast Guard museum. In 1602, Monterey Bay was "discovered" and named by Spanish explorer Sebastian Vizcaino. The area at the time was well established by nomadic communities of Ohlone Indians, also called the Costanoans, who had lived in the Monterey Bay area at least a thousand years before the arrival of the Spanish. Vizcaino named the southern tip of Monterey Bay *Punta de Pinos*, "Pine Point." This rocky, low-lying point backed by dune is a refuge for marine life. Snails, sea stars, and black abalones inhabit the tide pools. Great numbers of pelagic red crabs are washed ashore here and on nearby beaches during El Niño years. Whales and pelagic birds can be seen from the point beginning in December and until mid-February. Crespi Pond, a freshwater pond and sanctuary for nesting birds, is on the edge of Point Pinos Lighthouse and to the adjacent golf course.

Lake San Antonio

Launch site 7, p. 142

Estimated Paddle Time: 2 hours

Trip Rating: SK 1

Special Hazards: Moderate afternoon winds

Launch Site: There is a boat ramp at the southern end of the lake. Take US 101 to Paso Robles and turn west on Interlake Road. Turn right on San

Antonio Road to the Harris Creek boat ramp. There is adequate parking. Monterey County Parks Department (831-647-7795).

Nearest Campsite: Lake San Antonio has several campsites (805-472-2311).

Best Paddle Time/Tide: Morning in spring and winter. Get off the water by midafternoon to avoid possible strong winds.

This enjoyable, 4-mile paddle is appropriate for beginners. As you paddle south toward the dam, the first inlet on your right is Harris Creek; poke inside. Lake San Antonio is home to migrating eagles, and they tend to gather in this protected inlet. Picnic on group tables near the ramp.

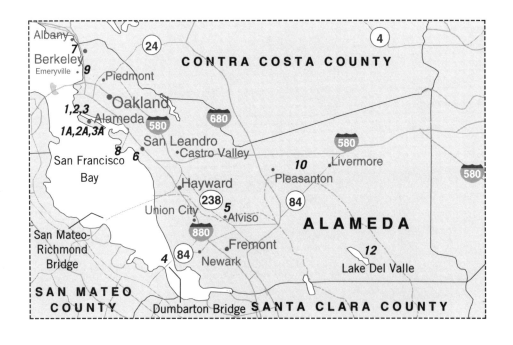

Alameda County

1. Jack London Square to Coast Guard Island

2. Jack London Square to Yerba Buena Island

3. Jack London Square to Alameda Island's Robert Crown Memorial State Beach

4. San Francisco Bay National Wildlife Refuge: Newark Slough

5. San Francisco Bay National Wildlife Refuge: Alviso Boat Ramp to Drawbridge Island

6. San Leandro Marina to Oyster Bay Regional Shoreline

7. South Sailing Basin (Berkeley)

8. Martin Luther King Regional Shoreline (Doolittle Beach)

9. Emeryville City Marina

10. Shadow Cliffs Regional Recreation Area

11. Full Moon Paddle at Lake Chabot

12. Lake Del Valle

Jack London Square to Coast Guard Island

Launch site 1, p. 152

Preferred NOAA Chart: 18649, "Entrance to San Francisco Bay"
Estimated Paddle Time: 3 hours
Trip Rating: SK 2
Special Hazards: Afternoon winds and chop; novice sailors in channel
Launch Sites: 1) The Jack London Square public launch dock is behind
   Scott's Restaurant, across from California Canoe and Kayak (510-893-
   7833) in Jack London Square. From Interstate 880 in Oakland, go west
   on Broadway Avenue and proceed to the end at Jack London Square.
   California Canoe and Kayak is on 400 Water Street. Put your boat near
   the dock and then park. The nearest parking is across the plaza in the
   Jack London Square Parking lot. 2) Another easy launch site is Estuary
   Park's boat launch at the intersection of Embarcadero and Oak Street,
   about ½ mile south of Jack London Square. Operated by the East Bay
   Regional Park District (510-562-PARK). *(1A)*
Nearest Campsite: Anthony Chabot Regional Park is 20 miles southeast of
   Oakland off Interstate 580 in Castro Valley. The park has several campsites
   and is managed by the East Bay Regional Park District (510-562-CAMP).
Best Paddle Time/Tide: Morning to early afternoon. Be sure to return be-
   fore midafternoon, when winds pick up and create intense chop until 6
   P.M. Channel is not strongly tide dependent.

Paddle out from the low dock to your left along Jack London Square. You'll pass
by a private marina and Heinhold's First and Last Chance Saloon, where Jack
London spent many hours listening to tales of the sea. Along the walkway is the
tiny sod-roofed cabin in which he lived during the Klondike Gold Rush in
Alaska. The cabin was brought here in 1969. After ½ mile, past the complex of
shops in Jack London Village, you come to Estuary Park. The park parallels San
Antonio Creek, which once drained Lake Merritt.

Enter Embarcadero Cove after another ½ mile, where the Oakland Estuary
widens around Coast Guard Island. Be careful of large-vessel traffic near the estuary ship slips. At the north end of the estuary's eastern arm, called South
Channel, you'll see the San Antonio fishing pier and lots of picnic tables. Most of
the estuary cove is lined with marinas and no public dock access to Estuary Park.

Coast Guard Island, headquarters for the captain of the port and the 11th
US Coast Guard District, looms closely on your right. Landing here is prohibited, so paddle by the shady picnic tables and the campuslike setting of buildings and well-planned walkways. There is little current flow near Coast Guard
Island, so paddling around it offers a protected area from which to observe the
egret and heron nests on the island and enjoy the view.

As you round the island, paddle back along the Oakland side of the estuary;

the Alameda harbors have much marine traffic and stronger currents. Be sure to return before 3 P.M. to avoid the very strong winds and chop in the Inner Harbor.

Jack London Square to Yerba Buena Island

Launch site 2, p. 152

Preferred NOAA Chart: 18649, "Entrance to San Francisco Bay"
Estimated Paddle Time: 4 hours
Trip Rating: SK 4
Special Hazards: Strong winds; steep waves
Launch Sites: Launch from Jack London Square or the alternate launch
   ramp (see launch description on p. 154). *(2) (2A)*
Nearest Campsite: Anthony Chabot Regional Park is 20 miles southeast of
   Oakland off Interstate 580 in Castro Valley. The park has several camp-
   sites and is managed by the East Bay Regional Park District (510-562-
   CAMP).
Best Paddle Time/Tide: Early morning; return in early afternoon to avoid
   midafternoon winds. Launch in slack or ending ebb; return in flood.

There are no immediate plans for public access to Treasure Island, so this trip's destination is Yerba Buena Island. Docking at the Treasure Island Marina is strictly forbidden, except for emergency bailout. A better option in emergencies is the Oakland Middle Harbor ship docks in the Inner Harbor Channel.

As you exit the Inner Harbor Channel, the fetch will pick up considerably to Yerba Buena, and you can expect 4-foot breaking waves, or higher. Paddle 2½ miles to the dock at the Yerba Buena Coast Guard Station, on the east side of the island. Expect some surf paddling with the prevailing west winds behind you to speed your return to the Inner Harbor Channel.

Yerba Buena is a natural island, called Goat Island until 1931. Miwok middens have been discovered on the island. Treasure Island is a man-made island, and was a northern addition to the island from landfill for the 1939–1940 Golden Gate International Exposition. Treasure Island was a navy base until recently and is undergoing a long planning process for public use at this writing.

Jack London Square to Alameda Island's Robert Crown Memorial State Beach

Launch site 3, p. 152

Preferred NOAA Chart: 18649, "Entrance to San Francisco Bay"
Estimated Paddle Time: 5 hours (one way)
Trip Rating: SK 3
Special Hazards: Strong afternoon winds and chop

Launch Sites: Launch from Jack London Square or the alternate launch site (see launch description on p. 154). *(3) (3A)*

The shuttle site is the parking lot at the Robert Crown Memorial State Beach at Alameda Island. From Jack London Square, take the Webster Street Tunnel to Alameda Island. Follow Webster Street until it ends adjacent to Robert Crown Memorial State Beach. Great views, swimming, and picnic tables. There is adequate parking along the northernmost tip of the beach park. For more information regarding Robert Crown Memorial State Beach, contact East Bay Regional Park District (510-562-PARK).

Nearest Campsite: Anthony Chabot Regional Park is 20 miles southeast of Oakland off Interstate 580 in Castro Valley. The park has several campsites and is managed by the East Bay Regional Park District (510-562-CAMP).

Best Paddle Time/Tide: Early morning. Land at your shuttle site by early afternoon. Winds pick up in the afternoon and create intense chop until 6 P.M. Launch in slack/beginning ebb.

This is a diverse and scenic 7-mile (one way) shuttle trip for intermediate paddlers. Paddling south from Jack London Square down the South Channel requires only that you pay attention to novice sailboats and large-ship traffic. From the tip of Alameda Island, rounding the island into San Leandro Bay requires moderate bracing due to the outflow of channel waters to the bay in beginning ebb tide. Oakland International Airport is a ½ mile south of Alameda Island.

Follow the island shoreline, which extends to mudflats on its west side, and paddle under the bridge. Continue north along the island. The west side of Alameda is shallow but does have visible pilings a few hundred yards along the shoreline. Land past the 2.5-mile-long, sandy swimmer's beach—Robert Crown Memorial State Beach. At its northern tip, a wooden wall separates the sandy beach from the sandy landing area. Do not land in the mudflats. This beach offers superb views of the city, but no surf. Enjoy a picnic here.

San Francisco Bay National Wildlife Refuge: Newark Slough

Launch site 4, p. 152

Preferred NOAA Chart: 18649, "Entrance to San Francisco Bay"
Estimated Paddle Time: 4 hours
Trip Rating: SK 1
Special Hazards: Narrow; tidally effected; mudflats
Launch Site: The Newark Slough boat ramp is in the Don Edwards San Francisco Bay National Wildlife Refuge (SFBNWR). From CA 84, at the east end of Dumbarton Bridge, exit at the Thorton Avenue/Paseo Padre Parkway. Travel south on Thorton Avenue for a mile to the refuge entrance on the right. Turn right into the refuge and park 100 yards past the entrance,

on the left side at the off-road parking area. Next to the parking area is a sign identifying the public launch ramp, operated by the refuge (you won't be able to see it, since it's on the opposite side of the road). The ramp is a graded, concrete ramp and is often very muddy. You will have gone too far from the entrance if you see the CITY OF FREEMONT sign. For more information call the SFBNWR Visitor Center (510-792-0222).

Nearest Campsite: Anthony Chabot Regional Park is 25 miles north of Newark off Interstate 580 in Castro Valley. The park has several campsites and is managed by the East Bay Regional Park District. For reservations, call 510-562-CAMP.

Best Paddle Time/Tide: Morning, in mid-high flood; return in slack. Moderately tide dependent.

Although there is a long carry down to launch, this is an excellent paddle for beginners. The slough offers protection from wind and waves, yet you'll learn a great deal about paddling in flood tides. This ramp offers a launch and return site that won't leave you stuck in the mud during ebb. Other slough-bank launch sites are environmentally prohibited or dangerously muddy (deep, porous swamp mud). Plan for about a four-hour paddle.

The refuge encompasses 19,000 acres of bay sloughs, salt ponds, marshes, and open water. Although nearby traffic rushes past, you'll be part of a habitat remote from its direct invasion. Great blue herons, egrets, and kites nest and hunt amid the narrow marshland tule grasses. Seals doze here in the afternoon before returning to their home in Mowry Slough, the next slough south.

Newark Slough curves around hills and meanders through the refuge's reclaimed salt ponds until it reaches the bay. The head of the slough has been an important local access point to the bay since the early 1800s, first as the main embarcadero for Mission San Jose and later as a landing for the growing port community of Newark.

Time your paddle in these lovely, protected, and warm waters; if you forget when you launched, you could get stuck in mud, ebb, and wind on your return. Since the bay is 4½ miles from the launch and you have to return with flood tide, don't plan on making it to the bay. Of course, you can paddle as close as you want, just don't lose track of time.

The farther along you paddle, the more wildlife you'll encounter. First you'll see egrets and shorebirds, then larger birds such as herons and endangered white pelicans, and finally along the bay banks you'll see some seals. The slough is also a fertile ground for the little critters: rabbits, mullets, and cacophonous crickets. Wear some bug repellent and sunblock—it gets sunny and hot, even on lovely winter paddles.

I particularly enjoy the wind rustling across the common tule grasses in the marsh. This grass, also called bulrush, is an abundant plant in brackish and freshwater marshlands. There are 17 species of tule in California. Ohlone Indians used tule for food, bait, and to build canoes. Scientists have found another use: Tule grasses remove metals from marsh waters and retain them in their root systems, making the marsh habitat safer for wildlife.

Before leaving, check out the visitor center at Newark Slough and the Hayward Shoreline Interpretive Center, on the way to the Dumbarton Bridge as you head west.

San Francisco National Wildlife Refuge: Alviso Boat Ramp to Drawbridge Island

Launch site 5, p. 152

Preferred NOAA Chart: 18649, "Entrance to San Francisco Bay"
Estimated Paddle Time: 7 hours
Trip Rating: SK 3
Special Hazards: Strong afternoon winds and chop; tidally affected channels; mudflats
Launch Site: There is a narrow concrete boat ramp and a low pier at the Alviso Marina, operated by Santa Clara County, 1195 Hope Street in Alviso (408-358-3741). For more information, maps, or to reserve a time for a ranger-led walking tour of Drawbridge Island, call San Francisco Bay National Wildlife Refuge (510-792-0222). No landing or entry on the island is permitted, other than with a ranger. Note that the town of Drawbridge is not identified for preservation purposes on SFBNWR or many local maps. Follow directions below for your destination.
Nearest Campsite: Sunol Wilderness Area, managed by the East Bay Regional Park District, is 15 miles east of Alviso, off CA 84 near Milpitas. For reservations, call 510-562-CAMP.
Best Paddle Time/Tide: Early morning in flood; return in beginning ebb. Strongly tide dependent.

On most maps, including the San Francisco Bay National Wildlife Refuge map, Drawbridge Island is called Station Island. This is done in part to keep Drawbridge a pristine area. Foot access is limited to ranger-led walking tours from May through October, because the salt marsh and wildlife surrounding Drawbridge are especially sensitive to human interaction.

Launching is fairly easy from the ribbed-concrete ramp or the adjacent pier. Keep in mind some landmarks near the entrance to the ramp as seen from the water, since you will be returning in flood. This is a seven-hour, 10-mile intermediate paddle.

The 5½-mile-long Alviso Slough is a protected calm paddle through a lush habitat of birdlife and a patchwork of mudflats and tule grasses. It is wide enough to catch a little wind, yet protected enough so you'll see stilts, oystercatchers, white and great blue herons, kites, and egrets foraging and nesting in their communities. Colorful ramshackle houseboats and private fishing boats reside in the slough. Boat traffic is rare, since the slough is accessible only at high tide. Kayaking, even during low tide, is easy through the slough. The water is warm and very shallow. On sunny days, be sure to use sunblock.

Many problems have plagued Alviso Slough, and they are worth noting for paddlers. Over many decades of filling the land and building levees, we contaminated the soil with high levels of asbestos. In 1984, Alviso qualified for a federal hazardous waste cleanup. While most land filling has been capped since the early 1990s, there is still a high level of airborne and water contaminants in the slough.

In the last ½ mile of the trip along the slough, as you head toward the mouth of the slough, you'll encounter some wind and slight chop. And as you head south along the mud and silt eastern bay shoreline to Drawbridge, moderately strong wind and a moderate chop will become evident. A current that goes against you circles the island. You'll notice utility towers to your left, and the Dumbarton Bridge in the distance on your ahead of you. As you paddle along the eastern shoreline to Drawbridge, you'll notice a narrow silted beach on your left. This is Triangle Marsh; you may land there and have a picnic. Be sure to get your boat off the silt and onto the grasses. Bailout points are muddy and will flood, but you can land along Triangle Marsh and find the bordering 2-mile trail to the Environmental Education Center.

After you pass Triangle Marsh, it's another hour to reach Drawbridge. The paddle between Triangle Marsh and Drawbridge, given the length of the paddle, will be a challenging part of the trip. Moderate chop combined with moderately strong late-morning wind will challenge you to keep going. It's not strong paddling you need to do here—you just need to keep paddling.

Some kayakers find this annoying, but there are rewards for paddling in this area: You'll see a runway and nesting sites on your left for endangered white pelicans, which are abundant and living well in this stretch. Station Island, on your left, is the first island that will give you some shelter from the wind as you paddle to your right along the shore. Then you'll see a railroad bridge above the water. There is no landing on this part of Station island, which includes the town of Drawbridge, nor are there any viable landing points. But as you paddle along the side, you'll catch a glimpse of its shacks.

The railroad leads into Drawbridge, whose entrance, as mentioned earlier, is restricted to ranger-led walks. This railroad was critical to the birth of Drawbridge. At only 20 feet above the water at high tide, this tiny barren mudflat, then called Station Island, did not appear to be an inviting place to live. But by 1876, when the South Pacific Coast Railroad was built, the new bridgetender, George Mandershied, began inviting friends to go hunting there. With a seemingly endless supply of ducks and many other seasonal wildlife, residents began clambering to Station Island by boat and rail and built homes. Pilings supported the houses high above the water, and raised wooden catwalks ran from doorsteps to the railroad bed, which soon became the main street. By the 1920s, the respectable Town of Drawbridge claimed 90 cabins made up of homes and hunting clubs. Most residents were middle to upper class, all living above the tides. Religion divided the town—Catholics were at the south end and Protestants were at the north end.

The fall of Drawbridge was due to industrialization and bay development in the 1930s and 1940s. Businesses were pumping freshwater from under the bay's aquifer, and the island slowly sank into the mud. Cabins and the railroad bed had to be continually jacked up. Fishing and hunting decreased as communities of the south bay dumped raw sewage into the water. Dikes were constructed for salt evaporation ponds, defeating the cleansing action of the tides. Both the water quality and the wildlife habitat deteriorated. By the 1940s, only 50 cabins were still inhabited. Shortly thereafter, the trains stopped making their regular stops. The buildings now rest on the mud among the pickleweed and cordgrass. I am reminded of Carl Sandburg's poem "Grass," in which he writes of time and nature's inevitable growth: "I am the grass. Let me work."

So Drawbridge is returning to its original architecture—pickleweed and cordgrass—and soon there will be no wooden facades to remind us of its unique cultural history. Although birdlife has significantly decreased since the town's heyday, ducks, pelicans, egrets, herons, stilts, oystercatchers, and avocets still live in the tidal flats and are especially seen in plenitude during winter migration.

Plan on a four-hour return to the Alviso launch ramp. Paddle along the opposite bank of the bay, where you will be sheltered from early-afternoon winds. While this makes your trip a little longer, it saves your paddle endurance for the middle of the bay, where the shoals and wind get strong. Cross directly into the Alviso Slough mouth, and be aware that there is occasional illegal fecal outflow in this area. The crossing into the slough mouth will be the most difficult part of the paddle, but can be easily accomplished by intermediate kayakers. Meandering back up through the slough will be a restful return to the Alviso Marina.

San Leandro Marina to Oyster Bay Regional Shoreline

Launch site 6, p. 152

Preferred NOAA Chart: 18651, "San Francisco Bay (Southern Part)"
Estimated Paddle Time: 3 hours
Trip Rating: SK 3
Special Hazards: Strong afternoon winds; moderate chop
Launch Site: There is a public launching ramp on South Dike Road in the San Leandro Marina. Take CA 880 west to Marina Boulevard. Head west on Marina Boulevard until it ends at the Marina. As you enter the San Leandro Marina, you'll be on Neptune Drive. Turn right on South

Dike Road to the public launching ramp, where there is adequate parking. San Leandro Marina (510-357-7447).

Nearest Campsite: Anthony Chabot Regional Park is 10 miles east of San Leandro, off Interstate 580 in Castro Valley. The park has several camp-sites and is managed by the East Bay Regional Park District. For reservations, call 510-562-CAMP.

Best Paddle Time/Tide: Early morning; return before midafternoon when winds pick up. Not strongly tide dependent.

This intermediate paddle presents a good view of south Oakland from the loud Oakland International Airport to sheltered embayments hosting many native plants and butterflies. You'll be paddling three hours.

Entering the mouth of the bay from the marina requires some caution: Watch the wind and chop. If you launch, as suggested, in the early morning, you'll encounter a calm-water paddle. Paddling ¾ mile north along the sheltered bay bordered by Neptune Drive, you'll see quiet, fertile grasslands. In late spring, a variety of beautiful of butterflies such as swallowtails, painted ladies, and California sisters reside in the grasses.

After another ¼ mile along this sheltered bay, you'll enter Oyster Bay Regional Shoreline. Kites, hawks, and ducks fish these shallow waters. Ebb tides make the shoreline muddy, but docking is still accessible. The Oyster Bay Regional Shoreline trails are worth exploring, and they feature fine picnic areas. Surprisingly, the park is built directly over a former garbage dump.

Avoid strong winds by returning before midafternoon.

South Sailing Basin (Berkeley)

Launch site 7, p. 152

Launch Site: Use the public launch docks in Berkeley Marina. From Interstate 580 east in Berkeley, turn west onto University Avenue. Drive to the end and follow the signs to the South Sailing Basin. Turn left and follow the signs to Cal Adventures (510-642-4000) and the South Sailing Basin docks. Parking is adjacent to the docks.

Nearest Campsite: Anthony Chabot Regional Park is 20 miles southeast of Oakland, off Interstate 580 in Castro Valley. The park has several camp-sites and is managed by the East Bay Regional Park District. For reservations, call 510-562-CAMP.

Best Paddle Time/Tide: Morning, before late afternoon. Windy area.

These kayak and windsurfing launch docks are semiprotected from the wind. Launching from this quieter area of the bay makes several destinations possible, including those listed below.

Emeryville Shoreline

Preferred NOAA Chart: 18649, "Entrance to San Francisco Bay"
Estimated Paddle Time: 3 hours
Trip Rating: SK 2
Special Hazards: Strong afternoon winds; moderate chop

This 2-mile flatwater stretch from the docks south along the grassy Emeryville shoreline is suited to beginners. Here kayakers can experience slight to moderate wind chop, a panoramic view of the Bay Bridge, and observe birdlife. Windsurfing traffic is limited mainly to the dock area.

Emeryville City Marina

Preferred NOAA Chart: 18649, "Entrance to San Francisco Bay"
Estimated Paddle Time: 3 hours
Trip Rating: SK 2
Special Hazards: Strong afternoon winds; moderate chop

For intermediate paddlers, this paddle from the docks to the marina will be an easy 5-mile paddle that includes birdlife, old docks with sculptures, and the marina. Follow the shoreline 2 miles to the public access shoreline near Charley Brown's restaurant in Emeryville. This access will be obvious when you see an abandoned pier; its pilings are topped by large sculptures, interesting, whimsical forms of people and birds. This pier is a few hundred yards before the dark wooden Charley Brown's restaurant on Emeryville Bay.

The public access shoreline adjacent to the abandoned pier—Emeryville Crescent—includes a small public beach where you can launch or picnic. It has a small parking area and picnic tables. This sliver of marsh has survived decades of metal sculpture making, illegal garbage dumping, and development proposals. Despite the constant roar of cars, thousands of egrets and herons stop here in the fall and early winter. In spring, nesting avocets forage along the banks, and killdeers call from the grass.

From the abandoned pier, paddle the shoreline to Charley Brown's and head to the more open shoreline and Emeryville City Marina. You'll be exposed to a little more wind on the leg to the marina, but the water is flat to a little choppy. If you round Point Emery heading north along the shoreline, be aware that winds are quite strong in the afternoons and will make the return paddle difficult. This area was saved by the Bay Conservation and Development Commission when it refused to permit the filling in of marsh for a large shoreline development.

As you return, beware of windsurfers speeding to the shore.

To the Bay Bridge

Preferred NOAA Chart: 18649, "Entrance to San Francisco Bay"
Estimated Paddle Time: 4 hours
Trip Rating: SK 4
Special Hazards: Strong afternoon winds; steep waves

Intermediate and advanced paddlers do this 7-mile trip in the early morning, when there is no wind and little chop. But be prepared for wind and chop, even on calm mornings. Most kayakers do this trip as a fast endurance paddle, to prepare for longer open-bay excursions.

As you paddle southwest to the beginning of the bridge by the Oakland radio towers, you'll be in mostly shallow water. Tides affect this area strongly. There are no observed routine strong currents here; however, with wind in a shallow marshland, you can get fast chop.

Dolphins have frequently been spotted a few hundred yards between Radio Point Towers and the midsection of this leg of the Bay Bridge. Radio Point Beach and its adjacent beautiful marshland is a bountiful nesting and feeding area for herons and egrets.

To the Berkeley Pier

Preferred NOAA Chart: 18649, "Entrance to San Francisco Bay"
Estimated Paddle Time: 4 hours
Trip Rating: SK 3
Special Hazards: Strong afternoon winds; chop; boat traffic

This paddle is best done in the early morning; get off the water by midafternoon to avoid strong winds, boat traffic, and chop. Paddle northwest along the shore and around the point for 1½ miles. As you reach the point you'll experience steady wind, which will be present as you prowl along the Berkeley Pier.

The City of Berkeley acquired the Pier in 1938 and rebuilt the first 3,000 feet in 1958 and again in 1961. Dangerous, submerged pilings extend out from the visible end of the pier by several hundred feet. While these pilings are a paddler's nuisance, biologists have shown that they serve as a perch for birds and as a nutrient-rich habitat for bay marine life.

To Brooks Island

Preferred NOAA Chart: 18649, "Entrance to San Francisco Bay"
Estimated Paddle Time: 5 hours
Trip Rating: SK 3
Special Hazards: Strong afternoon winds; chop

This trip is best undertaken by intermediate paddlers and started early in the morning to avoid midafternoon wind and chop; or plan your return for after 5 P.M. Although it's listed as an 11-mile paddle, it would be better as two one-way trips or even as a one-way shuttle trip. Picnic at Brooks Island or picnic/lunch at Richmond Harbor. Be prepared for strong winds and chop and watch out for boat traffic to and from Berkeley Marina.

Martin Luther King Regional Shoreline (Doolittle Beach)

Launch site 8, p. 152

Launch Site: There is a bank launch at the Martin Luther King Regional Shoreline Park. From Interstate north in San Leandro, turn east onto Davis Street, then north onto CA 61 (Doolittle Drive). Follow the signs to Martin Luther King Regional Shoreline Park, on the right side of the road. Parking is adjacent to the bank launch. Operated by East Bay Park and Recreation Department (510-562-PARK). Aolian Yacht Club (510-523-2586).

Nearest Campsite: Anthony Chabot Regional Park is 20 miles southeast of Oakland, off Interstate 580 in Castro Valley. The park has several campsites and is managed by the East Bay Regional Park District. For reservations, call 510-562-CAMP.

Best Paddle Time/Tide: Morning, before late afternoon.

Below you'll find two good paddles for beginners from an easy bank launch at the very underused Doolittle Beach in Martin Luther King Regional Shoreline Park. This park has adequate parking, picnic facilities, and even a café. The easiest place to launch is from the low sloping banks across from the park's Beach Café. Watch for jet-skiers, who are permitted to ski to the right of you in unprotected marsh areas.

This narrow channel, called Airport Channel, is a flatwater paddle to other marsh areas and to Alameda. Buoys mark the channel's traffic lanes.

To Damron Marsh

Preferred NOAA Chart: 18649, "Entrance to San Francisco Bay"
Estimated Paddle Time: 5 hours
Trip Rating: SK 2
Special Hazards: Afternoon winds; tidally affected channel

This beginner's paddle can be done in four to five hours, including a picnic lunch. Although it's 8 miles long, you'll be hugging the marsh coastline and paddling in protected areas with little tidal or current effects.

From the launch site, head northeast to Arrowhead Marsh, the peninsula on the other side of the channel. Arrowhead is a large protected wildlife area in which to view egrets, herons, and kites nesting and feeding in the grasses. Hug around the tip of Arrowhead Marsh peninsula and south into San Leandro Creek, the narrow creek at the end of the marsh. From the San Leandro Creek mouth, paddle across the Elmhurst Creek mouth. If you have time and interest, these smaller creek mouths are worth paddling for fauna.

From Elmhurst Creek, the shore you'll be paddling runs parallel to the Elmhurst Creek Trail. You can easily land along the banks and enjoy lunch on picnic tables by the trail. Then paddle west to Garretson Point and tiny Damron Slough and Damron Marsh.

Your return will be quicker if you paddle across the bay to Arrowhead Marsh, a distance of 1 mile, or about 45 minutes, if there is little or no wind and it is still well before midafternoon. If you are heading back later, paddle back alongshore, following the Elmhurst Creek Trail to Arrowhead Marsh, and back to Doolittle Beach.

To Alameda Island's Aolian Yacht Club
Preferred NOAA Chart: 18649, "Entrance to San Francisco Bay"
Estimated Paddle Time: 2 hours
Trip Rating: SK 3
Special Hazards: Strong afternoon winds and chop

If you head out on a calm morning and return before early afternoon, this is a two-hour paddle for beginners. It is 4 miles long. Airport Channel is not strongly affected by tides or currents. Do watch for jet-skiers in areas not restricted by marshland protection.

Paddle north along the shore of Doolittle Beach for a mile and a half. As you make your way up the beach and out Airport Channel, you'll encounter small chop at the channel mouth when you cross to Alameda Island. Head toward the tip of Alameda, where you see the harbor of the Aolian Yacht Club. Land at the dock and picnic area, or return to Doolittle Beach and the Beach Café. Be back at Doolittle Beach before midafternoon to avoid strong winds.

Emeryville City Marina

Launch site 9, p. 152

Preferred NOAA Chart: 18649, "Entrance to San Francisco Bay"
Estimated Paddle Time: 2 hours
Trip Rating: SK 2
Special Hazards: Afternoon winds; moderate chop
Launch Site: There is a public launching ramp in the Emeryville Launching
    Facility, operated by the Emeryville Park and Recreation Department at

3310 Powell (510-596-4395). From Interstate 80, turn west on Powell Street and follow the signs to the EMERYVILLE CITY MARINA. The marina has rest rooms, picnic tables, and adequate parking. Emeryville City Marina (510-596-4330).

Nearest Campsite: Anthony Chabot Regional Park is 20 miles southeast of Emeryville off Interstate 580 in Castro Valley. The park has several campsites and is managed by the East Bay Regional Park District. For reservations, call 510-562-CAMP.

Best Paddle Time/Tide: Morning to early afternoon.

This is a fun beginner's paddle inside the marina. Outside the marina, the bay is very gusty from midmorning onward, and I don't recommend it. There's also a lot of sailboat traffic out there. The marina itself is clean and new, and it's always fun to poke around the boats. Watch for boat traffic—everyone's moving pretty slowly, but there's not much maneuvering room.

Shadow Cliffs Regional Recreation Area

Launch site 10, p. 152

Estimated Paddle Time: 2 hours
Trip Rating: SK 1
Special Hazards: Afternoon winds
Launch Site: There is a public launch ramp at Shadow Cliffs. From Interstate 680 take the Pleasanton exit and turn west onto Main Street and then right onto Stanley Boulevard. Drive 1 mile east on Stanley Boulevard to the Shadow Cliffs Regional Recreation area entrance and proceed along the entrance road for 2 miles southeast to the boat ramp. Parking is available adjacent to the boat ramp. Day-use parking and launch fees are charged. Owned and managed by East Bay Regional Park Department 510-635-0135). Kayak length limit is 17 feet.

Nearest Campsite: Anthony Chabot Regional Park is 20 miles north of Pleasanton off Interstate 580 in Castro Valley. The park has several campsites and is managed by the East Bay Regional Park District (510-562-CAMP).

Best Paddle Time/Tide: Morning and afternoon. Not tide dependent.

You can combine this 1½-mile-long beginner's paddle with hiking and a picnic for a great day for the family. The waters are warm and quiet, without jet-ski traffic. Paddle around the main lake and you might even see trout and catfish. This is a peaceful retreat on a hot summer day.

Full Moon Paddle at Lake Chabot

Launch site 11, p. 152

Estimated Paddle Time: 3 hours
Trip Rating: SK 1
Special Hazards: Cold night temperatures
Launch Site: Public boat ramp in Anthony Chabot Regional Park. This trip is led exclusively by the East Bay Regional Park District; fee is $50 per person. Call East Bay for reservations (510-636-1684).
Nearest Campsite: Anthony Chabot Regional Park has several campsites and is managed by the East Bay Regional Park District. For reservations call 510-562-PARK.
Best Paddle Time/Tide: Full moon, with ranger-led tours only through East Bay Regional Park District.

There is nothing like the stillness of a moonlit night, with the moonlight reflected on the hills and water. This quiet-water trip lasts three hours and is perfect for beginners and families. Tours led by the East Bay Regional Park District include all equipment. This 4,600-acre park was named after Anthony Chabot, the pioneer Californian philanthropist who built Lake Chabot by constructing an earth-fill dam. Miwok collected acorns and other staples here.

Lake Del Valle

Launch site 12, p. 152

Estimated Paddle Time: 2 hours
Trip Rating: SK 1
Special Hazards: Afternoon winds; moderate chop
Launch Site: There is a public launch ramp in Del Valle Regional Park. From CA 580 in Livermore, turn north at the North Livermore Avenue exit. Proceed 2 miles on North Livermore, then turn east onto Mines Road, which becomes Del Valle Road for 7 miles. At the entrance to the reservoir, turn right and drive 1 mile to the launch. Day-use fee of $4 on weekdays, $5 on weekends, plus a $2 charge per kayak. Parking available at the launch. Lake Del Valle Visitor Center (510-373-0332).
Nearest Campsite: Del Valle Park has several campsites (510-373-0332).
Best Paddle Time/Tide: Morning to midafternoon. Not tide dependent.

This lake is the last in a series of excellent Alameda County waters for beginners and families. Five miles long, Del Valle boasts a tree-shaded shoreline, picnic areas, swimming, and trails. Summer boaters are busy here, especially windsurfers. It gets windy in the afternoon.

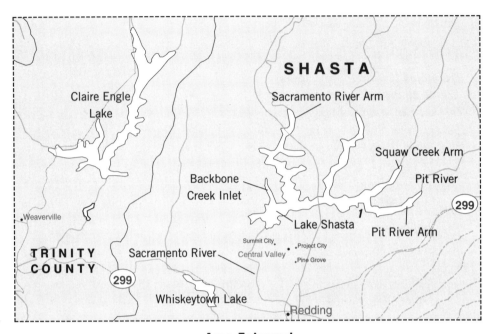

Area Enlarged

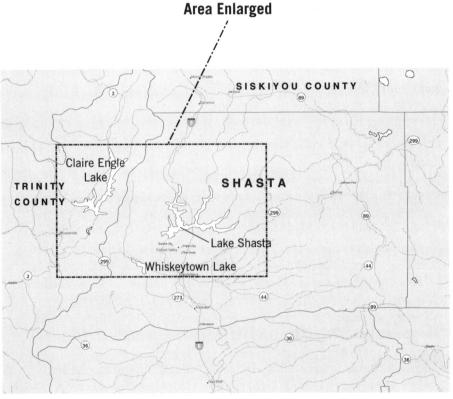

Shasta County

1. Lake Shasta: Pit River Arm

Lake Shasta: Pit River Arm

Launch site 1, p. 168

Estimated Paddle Time: 2 hours

Trip Rating: SK 2

Special Hazards: Submerged tree limbs; moderate afternoon winds

Launch Site: There is a boat ramp with an adjacent parking lot, identified as the Public Launch Ramp of Arbuckle Flat Campground in Lake Shasta. There is a $2 day-use fee. Take Interstate 5 to the south end of Lake Shasta. Turn off the Oasis Road exit and proceed east 10 miles to the Arbuckle Flat Public Boat Ramp. For information, including a list of all six public launching ramps and maps, contact the Shasta Lake Information Center, 14225 Holiday Road, Redding, CA 96003 (530-275-1589).

Nearest Campsite: The Pit River Campsites are boat-access only. Many other public and private access campsites in Lake Shasta are available. For public campsite permits and camping information, call Shasta Lake Information Center, 14225 Holiday Road, Redding, CA 96003 (530-275-1589).

Best Paddle Time/Tide: Morning and afternoon are both fine. Not tide dependent.

Lake Shasta attracts many jet-skiers and powerboaters; fortunately, however, the Pit River Arm is off-limits to motorized craft. This arm of the lake is very calm and is protected from winds in the morning and afternoon. Lake Shasta is 371 square miles and is 517 feet deep at its deepest point. With more shoreline than San Francisco Bay, Lake Shasta is the largest reservoir in California. The lake is primarily fed by the Sacramento, McCloud, and Pit Rivers and Squaw Creek. Each of these feeders makes up a separate arm of the lake. There are 16 species of fish in Lake Shasta, including rainbow trout, brown trout, and bass.

After launching from the Pit River Arm Public Access Boat Ramp in Arbuckle Flat, head east along the south end of the river arm. You'll discover numerous small arms in which to poke around. The water is calm, but expect a slight wind in the morning. There are snags and tree stumps the farther east you go, so be mindful of these nuisances.

The fish habitat is excellent, so if you like to fish, whether from your boat or the bank, you're in for a treat—but keep those snags in mind.

Area Enlarged

Eldorado County

1. Lake Tahoe: Camp Richardson to Emerald Bay

2. Lake Tahoe: Sand Harbor, Nevada, to Deadman's Point, California

3. Loon Lake Boat Ramp to Pleasant Campground

Lake Tahoe: Camp Richardson to Emerald Bay

Launch site 1, p. 172

Estimated Paddle Time: 2 hours (one way); 4 hours (round trip)

Trip Rating: SK 2

Special Hazards: Gusty afternoon winds; jet-skis

Launch Sites: Public boat ramp and beach launch at Camp Richardson. From CA 89 or Emerald Bay Road in South Lake Tahoe, turn north onto Jameson Beach Road to Camp Richardson. Parking is adjacent to the launch site. For more information, call Kayak Tahoe (530-544-2011), which is at the beach at Camp Richardson.

Nearest Campsite: Emerald Bay State Park has one campground for boaters and one for campers arriving by car. Boat-in campsites are available on a first-come, first-served basis, but they are rarely filled. Call ahead to be sure. Look for the pier and mooring buoys on the north side of Emerald Bay. If coming by car, take CA 89 and US 50 in South Lake Tahoe and drive 8 miles north on CA 89 to the park headquarters and campgrounds. Emerald Bay State Park (530-541-3030).

Best Paddle Time/Tide: Morning. Not tide dependent.

This trip can be taken as a 3-mile (round trip) paddle or as a 2-mile paddle (one way), with fantastic views of Mt. Tallac. Both are beginner's trips.

Paddle two hours northwest to gorgeous Emerald Bay. On weekend afternoons in the summer, powerboaters and jet-skiers make the mouth of Emerald Bay moderately choppy. Hug the banks for a safe and visible route. It's best to make this trip in the morning. The bay is sheltered from the wind and the powerboaters, so you can work your way back to Camp Richardson at your own pace. Picnic and launch areas are plentiful along the banks of Emerald Bay.

In the early 1900s, Emerald Bay was a resort, saved from Tahoe clear-cutting during the Comstock era. Today, birdlife is abundant, featuring eagles, hawks, herons, and egrets. Large Ponderosa, sugar, and Jeffrey pines grow in this area. There are also three species of sequoias found nowhere else in the Tahoe area. Ospreys nest here and feed on fish in the lake and in surrounding streams. Common mergansers also nest along the lake and are permanent residents. Canada geese Emerald Bay depend on the upland meadows for their dinner. Coyotes and bears inhabit this area, so be sure to use good campground sense and hang your food in a bear bag. Bald eagles are common in the winter months.

Emerald Bay State Park boat-in campsites are very safe and clean. It's lovely to camp there, and at night to paddle to the Emerald Bay Island's Tea House. This lovely structure is nestled in the southwest corner of Emerald Bay on top of little Fanette Island. Early-morning sunrise paddles are good for photographing the mountains and the geese.

The wind on Lake Tahoe is generally out of the west, northwest, or southwest from June to mid-September. There are only a few days when these winds are strong enough to make paddling along the west shore difficult. The east shore is prone to 2- to 3-foot waves in the afternoon, and they can get much larger. The west shore gets waves only during thundershowers and winter weather. Thundershowers occur about every two weeks during the summer, when west-shore paddles are ideal. Fall and spring weather can bring east winds and small waves, and the temperature is cool for paddling. In winter, make sure you end your trip before the sun sets; it gets very cold here at night. Bald eagles, ospreys, and geese are abundant in winter, and you are likely to have the lake to yourself then. There are no other boats, and paddling in the glassy-calm water is unforgettable.

Lake Tahoe: Sand Harbor, Nevada, to Deadman's Point, California

Launch site 2, p. 172

Estimated Paddle Time: 4 hours
Trip Rating: SK 3
Special Hazards: Strong afternoon winds
Launch Site: Public boat ramps at Sand Harbor Marina in Sand Harbor, Nevada, 4 miles south of Incline Village (702-831-0494). Parking is available next to the boat ramps. From US 50 east in South Lake Tahoe, drive 20 miles to NV 28 north, to Sand Harbor. For more information, call Kayak Tahoe (530-544-2011).

It's 10 miles to Deadman's Point and back; this is an intermediate paddle.

Head south along the eastern lake shore and you'll see lush vegetation, neat little harbors such as Secret Harbor and Skunk Harbor, and beautiful sandy beaches. The beaches are not crowded because they are far from the roads. Although Sand Harbor's beach is off-limits, the beaches south along this paddle are public access. Taking this shoreline route will shelter you from the wind. The water is cold and deep green, and you'll see a variety of birdlife.

Loon Lake Boat Ramp to Pleasant Campground

Launch site 3, p. 172

Estimated Paddle Time: 3 hours
Trip Rating: SK 1
Special Hazards: Submerged tree limbs
Launch Site: There is a boat ramp at Loon Lake, 30 miles southwest of Tahoe. From Lake Tahoe, take US 50 west 30 miles to Crystal Basin/Ice House Road and proceed 29 miles until you see signs for the Loon Lake

Public Boat Ramp. Follow the signs and proceed 1 mile to the ramp. There is a big parking lot adjacent to the ramp. Due to late spring runoffs, call ahead to verify that the ramp is open. For information, call the Eldorado National Forest Information Center (530-644-6048).

Nearest Campsite: Beach camping is available wherever you would like to stop, provided you have a campfire permit from the Eldorado National Forest. Pleasant Campground is a boat-in-only area. There is no fee for beach camping or for Pleasant Campground. Call the Eldorado National Forest Information Center main office at 530-644-6048 or their satellite site, the Pacific Ranger Station at Pollock Pines, CA 95726, at 530-644-2349. Loon Lake is open from June through September.

Best Paddle Time/Tide: To paddle to the boat-in campsite, begin your paddle in midmorning to avoid gusty midafternoon winds. Not tide dependent. June through September only.

Be sure to wear your farmer johns on this pleasant beginner's paddle; the water is very cold. Loon Lake is at an elevation of 6,500 feet in Eldorado National Forest. This high mountain lake, with its sublimely clear water and striking geology, always looks to me as if it were carved out of granite.

From the Loon Lake Boat Ramp, paddle northeast along the banks to Pleasant, the boat-in-only campsite. The 3-mile journey to Pleasant Campground will take you an hour and a half if you have little or no wind. It's best to paddle in midmorning to avoid the gusty winds, which usually pick up between 2 and 3 P.M., and to take advantage of the mild summer morning temperatures. Paddling along the pristine beaches and banks you will be treated to spectacular mountain vistas. Bird-watchers will enjoy nesting eagles, as well as resident jays, warblers, and woodpeckers. Plan to picnic at one of the many beaches and to return before the afternoon wind picks up or to make camp at Pleasant Campground or anywhere along the shore.

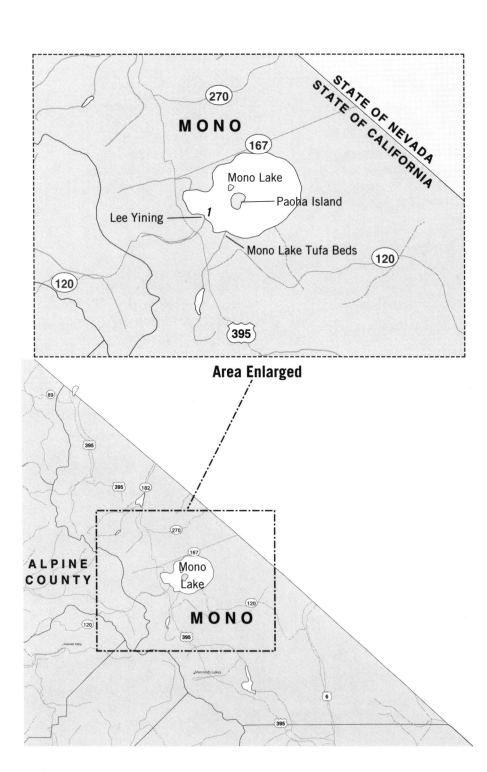

Area Enlarged

Mono County

Mono Lake Picnic Grounds to Paoha Island

Launch site 1, p. 178

Estimated Paddle Time: 4 hours

Trip Rating: SK 2

Special Hazards: Windy; get off the water by noon. Due to strong alkaline winds, bring protective eyewear such as ski goggles or sport sunglasses.

Launch Site: There is a boat ramp at the dock north of Lee Vining Road, 2 miles off US 395. From Lee Vining near the high school, head 1 mile north and turn right on the unidentified gravel road. Proceed down this gravel road 1½ miles. Before the creek crosses this road, turn left and proceed for ½ mile. Park in the parking lot adjacent to the dock. Mono Lake information: Mono Lake Committee Information Center and Bookstore (760-647-6386). Visit the Information Center to confirm conditions before starting your paddle.

Nearest Campsite: Aspen Grove Campground in Mono County Parks Department is 6 miles west of the Town of Lee Vining on CA 120 (760-932-5248).

Best Paddle Time/Tide: Morning to early afternoon. Not tide dependent.

Paddling here is a fascinating tour in contrasting environments. Do this beginner's trip early in the morning and get off the lake before noon. The winds pick up in late morning and blow all day. Alkaline water in your eyes will sting and make it difficult to see, and swallowing this heavily mineralized water will make you gag. Trust me on this!

The west side of the lake is at the foot of the Sierra Nevada, while the east side is high desert. Powerful dust storms blow around the shoreline, because there is no vegetation to protect the soil, but round a point and you'll see plants and trees growing along a creek that flows into the lake. The water is alkaline and supports brine shrimp, which are food for millions of birds that pass through on their annual migrations. The water is very clear but looks oily, the result of brine shrimp congregating to feed near the surface in areas where freshwater and lake water mix.

Among this lake's most extraordinary features are the *tufas*, which stick up from the water's surface and dot the shoreline. These columns of mineral deposits—mostly calcium carbonate—originate in the mineral springs in the lake bottom. Typically, tufas grow only to the water's surface, but because the water level today is 30 to 40 feet below its former level, some rise as much as 20 to 30 feet above the surface.

One more tip: Wash all your gear as soon as possible after paddling; the minerals dissolved in the water of Mono Lake are corrosive.

≋ Surf Kayaking: 11 Hot Spots

Advisory warning: Conditions change radically with increasing wave size. A beginner location can quickly become an advanced surfer area. Beginners should not attempt to surf waves more than 3 feet high. Tide levels dramatically affect waves and surfing conditions. Observe the surf for a long time before you launch and access your skills honestly with your fellow paddlers.

Marin County: Bolinas Lagoon

Launch Site: This is an easy launch from a lagoon bank next to the roadside on CA 1. Take CA 1 four miles west of Stinson Beach to Audubon Canyon Ranch. All along the lagoon side of CA 1 across from the ranch is public access. Launch where there is parking and good (not muddy) access to the lagoon. The most feasible off-road parking and launching access is just across from Audubon Canyon Ranch.

Long rides are common here, and there is a good peeling right. Bolinas wave breaks are safe and forgiving, making this lagoon a natural for beginning and intermediate surf kayakers.

City and County of San Francisco: Ocean Beach

Launch Site: Ocean Beach is on CA 1 in San Francisco, across from Golden Gate Park. There are several parking lots adjacent to the beach. Watch the wave breaks to choose where sets are safest.

For intermediate surf kayakers only. Best in 3- to 6-foot waves. Sets roll in a few hundred feet from shore. Nice long rides, but avoid the tide rips.

San Mateo County: Pacifica State Beach—Linda Mar

Launch Site: The beach launch is at Linda Mar Beach in Pacifica, off CA 1. Parking is available at Pacifica State Beach. Operated by city of Pacifica (415-875-7380).

Linda Mar is best in 4- to 6-foot waves. Larger waves become dumping waves on shore, and they're not fun to surf. For beginning and intermediate surf kayakers.

San Mateo County: Princeton Harbor to the Inside Reef near the Mavericks

Launch Site: This is a beach launch in a protected harbor along the beach next to California Canoe and Kayak in Princeton (650-728-1803). From CA 1 at Princeton, turn west onto Harbor Drive. Turn onto Princeton Avenue (there is only one way to turn). Follow the signs to California Canoe and Kayak at 214 Princeton Avenue, at its intersection with Vassar Street. California Canoe and Kayak shares the building with the Half Moon Bay Yacht Club.

Paddle across the harbor to your right and portage over to the ocean side. Stay inside the tower rock formation, inside the reef. Do not paddle outside this rock formation near the Mavericks, a world-renowned big-wave surf spot. The Mavericks are a dangerous place for big waves.

The 4- to 8-foot high waves, locally called microwaves, are particularly fun. After riding the wave out, you're still in a deep channel. This makes it easy and fast to paddle back out.

A beginning surf kayaker's beach is just south of the breakwater, and it's the place to learn how to launch and land in small to moderate surf.

San Mateo County: Gazo's Creek

Launch Site: This is a creek launch on the west side of CA 1 at Gazo's Creek, 18 miles south of Half Moon Bay. Follow the overpass sign identifying Gazo's Creek. Park in parking lot.

Gazo's Creek is an intermediate surfer site only when all the other spots are running little to no surf. This spot frequently has dumping waves that are not surfable, and it's a dangerous place when the surf is big. Heavy rip currents work north to south. This site is best in small to medium waves. Anything larger than that makes it much too dangerous.

Santa Cruz County: Davenport

Launch Site: This is a beach launch on the west side of CA 1 in Davenport, 12 miles north of Santa Cruz.

Davenport Beach changes radically day to day; it's for advanced surf kayakers only. Davenport offers two breaks, the Point Break in big waves and the Lower Reef in small to medium waves. Davenport offers a mushy type of wave, fun for surf kayakers but not for board surfers—so advanced surf kayakers have this spot all to themselves. When the waves break in large sets, and board surfers are here, some get aggressive and often exceed their allotted shared space. Avoid them. Be aware of the close-out onto the submerged ledge at South Break.

Santa Cruz County: Greyhound Rock Beach

Launch Site: Greyhound Rock Beach is 6 miles north of Davenport. Follow signs on the west side of CA 1. There is off-road parking.

Greyhound Rock is good for beginning and intermediate surf kayakers. It has a deep channel with breaks on either side of the rock, which can make for steep waves with a hollow form. Greyhound Rock works up to about a 6-foot wave. At that point, surfing can get very dangerous, very quickly. Greyhound Rock is best at high tide. It has long, open beaches with few if any surfers. Except for the long hike down to Greyhound Rock, this is a good spot for kayak surfing: no surfers, several breaks (right and left), sandy open beaches, and it's great in small to medium waves.

Santa Cruz County: Steamer Lane

Launch Site: This beach launch is at Steamer Lane in Santa Cruz, on the west side of CA 1. Park on West Cliff Drive.

Steamer Lane is for advanced sea kayakers and is among the best-known surfing locales on the West Coast. On any given day, board surfers don't want anything to do with kayakers. They are verbal and have been known to become physical. If you surf here, you must have great boat control. Very long rides are possible. Start at Cowell Beach and become proficient there before you move on to Steamer Lane. I advise gradually learning to control your boat in larger waves. Good luck, and be safe!

Santa Cruz County: Pleasure Point

Launch Site: This beach launch is at Pleasure Point, along CA 1 in Santa Cruz. There is an adjacent parking lot and off-road parking.

Pleasure Point is a runner-up to Steamer Lane and a good intermediate surf kayaker's spot. A shallow kelp shelf creates a main break with several smaller breaks all the way to Capitola. Pleasure Point works in all conditions. If the waves get too big, just tuck around the point for protection. Surfers can be aggressive and territorial, so beware.

Monterey County: Moss Landing State Beach

Launch Site: There are two launch sites at Moss Landing:

1. There is a launch ramp a few hundred feet north of the entrance to Elkhorn Slough, on the west side of CA 1, at Moss Landing Harbor District Launch Ramp.
2. Kirby Park has a bank launch off CA 1 west on Dolan Road, which is ¼ mile south of Elkhorn Slough. Follow Dolan Road to Kirby Park. Parking and rest rooms are available. Elkhorn Slough Nature Conservancy (408-633-5555). Elkhorn Slough National Estuarine Research Reserve Visitor Center, 1700 Elkhorn Road (408-728-2822).

The beach break here is gentle, in small waves, but will kick you out when waves get any bigger. Moss Landing has open sandy beaches and is a fine place to learn surf kayaking in small to medium waves. Monterey Bay sand deposits create the beach break here. For beginning and intermediate surf kayakers.

Monterey: Sand Dollar Beach

Launch Site: This beach launch is on the west side of CA 1. Sand Dollar beach is 11 miles south of Lucia. Parking is 100 yards from the launch.

Except for the long hike down to the beach, Sand Dollar is ideal, with beautiful sandy beaches, several reef breaks, and few board surfers. The water is often very clear and excellent for diving. Beginning and intermediate surf kayakers will enjoy the easy, gentle break. It works well in small to medium surf.

⟩⟩⟩⟩⟩ Part 3
Resources

Guided Tours, Classes, and Rentals

Adventure Rents
39175 Highway 1
Gualala, CA 95445
(888) 881-4386
Rentals: For self-guided trips on the Gualala River
Classes: Basic
Trips: Family trips on the Gualala River
Special Interests: Self-guided, easy tours that are fun for the whole family
Notes: Aventure Rents also rents mountain bikes for the trails around Mendocino County and can offer great advice on easy trails for family trips.

Blue Waters Kayak Tours
Kate McClain
P.O. Box 893
Inverness, CA 94937
(415) 669-2600
Trips: Tomales Bay/Estero de San Antonio/Las Gallinas/Corte Madera Creek/Brooks Island/Marin Islands/Cosumnes River Nature Conservancy Preserve/Big River/China Camp/Monterey Bay/Lake Tahoe's Emerald Bay and Richardson Bay; Tiburon/Sacramento River/Mono Lake; customized trips
Special Interests: Bird-watching/marine life guided tours; protected bays and estuaries
Notes: Kate and her guides are excellent professional nature guides, great cooks, and ACA certified, and they make great half-day to week-long trips. She leads trips for people who have had no experience kayaking and for all beginners and intermediate paddlers. She rents boats and all equipment, and provides training for her trips.

Cal Adventures
2301 Bancroft Avenue
Berkeley, CA 94720
(510) 642-4000
Rentals: Complete rental equipment
Classes: Basic to expert
Trips: Day and weekend trips
Special Interests: Varies with group
Notes: A good series of inexpensive classes and trips. Call ahead for a schedule. Located in the Berkeley Marina and associated with UC Berkeley, Cal Adventures provides a marina for sailing, windsurfing, and sea kayaking. Their one-day introductory course allows you to purchase a three-month unlimited kayak rental pass. This year, Cal Adventures led paddles to Mono Lake, Tomales Bay, and Bolinas.

California Canoe and Kayak (Princeton)
214 Princeton Avenue
Princeton, CA 94018
(650) 728-1803
California Canoe and Kayak (Oakland)
409 Water Street
Oakland, CA 94607
(510) 893-7833
California Canoe and Kayak (Sacramento)
11257 South Bridge Street
Rancho Cordova, CA 95670
(916) 631-1400
Rentals: Complete equipment
Classes: Beginner to expert
Trips: Brooks Island, Treasure Island, Alameda Island, surfing, rock gardens, youth programs, California

Kayak Kids, Mendocino, Big Sur, Golden Gate, Point Lobos, Drakes Estero, Tomales Bay, Kayak Diving, Elkhorn Slough, Sunset and Full Moon Paddles, Salinas River, Lake San Antonio, Santa Cruz, Tule Lake, customized trips

Special Interests: To provide specialized individual and group attention in all classes and trips. Great with kids and families, too.

Notes: California Canoe and Kayak is a wonderful center for all kayak activities. A full spectrum of classes from basics, tide rips, surfing, and diving to open coast is offered for much of the year. Their trip schedule is diverse and complete and well worth the trip rates.

Center Activities

Humboldt State University
Arcata, CA 95521
(707) 826-3357

Rentals: Complete equipment. Open-ocean rentals (for groups of up to 10) are contingent upon experience and manager's approval.

Classes: Basic to expert

Trips: Humboldt Bay to San Francisco Bay

Special Interests: Public awareness and education center for all paddling development skills

Notes: Humboldt State University (HSU) teaches sea kayaking skills step by step. Their excellent trips, like Outdoors Unlimited's, are staffed by volunteers. HSU also operates a marine laboratory.

Chris Baltz Kayak School

2305 River Road
Modesto, CA 95351
(916) 537-9530
Rentals: For classes only

Classes: Basics to expert

Notes: This newly opened kayaking school enthusiastically welcomes and trains both new and experienced paddlers.

Current Adventures

Dan Crandall, ACA-certified sea kayaking instructor
18000 Twitchell Road
Placerville, CA 95667
(530) 642-9755

Classes: Kids' programs; safety and rescue; racing; ACA instruction

Trips: Customized to individuals and groups

Special Interests: Kids, families, serious racers, and trainers

Notes: Dan is an active racer and knows how rough the water can get. His kids' and safety programs are excellent.

Environmental Travelling Companions

Fort Mason, Building C
San Francisco, CA 94123
(415) 474-7662

Trips: San Francisco Bay

Special Interests: Special-needs populations

Notes: This outfit does a superb job leading trips for special-needs individuals and groups. A great place to volunteer.

ESKAPE! SeaKayaking

Roger Schumann, ACA-certified sea kayaking instructor
415 Windsor Avenue, Suite B
Santa Cruz, CA 95062
(408) 427-2297

Rentals: For trips/classes only

Classes: Beginning, intermediate, and expert paddlers. Some skills training (reading the water, bracing, surfing) are taught during trips.

Trips: Surf kayaking; rock gardens; paddling under the Golden Gate; Elkhorn Slough; Angel Island; Point Lobos; Big Sur; custom trips

Special Interests: Teaching beginning and intermediate paddlers what they'd like to learn while offering them a great trip

Notes: Roger Schumann is an excellent kayaking teacher and guide who leads instructive trips. You can learn at your own pace, become a more competent paddler, and have a great trip. Roger and his guides are all ACA certified. Especially for beginning and intermediate paddlers. Reasonable rates.

Force Ten
P.O. Box 167
Elk, CA 95432
(707) 877-3505
Rentals: For classes/tours only
Classes: Basic to expert
Trips: Throughout Northern California
Notes: Force Ten does a great job teaching individual and group classes at all levels and provides guides for trips throughout Northern California.

Great Expeditions
Greg Myers, ACA-certified sea kayaking instructor
253 Moore Street
Santa Cruz, CA 95060
(408) 425-5015
Rentals: For trips/classes only
Classes: Basic skills
Trips: Tomales Bay; Lake San Antonio; Elkhorn Slough; Salinas River; Drakes Bay; Bolinas; Morro Bay; campouts; customized trips
Special Interests: Natural history and nature preservation

Notes: Great Expeditions leads fascinating nature trips. Greg is a trained environmental biologist and guides individuals and groups.

Hum-boats (Eureka Area)
At the office:
P.O. Box 503
Eureka, CA 95502
(707) 443-5157
Trips: Humboldt Bay National Wildlife Refuge, especially Indian Island, Hookton Slough, Eureka Slough, Madrone Slough, Eel River; sunset and full moon paddles; sunrise paddles; high- and low-tide paddles; trips geared toward special-needs paddlers, kids, families, and special events
Special Interests: Humboldt Bay marine and bird habitat education and preservation; customizing trips for kids, families, and groups of up to 10 paddlers
Notes: Hum-boats does a wonderful beginning nature paddle in selected areas of Humboldt Bay. The trips are geared toward groups. Guides are especially insightful on training paddlers on specific Humboldt Bay tidal and weather conditions.

Kayak Connection (Santa Cruz Harbor)
413 Lake Avenue
Santa Cruz, CA 95060
(408) 479-1121

Kayak Connection (Moss Landing)
P.O. Box 691, 2370 Highway One
Moss Landing, CA 95039
(408) 724-5692
Rentals: Complete equipment
Classes: Basics to expert
Trips: Santa Cruz coast; sunset and full moon paddles in Santa Cruz; Elkhorn Slough; Elkhorn Slough full moon paddle; Salinas River

Special Interests: Santa Cruz; guided tours focusing on nature education in protected bays; kids' and family trips

Notes: Kayak Connection helps paddlers learn in increments, get to know the marine environment, and have fun doing it. It's a premier paddle class, sales, and rental center for the Santa Cruz area.

Kayak Tahoe

Dock location:
Timber Cove Marina
3411 Highway 50
Tahoe, CA 96150
(530) 544-2011
Mailing address:
Kayak Tahoe
P.O. Box 11129
Tahoe Paradise, CA 96155
Rentals: Complete equipment
Classes: Basic to expert
Trips: Lake Tahoe
Special Interests: Families and kids
Notes: Located at the end of the dock at Camp Richardson in Lake Tahoe, Kayak Tahoe offers a variety of surf ski and touring-boat rentals. They know Lake Tahoe very well and have paddled it in all seasons. They offer guided, one-day Tahoe tours, sunset and full moon paddles, as well as special events.

Mark Rauscher, ACA-certified sea kayaking instructor

15325 La Arboleda Road
Morgan Hill, CA 95037
(408) 779-0710
Rentals: For classes only
Classes: Individual paddle and roll instruction
Special Interests: Customized instruction for the beginning, individual paddler

Notes: A really wonderful, patient, energetic teacher, Mark has taught hundreds of paddlers for 14 years and finds that individualized lessons are the key to giving his students the skills and confidence they need to enjoy themselves safely on the water. You can learn bracing and roll skills in a safe, warm pool or at the site of your choice.

Monterey Bay Kayaks

693 Del Monte Avenue
Monterey, CA 93940
(408) 373-KELP
(800) 649-KELP
Rentals: Complete equipment
Classes: Beginner to expert
Trips: Monterey Bay; Elkhorn Slough; sunset and full moon paddles; Salinas River; Point Lobos
Special Interests: Monterey Bay preservation, kids' and family paddles, and thorough paddle instruction
Notes: Classes include basic skills, surf kayaking, advanced rescues, and more. Excellent skills training, service, and full equipment sales.

North Coast Adventures

Lowell Cottle, ACA-certified kayaking instructor
P.O. Box 939
Trinidad, CA 95570
(707) 677-3124
Classes: Basic to expert
Trips: Trinidad; whale-watching paddles in Trinidad Bay; Mendocino rock gardens and caves; estuaries and inland lakes
Special Interests: Beginner and family-oriented open-coast trips
Notes: Lowell takes groups of up to eight people, including kids, to the Mendocino rock gardens and caves, Trinidad Bay, and Patrick's

Point, and leads whale and coast sightseeing trips. He has open-deck boats and gives you lessons before launching. His open-coast trips are designed for beginner and intermediate paddlers.

Ocean Kayak, Inc.
P.O. Box 885
Stinson Beach, CA 99470
(415) 868-9603
Notes: Kayak tours and instruction by local Stinson Beach kayaker Scott Tye. Call or write for a brochure.

Otter Bar Kayak School
Otter Bar Lodge
Box 210
Forks of Salmon, CA 96031
(530) 462-4772
Classes: Extreme rough-water paddling for experts
Special Interests: Pushing the envelope
Notes: A raucous and highly energetic bunch of very athletic paddlers, Otter Bar prides itself in extreme rough-water survival paddling.

Outdoors Unlimited (UCSF)
Rental office:
530 Parnassus Street
San Francisco, CA 94143
(415) 476-2078
Rentals: Complete equipment
Classes: Basic to expert
Trips: Day, weekend, and week-long trips
Special Interests: Student/nonstudent; volunteers participate in all aspects of trip planning, guiding, coordinating, etc.
Notes: Call ahead, or get a quarterly trip schedule by sending a large SASE envelope with 55-cent stamp per each schedule to: Outdoors Unlimited, UCSF, P.O. Box 0234A, San Francisco, CA 94143; (415) 476-2078. Excellent skills instructors. Classes and trips are reasonably priced. A great place to meet new people and to volunteer. Although affiliated with UC San Francisco, Outdoors Unlimited welcomes everyone from the community.

Outside Sports
584 Castro Street
San Francisco, CA 94114
(415) 864-7205
Rentals: For tours only
Trips: Tomales Bay; Bodega Bay; Estero de San Antonio; China Camp; Angel Island
Special Interests: Combined camping, biking, and kayaking trips
Notes: Combined kayak and bike touring in Tomales Bay, Bodega Bay, Estero de San Antonio, China Camp, Angel Island, etc.

Pacific Currents
Mailing address:
P.O. Box 210
Olema, CA 94950
(800) GO-KAYAK
On the water:
10155 State Highway 1
Olema, CA 94950
Rentals: Complete equipment
Classes: Basic to advanced
Trips: North Bay; Point Reyes; Tomales Bay
Special Interests: Kayaking and biking tours
Notes: Pacific Currents can combine bike riding, camping, and kayaking on their trips—a great way to explore the coast with wonderful guides. All classes are all taught by ACA-certified kayaking instructors.

Riptides and Rapids

1220 Pear Avenue, Suite D
Mountain View, CA 94043
(650) 961-1240
(650) 988-9089 (fax)
Notes: Riptides and Rapids leads a variety of trips and will customize trips for anyone, including beginning and advanced paddlers and families. Their diverse trip schedule encompasses the entire San Francisco Bay area. They also offer basic skills classes.

Sea Trek

P.O. Box 561
Woodacre, CA 94973
In the office: (415) 488-1000, weekdays
At the dock at Schoonmaker Point in Sausalito: (415) 332-4465, weekends
Rentals: Complete equipment and three-month unlimited rental passes
Classes: Basic to expert
Trips: San Francisco Bay area, including special events and kids' paddles
Notes: Sea Trek does an excellent job teaching sea kayaking skills step by step. Located in Sausalito, they have the perfect bay environment to train paddlers in basic skills, beginning surf skills, and expert rough-water paddling. The oldest in the Bay Area.

Stinson Beach Health Club

P.O. Box 635, 3605 Highway 1
Stinson Beach, CA 99470
(415) 868-2739
Notes: Kayak rentals and some tours in Tomales Bay

Tamal Saka or Tomales Bay Sea Kayaking

P.O. Box 833
Marshall, CA 94940
(415) 663-1743
Notes: Tamal Saka offers a variety of Tomales Bay tours and classes in photography, yoga, and culinary experiences, navigation, basic skills, and rescue skills on Tomales Bay. They also offer Tomales Bay, Drakes Estero, Estero Americano, and Mono Lake guided tours, including some for the whole family. Of particular interest is the storytelling kayak trip, which includes Miwok and Pomo settlement history in Tomales.

Wilderness Sports

11327 Folsom Boulevard
Rancho Cordova, CA 95742
(916) 852-5000
Rentals: For classes/trips only
Classes: Basic instruction on Lake Natoma
Trips: Lake Natoma and other nearby sites
Special Interests: Focuses on basic skills classes.

You Wan Tu Canoe

Bill Davis
P.O. Box 474
Chico, CA 95927
(916) 891-1424
Rentals: For classes/trips only
Classes: Basic to expert
Trips: Sacramento River and Delta; other local spots
Special Interests: Local outings

Kayaking Clubs

These clubs are a useful resource. Pick up their newsletters, check out their Web sites with your search engine, or call to find out their current trip schedules—which may cover much of Northern California.

Sonoma County

Force Ten
P.O. Box 167
Elk, CA 95432
(707) 877-3474
For expert paddlers into big surf kayaking, rock gardens, caving, and rough open coast. Membership by invitation only.

Marin County

Slackwater Yacht Club
B37 Gate 6 Road
Sausalito, CA 94965
For beginning and intermediate paddlers. Write for member information.

City and County of San Francisco

Bay Area Sea Kayakers (BASK)
229 Courtright Road
San Rafael, CA 94901
(415) 457-6094
A mixture of beginning, intermediate, and expert paddlers. Gives great classes for members in basic skills, tide rips, and surf zones. Trips throughout Northern California and beyond. Member driven. Fun monthly meetings with trips, slide shows, annual swap meets, and food. Reason-able membership fee. Insightful and witty monthly newsletter.

Environmental Traveling Companions (ETC)

Fort Mason Center, Building C
San Francisco, CA 94123
(415) 474-7662
A nonprofit, volunteer-driven organization offering outdoor experiences and skills to persons with special needs, including people with developmental and other disabilities, those with chronic illnesses, and disadvantaged youth. Sea kayaking is one of their specialties. ETC sponsors great trips and helps people learn physical empowerment and leadership. Small membership fee. Volunteer now! Newsletter.

Santa Clara County

Western Sea Kayakers
P.O. Box 59436
San Jose, CA 95159
(408) 984-7611 (Western Mountaineering)
A low-key, friendly, and entertaining mixture of beginning, intermediate, and expert paddlers. Fun, social monthly meetings. Skills development sessions for beginning and intermediate paddlers. Great trips throughout Northern California, from Point Lobos to Mono Lake. E-mail network is a blast. Reasonable membership fee. Irregular newsletter.

San Mateo County

Miramar Beach Kayak Club
Number One Mirada Road
Half Moon Bay, CA 94109
(650) 726-2748 (Michael Powers)
For beginning to advanced surf kayaking and open-coast paddles around Half Moon Bay. Membership fee.

Tsunami Rangers
c/o Eric Soares
P.O. Box 339
Moss Beach, CA 94038
(650) 728-5118
Small, free-spirited, expert paddling
group devoted to master surfing,
caving, and rock gardens. Membership by invitation only.

Santa Cruz County

Santa Cruz Kayak Club
P.O. Box 7228
Santa Cruz, CA 95061-7228
(408) 464-2406
A terrific combination of beginning,
intermediate, and expert paddlers.
Sponsors great classes, trips
around Santa Cruz and Elkhorn
Slough, and really fun special
events. Open-coast and surf
kayaking, and environmental
protection events of special
interest. Reasonable membership fee. Huge, fun bimonthly
newsletter.

Shared Adventures
Foster Anderson, Director
918½ Windham Street
Santa Cruz, CA 95062
(408) 458-9121
Shared Adventures is a fun, new paddling group in the Santa Cruz area
that sponsors trips throughout
Northern California for paddlers
with special needs. Newsletter.

Alameda County

**Sea Kayakers of Alternate Persuasion
(SKOAP)**
1313 Hale Drive
Concord, CA 94518
For beginning and intermediate gay
and lesbian paddlers—part fun,

part skills, part social group.
Fun trip planning meetings and a
quarterly newsletter. Small membership fee.

Shasta County

Shasta Paddlers
c/o North Country Canoe and Kayak
2515 Park Marina Drive #104
Redding, CA 96001
This new group of paddlers is looking
for members of all skill levels.
Trips in Northern California.
Newsletter.

El Dorado County

Gold Country Paddlers
P.O. Box 1721
Fair Oaks, CA 95628
Group-oriented lake and river pad-
dlers in the Gold Country.
Reasonable membership fee.

Reporting Pollution

BayKeeper Hotline
(800) KEEP-BAY
Report pollution, oil or hazardous
material spills, toxic discharge, or
dumping.
http://www.baykeeper.org

**California Department of Fish and
Game Hotline**
(800) 952-5400
Report poaching, creek pollution,
habitat destruction, and fish or
bird kills.

**Lindsay Museum Storm Drain Pollu-
tion Hotline**
(510) 935-1978
Report toxic spilling into storm
drains.

San Francisco Bay Area Regional Quality Control Board
(510) 622-2300
Report San Francisco Bay area spills and water-quality problems.

San Francisco Bay Conservation and Development Commission
(415) 557-3686
Report suspected illegal shoreline and wetland fill or construction in San Francisco Bay.

Surfrider Foundation
(831) 476-POOP
Report pollution or check daily water-quality report.

United States Army Corps of Engineers
(415) 332-0334
Report large submerged objects that are hazardous to navigation.

United States Coast Guard
(510) 437-3073 or (800) 424-8802
Report oil or hazardous materials spills, 24 hours a day.

United States Environmental Protection Agency, Region 9
(415) 744-2000
Report oil or hazardous material spills to this hotline number 24 hours a day.

Waste Alert Hotline
(800) 69-TOXIC
Report suspected environmental crimes and improper disposal of hazardous materials in California.

Reporting Sick or Stranded Wildlife

California Marine Mammal Center, Marin County (marine mammals only)
(415) 289-7325

Lindsay Museum, Walnut Creek
(510) 935-1978

Wildcare Terwilliger Nature Education and Wildlife Rehabilitation
(415) 456-SAVE
Report sick or stranded wildlife in the San Francisco Bay Area.

North Coast Marine Mammal Rehabilitation Center
(707) 465-6265 or (707) 465-MAML
Report stranded or entangled marine mammals in Del Norte and Humboldt counties.

Marine Mammal Center in Marin County
(415) 289-7325 or (415) 289-SEAL
Report stranded or entangled marine mammals from Mendocino to San Luis Obispo counties.

Marine Sanctuary Watch Hotline, Save Our Shores
(800) 9-SHORES
Report a mammal in distress or mammal habitat destruction.

Monterey Bay Aquarium
(408) 648-4888
Report a mammal in distress or mammal habitat destruction.

Preservation

Bay Model
(415) 332-3870
View a working model of the San Francisco Bay.

Save S. F. Bay Association
(510) 452-9261
Work with San Francisco Bay preservation on water quality, shoreline, and mammal and bird habitat issues.

SEALS Volunteer Coordinator, Farallones Marine Sanctuary Association
P.O. Box 29386
The Presidio
San Francisco, CA 94129
(415) 561-6625
Help record harbor seal behavior and haulout patterns in the bays.

Surfrider Foundation
P.O. Box 3203
Santa Cruz, CA 95063
(831) 476-POOP
Issue Hotline and Member Information (800) 743-7873
Report water-quality problems such as illegal dumping, to check on the day's water-quality forecast for your area for surfing and kayaking, and to get involved with a local water-quality advocacy group that works directly on its own research and monitors water-quality testing of municipalities in your area. This group runs the offshore water-quality testing facility Blue Water Task Force, which does lab testing at 10 sites along the coast. Fights for strong water-quality legislation in the state assembly and congress. Other chapters: Humboldt Chapter, P.O. Box 4605, Arcata, CA 95521; (707) 445-1336. San Francisco Chapter; (415) 665-4155.

Volunteer Opportunities

Bay Institute of San Francisco
(415) 721-7680

BayKeeper
(800) KEEP-BAY
(415) 567-4401

California Coastal Commission
Adopt-A-Beach Program
(800) 262-7848

California Department of Parks and Recreation
(415) 831-2700

Center for Marine Conservation
(408) 375-4509

Citizens for a Better Environment
(415) 243-8373

Ecology Action
(408) 426-5925

Farallones Marine Sanctuary Association
(415) 561-6625

Friends of the River
(916) 442-3155

Humboldt Bay National Wildlife Refuge
(707) 733-5406

Monterey Bay National Marine Sanctuary
(408) 647-4201

Paint the Drain Campaign Estuary Project
(510) 622-2465

San Francisco Bay National Wildlife Refuge
(510) 792-0222

Save Our Shores
(800) 9-SHORES

Save San Francisco Bay Association
(510) 452-9261

Surfrider Foundation
P.O. Box 3203
Santa Cruz, CA 95063
(831) 476-POOP
Humboldt Chapter
(707) 445-1336
San Francisco Chapter
(415) 665-4155
Issue Hotline and Member Information (800) 743-7873

Urban Creeks Council
(510) 540-6669

Books

The Basic Essentials of Sea Kayaking, by Mike Wyatt. Merrillville, IN: ICS Books, Inc., 1990.

The Bombproof Roll and Beyond!, by Paul Dutky. Birmingham, AL: Menasha Ridge Press, 1993.

California Camping: The Complete Guide to More Than 50,000 Campsites for Tenters, RVers, and Car Campers, 9th edition, by Tom Stienstra. San Francisco, CA: Foghorn Press, 1996.

California Coastal Access Guide, 5th edition. Erin Caughman and Jo Ginsberg, editors. California Coastal Commission. Berkeley, CA: University of California Press, 1997.

California Coastal Resource Guide. Madge Caughman and Joanne Ginsberg, editors. Berkeley, CA: University of California Press, 1987.

Cal/North Boating/Fishing/Diving Directory. San Francisco, CA: Cal/North Publishing Company, 1998.

The Coastal Kayaker's Manual: The Complete Guide to Skills, Gear, and Sea Sense, 2d edition, by Randel Washburne. Old Saybrook, CT: The Globe Pequot Press, 1993.

Complete Book of Sea Kayaking, 4th edition, by Derek Hutchinson. Old Saybrook, CT: The Globe Pequot Press, 1995.

Complete Folding Kayaker, by Ralph Díaz. Camden, Maine: Ragged Mountain Press, 1994.

Complete Sea Kayak Touring, by Jonathan Hanson. Camden, Maine: Ragged Mountain Press, 1998.

The Essential Sea Kayaker: A Complete Course for the Open Water Paddler, by David Seidman. Camden, Maine: Ragged Mountain Press, 1992.

Fundamentals of Kayak Navigation, 2d edition, by David Burch. Old Saybrook, CT: The Globe Pequot Press, 1993.

Guide to Expedition Kayaking on Sea and Open Water, 3rd edition, by Derek Hutchinson, 1995. Old Saybrook, CT: The Globe Pequot Press.

The Hidden Coast: Kayak Expeditions from Alaska to Mexico, by Joel W. Rogers. Seattle, WA: Alaska Northwest Books, 1991.

Kayak: A Manual of Technique, by William Nealy. Birmingham, AL: Menasha Ridge Press, 1986.

Kayak Touring, by William Sanders. Mechanicsburg, PA: Stackpole Books, 1998.

Pacific Boating Almanac 1997: Northern California. Peter L. Griffes, publisher and editor. Marina Del Ray, CA: ProStart Publications, Ltd.

Paddle America: A Guide to Trips and Outfitters in All 50 States, 3rd enl. rev. ed., by David Shears and Nick Shears. Washington, DC: Starfish Press, 1996.

Paddling the Gate: A Kayak Trip on San Francisco Bay, by Paul Kaufmann. San Francisco: Mara Books, 1980.

Performance Kayaking, by Stephen B. U'Ren. Mechanicsburg, PA: Stackpole Books, 1990.

Recreation Lakes of California, 11th ed, by D. J. Dirksen. Santa Cruz, CA: Recreation Sales Publishing, 1996.

San Francisco Bay Shoreline Guide, California State Coastal Conservancy staff. Berkeley, CA: University of California Press, 1995.

Sea Kayaker's Deep Trouble, by Matt Broze and George Gronseth. Edited by Christopher Cunningham. Camden, Maine: Ragged Mountain Press, 1997.

Sea Kayaking: A Manual for Long-Distance Touring, expanded rev. ed., by John Dowd. Seattle, WA: University of Washington Press, 1997.

Tidelog 1998: Northern California Edition. Bolinas, CA: Pacific Publishers, 1998.

Waterproof Chart #52. San Francisco Bay International Sailing Supply. Punta Gorda, FL.

The Whole Paddler's Catalog, edited by Zip Kellogg. Camden, Maine: Ragged Mountain Press, 1997.

Periodicals

Canoe & Kayak
P.O. Box 3146
Kirkland, WA 98083-3146
(206) 827-6363

EcoTraveller
9560 S.W. Nimbus Avenue
Beaverton, OR 97008
(503) 520-1955

Headwaters
Friends of the River
Membership Department
128 J Street, 2nd Floor
Sacramento, CA 95814
(916) 442-3155

Outside Magazine
P.O. Box 51733
Boulder, CO 80321-1733
(303) 604-1464

Paddler
P.O. Box 775450
Steamboat Springs, CO 80477
(703) 455-3419

Sea Kayaker Magazine
P.O. Box 17170
Seattle, WA 98107-0870
Subscriptions: (206) 789-9536

Wave-Length
Site 17 Gabriola Island
BC, Canada V0R 1X0
E-mail: WaveNet@web.apc.org

Cool Web Sites

Note: Membership in kayaking clubs may include an E-mail bulletin board of upcoming group events. Using a search engine, you can find hundreds more Web sites on Northern California sea kayaking, skills diagrams, and tour ideas.

Gold Country Paddlers
http://www.best.com/~mbean/gcp/
    index.html

Monterey Bay Kayaks
http://montereykayaks.com

San Francisco Bay Area Kayak Schools
http://www.sunshinedaydream.com/
    water/seakayak/learningcurve/
    map.html

San Francisco Bay Area Sea Kayaking
http://www.bask.org

Videos

You can purchase these videos from most outdoor retailers who sell kayaking supplies.

"Grace Under Pressure"
Joe Holt Productions
Rapid Progression
P.O. Box 97
Almond, NC 28702

"1997 Santa Cruz Kayak Surf Festival"
Gecko Studios
234 Alta Vista Drive
Santa Cruz, CA 95060
(408) 427-2856

"Over and Out"
Distributed by Riptides and Rapids
1220 Pear Avenue, Suite D
Mountain View, CA 94043

"Performance Sea Kayaking: The Basics and Beyond"
Produced by Kent Ford and John Davis
Performance Video and Instruction, Inc.
550 Riverbend
Durango, CO 81301
(970) 259-1361

"Sea Kayaking: Getting Started"
Larry Holman
Moving Pictures
317 Tamalpais Drive
Corte Madera, CA 94925

"Surf Kayaking Fundamentals"
John Lull
P.O. Box 564
El Granada, CA 94018

"Tsunami Rangers Guide to Ocean Adventure Kayaking"
"Adventures of the Tsunami Rangers"
"Tsunami Ranger Anthology"
Eric Soares
Tsunami Rangers
P.O. Box 339
Moss Beach, CA 94038
(415) 728-5118

Events Calendar

February

Newport Bay 10K
(714) 646-7725

Round the Rock Kayak Race
Friends of the River Annual River Festival

San Francisco
Friends of the River
(916) 442-3155

March

Santa Cruz Surf Festival
(408) 479-1121

April

Russian River Marathon
Contact local kayak shops for further
information.

**SCOOP Santa Cruz Open Ocean
Paddlefest**
Kayak Connection
(408) 479-1121

May

Pacific Ocean Kayaking Conference
Half Moon Bay
California Canoe and Kayak
(800) 366-9804

July

Coastal Cleanups
Summer and fall weekends. Call for a
beach schedule and nearest
chapter.
Surfrider Membership Information
(800) 743-7873

Eppies Great Race Triathalon
(707) 672-1551

Race for Treasure
Oakland
California Canoe and Kayak
(800) 366-9804

August

Kayak Surf Competition
Moonstone Beach
Trinidad, CA
Northern Mountain Supply
(707) 445-1711

**Lake Tahoe Classic Race, North
Shore**
(916) 642-9755

Treasure Island Race
Contact local kayak shops for further
information.

September

Kayak Tahoe Blue Classic
Kayak Tahoe
(916) 544-2011

Tahoe Canoe and Kayak Classic
Kayak Tahoe
(916) 544-2011

October

**CCK "Get Your Boat Salty" Annual
Kayak Surf Contest**
Pacifica State Beach at Linda Mar
California Canoe and Kayak
(800) 366-9804

**Elkhorn Slough Canoe and Kayak
Race**
Elkhorn Slough
Kayak Connection
(408) 479-1121

Sea Trek/ETC Annual Regatta
Sausalito
Sea Trek
(415) 488-1000